INTERMEDIATE
Teacher's Guide

INTERMEDIATE
Teacher's Guide

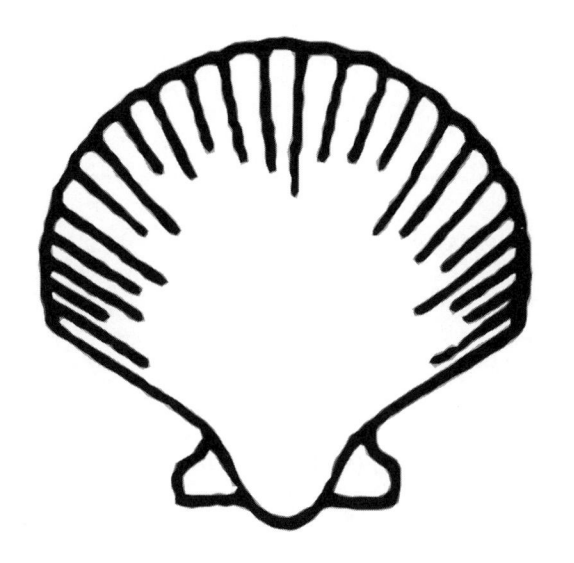

Center for the
Ministry of Teaching

MOREHOUSE PUBLISHING

©1994 By Virginia Theological Seminary and Morehouse Publishing

Revised edition, 2000

All rights reserved. No part of this book may be reproduced, stored in a retrieval system, or transmitted in any form or by any means, electronic, mechanical, photocopying, recording, or otherwise, without the written permission of the publisher.

Developed by
Virginia Theological Seminary
Center for the Ministry of Teaching
3737 Seminary Road
Alexandria, VA 22304

Published by
Morehouse Publishing
P.O. Box 1321
Harrisburg, PA 17105
Morehouse Publishing is a division of *The Morehouse Group.*

Locke E. Bowman, Jr., Editor-in-Chief

Amelia J. Gearey, Ph.D., Associate Editor

The Rev. George G. Kroupa III, Associate Editor

Judith W. Seaver, Ph.D., Managing Editor (1990-1996)

Dorothy S. Linthicum, Managing Editor (current)

Consultants for the Shell Year, Intermediate
    The Rev. William L. Evans, Alexandria, VA
    The Rev. David A. Scott, Ph.D., Virginia Theological Seminary
    The Rev. Benjamin E.K. Speare-Hardy II, Christchurch, VA
    Jackie H. Stanley, Chapel Hill, NC
    The Rev. Anne O. Weatherholt, Frederick, MD

Community Times, student newspaper, designed by Jan E. Moffatt.
Art by Bobbi Tull and Jan E. Moffatt, Alexandria, VA

Symbol Card art and Shell Year Treasurebook designed by Jan E. Moffatt.

For additional copies, contact:

MOREHOUSE PUBLISHING

Toll Free: 1-800-877-0012   Fax: 717-541-8128
www.morehousegroup.com
ISBN: 0-8192-6015-0

Printed in the United States of America
04 03 02   10 9 8 7 6 5

CONTENTS

BACKGROUND FOR TEACHERS
    The Teaching Ministry in Episcopal Churches 1
    Understanding Intermediate-Age Students 9
    Using the Curriculum 15
    Teaching Strategies and Resources 19

UNIT I: COVENANT
    Letter to Parent 35
    Session 1. God Preserves Creation 37
    Session 2. God Calls a People into Covenant 41
    Session 3. Moses Receives the Commandments 45
    Session 4. God Provides Leaders 49
    Session 5. A Place for the Ark of the Covenant 53
    Session 6. Covenant People Divided 57
    Session 7. Covenant People in Exile 61
    Session 8. Covenant People Return 65
    Session 9. All Saints 69

UNIT II: MIRACLES
    Letter to Parent 73
    Session 1. Prophets' Vision: A New Covenant 75
    Session 2. Isaiah's Vision: Salvation 79
    Session 3. Gabriel Speaks of Visions Fulfilled 83
    Session 4. Mary's Song for Christmas 87
    Session 5. Magi Seek the Christ Child 91
    Session 6. Blind Bartimaeus 95
    Session 7. Healing the Paralytic 99
    Session 8. Cleansing of the Ten Lepers 103
    Session 9. Raising of Lazarus 107

UNIT III: BAPTISM: NEW LIFE

Letter to Parent 111
Session 1. The Baptism of Jesus 113
Session 2. Baptism and Our Beliefs 117
Session 3. Baptism and Our Living 121
Session 4. Baptized by Water and the Spirit 125
Session 5. Receiving the Newly Baptized 129
Session 6. Jesus is Servant 133
Session 7. Jesus Was Crucified 137
Session 8. Jesus Was Raised from the Dead 141
Session 9. Jesus Offers New Life 145

UNIT IV: THE APOSTLE PAUL

Letter to Parent 149
Session 1. Paul the Hebrew 151
Session 2. Paul the Convert 155
Session 3. Paul the Apostle 159
Session 4. Paul the Traveler 163
Session 5. Paul the Missionary 167
Session 6. Paul the Writer 171
Session 7. Paul the Leader 175
Session 8. Paul the Pastor 179
Session 9. Pentecost: Festival of the Spirit 183

FOUNDATION PAPER 187

BACKGROUND FOR TEACHERS

THE TEACHING OF MINISTRY IN EPISCOPAL CHURCHES

Jesus, the Son of God, lived among us as a teacher, preacher, and healer. Through his powerful example, Christians have come to understand that the act of teaching is basic to our faith.

All Christians are teachers. Our daily lives bear witness to what we believe and treasure. Christians are also learners for life. We never "graduate" or "pass the test."

No precise definition or set of rules governs teaching in the church. For all ages, as teachers and learners come to know one another, a special relationship develops. What transpires between them becomes a kind of "spiritual staff of life"—organic, dynamic, wonderful, and meaningful.

The Children's Charter for the Church, developed by the Office of Children's Ministries and a number of dioceses, calls for three responses to the children in our care: Nurture of the Child—to treasure each child as a gift from God; Ministry to the Child—to recognize and foster children's spirituality and unique gifts; and Ministry of the Child—to appreciate children's abilities and readiness to represent Christ and his church. All three responses will have an impact on relationships between teachers and students.

Teaching Is a Ministry

Students and teachers in the church share a singular experience that goes beyond the facts and strategies of the moment. Every encounter between teachers and students is important—a possibility for connection and meaning. Teaching is a ministry involving:

Hospitality—Teachers and learners share time and activity. There is a mutual sense of satisfaction in being together at this time and in this place.

Presence—Teachers and students listen to and care about each other. Not only do we hear each other speaking, but also we feel the underlying emotion, tuned in to the meaning of conversations.

Participation—Teachers and learners engage each other in a mutual spirit of inquiry, an interactive relationship. Roles are flexible.

Imagination—For teachers and students, the choreography of the "dance of learning" is nourished by spirit and grace. Teaching and learning change those who teach and those who learn.

Christian formation is a lifelong process. Often the metaphors of journey or pilgrimage are used to describe these formations. The facts of our faith will be encountered again and again. From this perspective, intermediate-age students are just beginning a lifetime quest. Consider, for example, how—over the course of a lifetime—we renew our acquaintance with the stories of the nativity and Passion of Jesus Christ. The details become familiar, but the emotional power of the events touches us again and again. Age and experience enrich us with new meaning.

A Tool for Teachers

The aim of the Episcopal Children's Curriculum (ECC) is to sustain and strengthen the ministry of teaching in the Episcopal Church. The Curriculums focus on classroom-based efforts does not deny the importance of other Christian education in a local congregation. It does reflect an intentional decision to affirm the act of teaching and spotlight the respective roles of teachers and learners.

The Curriculum is a tool for teachers. It serves as a resource to help teachers formulate answers to three pivotal questions:

What do I teach?

The Curriculum offers a reasonable embodiment of the "data of our faith." Teachers using the materials are expected to pursue actively an adult-level understanding of the content of the session outlines, taking seriously their own roles as learners.

Whom do I teach?

At every age level, teachers are challenged to adapt to both the developmental characteristics of the group as well as the particular interests of each individual. The ECC addresses issues of developmental differences from two important perspectives. Content is approached differently at each of the three age levels—preschool/kindergarten, primary, and intermediate. Then, within each session outline at every age level, provision is made in activity suggestions for varying degrees of skill and learning styles among students.

How do I teach? The Curriculum was written for teachers by teachers. Workability is essential. Options and guidelines to help teachers make adjustments to fit local circumstances are invaluable. In addition to a variety of activity suggestions for every session, there are practical comments and specific tips to guide learning.

It is hoped that teachers who use the ECC will be nurtured, inspired, and enriched personally as they prepare to teach and learn, and reflect on their efforts.

Teachers will find that the session outlines in this guide provide support and structure for the inexperienced, and challenge and flexibility for the more confident. It is highly recommended that every teacher have access to a Bible (NRSV), *The Book of Common Prayer*, and *The Hymnal 1982*. The Access Bible (NRSV) provides commentary, study tips, maps, and a concordance. At every age level, teachers can expect to find support for their preparation and planning. Every Intermediate session outline includes the following:

• *Unit Introduction,* to show how the sessions relate to the Unit theme. This is presented in a letter format that can be reproduced for parents/guardians of students in the class.
   • *Focus statement,* to state the concepts along with objectives.
   • *Getting Ready,* to provide factual background and personal inspiration.
   • *Teaching Tip,* to offer useful information about working with this age group.
   • *Teacher's Assessment,* to prompt thinking back over the session.
   • *Looking Ahead,* to preview upcoming concepts.

The Episcopal Perspective

The theological foundation of the Episcopal Children's Curriculum is set forth in a Foundation Paper (January 1990). This document is reproduced on the last pages of this Teacher's Guide. Teachers are urged to read the complete statement. Repeated below are the first few lines:

"The aim of Christian education in Episcopal Church parishes and congregations is to assist every member in living out the covenant made in Holy Baptism (BCP, p. 304). Hence the common ministry of teachers and learners focuses on matters of both faith and practice."

Baptism confers full participation in the Episcopal Church. The ECC sets forth a framework for helping all who teach and learn to grow in their understanding of the meaning of sacramental experiences. At every age, we are people of faith whose lives offer legitimate testimony to our baptismal promises. At every baptism, we are called to renew our commitment to these promises, in an unending, ever-enlarging circle of affirmation and action.

In describing ECC, these terms are key: "biblically based" and "liturgically oriented." The Curriculum is designed to follow the Bible in ways understood by young students. But the presence of biblical material does not mark the ECC as distinctively Episcopal. Like all Christians, we look to Holy Scripture for the content of our faith and practice. We view the Bible as the written Word of God.

Our Episcopal liturgy, set forth in *The Book of Common Prayer* and supported by *The Hymnal 1982,* invites each of us to enter into a relationship with God's Word. The three-year cycle of the Eucharistic Lectionary (appointed readings) and the seasons of the Church Year provide the pattern for worship. For Episcopalians, the Lectionary cycle ensures two things—fullness and context. Every year we hear the biblical witness to our salvation history.

Liturgy, defined as "the work of the people," brings us together as a congregation. We are invited to be active, not passive. In a deeply personal way, we encounter God's Word. We listen, seeking to hear God speaking to us through Scripture. As we hear—at whatever level of understanding—we are touched, informed, instructed, healed, and transformed. The liturgy provides a structure for this life-changing encounter. It is worship that establishes the "Episcopal" affirmation of Scripture.

Conscious of this role of liturgy, the editors and writers of the ECC have structured classroom experiences based on the general pattern of our Episcopal liturgy. We come together; we hear the Word, along with an explanation, and we go forth to live in the world. In ways appropriate for each age level, the Curriculum sessions prescribe a parallel pattern. At the intermediate-age level, the three essential activities are titled: Gathering, Introducing the Story, and Going Forth.

Students are encouraged through exposure and experience to learn words and actions for participation in worship and liturgy. The illustrations used in the ECC are specifically appropriate for Episcopalians. Clergy, churches, liturgical actions, text, and language are all used and portrayed as young people in Episcopal settings are most likely to experience them.

Selections from *The Book of Common Prayer* are incorporated into every session. Collects, prayers, and thanksgivings are included in every session. The music used in the ECC is found in *The Hymnal 1982,* and frequently appears also in the children's hymnal, *We Sing of God.* As students learn or listen on the *Children Sing!* tape to the suggested hymns, they will be acquiring words and melodies to help them participate in the Church's worship.

Background

The Episcopal Children's Curriculum

The Curriculum uses a cumulative framework of age levels, years, units, and sessions. The three age levels of the Curriculum are Preschool/Kindergarten, Primary, and Intermediate. At each age level, there are three separate years of material. A total of nine years' worth of material is provided—three years at each of the three age levels.

Unit I	Unit II	Unit III	Unit IV
Old Testament Themes	New Testament Themes	Sacraments —Baptism —Eucharist —Worship	Church Themes

Within each age level, the three years of material are designated by symbols linked to the Sacrament theme of each year: Shell (Baptism), Chalice (Eucharist), Cross (Worship).

The use of symbols to identify years at each age level is a deliberate attempt to move away from a designation (such as grades or numbers) that would signal a particular order for the sequence of the years of material at each age level. Symbols also avoid confusion with the A, B, or C designations for Lectionary years.

The content of the Episcopal Children's Curriculum focuses on four areas: Old Testament (Hebrew Scriptures), New Testament, Sacraments, and the Church. The basic building block of the Curriculum is the Unit. Each year's 36 sessions of Curriculum materials are written in four Units of nine sessions each, representing the four areas.

The organization is intended to be sequential, cumulative, and consistent over the scope of the Curriculum. In the overall ECC framework, the content focus broadens and deepens as students advance through the Curriculum. A child beginning the Episcopal Children's Curriculum at the age of three and proceeding forward for nine years will revisit Unit themes but will not actually repeat any material. Each level is a blend of the familiar and the new.

The accompanying three age-level charts provide an overview of the Unit themes within an age level, and help to explain how each of the four content areas unfold. We can see how the students are immersed, over and over, in the content of our faith and practice in ways most appropriate for their age levels. The approaches to teaching are different at each level.

Preschool/Kindergarten — Stories

Shell	Creation	Jesus: Son of God	Baptism: Belonging	We Are the Church
Chalice	Promise	Jesus: Storyteller	Eucharist: Sacred Meal	The Church Prays
Cross	Shepherd	Jesus: Teacher	Worship: Environment	The Church Sings

Preschool/Kindergarten. Written for three-through five-year-olds, this level of the Curriculum emphasizes the telling of stories as the principal experience for teaching and learning. Children this age come to know about their world primarily through stories. The Old Testament thread focuses on the stories of key figures in the Bible. Unit II tells stories of Jesus' birth and ministry. Unit III looks at Sacraments through stories of personal participation and experience. Unit IV recounts stories of the early Church.

Primary — People in Relationship

🐚	Pentateuch	Jesus: Healer	Baptism:People in Covenant	The Church in the New Testament
🍷	Judges/Kings	People in Parables	Eucharist: People in Communion	The Church in the Prayer Book
✝	Stories	Sermon on the Mount	Worship: People in Community	Saints of the Church

Primary. Planned for children in Grades 1-3, the Curriculum continues the emphasis on stories with particular attention paid to people and relationships. The goal is to make the people of the Bible and the Church come alive for young learners. This is consistent with a belief that the Christian faith is nurtured through relationships. Each of the themes involves a revisiting and expansion of the stories first encountered at the Preschool/Kindergarten level. In Unit I, Old Testament sessions all focus on specific people, their families, their actions, and the events in their lives. In Unit II, we look more deeply at Jesus' life among us, the people he taught, preached to, and healed. The Sacrament Units consider people in relationship to the Sacrament and to one another. The Church Units (IV) emphasize people—stories from the early Church in the Bible, the Church at prayer, and the lives of saints.

Intermediate — Symbols

🐚	Covenant	Miracles	Baptism: New Life	The Apostle Paul
🍷	Prophecy	Parables of Promise	Eucharist: Shared Life	The Catechism
✝	Psalms and Wisdom	The Reign of God	Worship	Church History

Intermediate. Students in Grades 4–6 are able to use and understand symbols for ideas and events they encounter. The stories, people, and relationships first met at earlier levels are recalled and examined through the increasing complexity of their perspective on the world. The Old Testament Units focus on the concepts of covenant, prophecy, psalms, and wisdom. Jesus' life and ministry are approached through miracles, parables, and the coming of God's kingdom. The Sacraments are examined in relationship to living out the gospel and creeds, and in Unit IV, Church history refers to the figures, events, and traditions of the Church both throughout history and today.

Background

Themes and the Calendar

The Unit organization of the Episcopal Children's Curriculum allows considerable flexibility for scheduling in local congregations. All sessions within a Unit are undated. Sessions within each Unit develop the thematic focus. There is an explicit connection, however, to the liturgical Church Year in the measured patterns of sessions within Units. Attention to major feast days is balanced with thematic development. In an important way, the Curriculum is seasonally compatible with our liturgy. Calendars for each year are available in the spring. Contact Morehouse or the Center for the Ministry of Teaching to receive one.

Scheduling Units and Sessions

The four Units are most appropriately used during specified Church Seasons. The chart below displays the pattern of seasonal connections for each Unit. Across all years and all age levels of the Curriculum, a clear, consistent pattern of Unit/Session connections to the Church Year has been preserved. Note that examples in the chart below are from the Intermediate Level—Shell Year. The Unit titles are from this Teacher's Guide.

Unit Title Intermediate Shell Year	I Covenant	II Miracles	III Baptism: New Life	IV The Apostle Paul
Church Calendar	Late Weeks after Pentecost	Advent/Christmas/ Epiphany	Lent/Easter	Easter/Early Weeks after Easter
Probable Months	September-November	December-February	February-April	April-May
Session Detail	#1-8—Old Testament Themes #9—All Saints	#1-4—Advent/Christmas #5—Epiphany #6-9—New Testament Themes	#1-5—Sacramental Themes #6-9—Lent, Holy Week Easter	#1-8—Church Themes #9—Pentecost

In order to take advantage of the thematic and liturgical sessions, church school leaders and teachers should plan a schedule that fits both their particular congregation's calendar and the yearly fluctuations in the liturgical calendar. Factors affecting scheduling variations are:
- different starting dates for local church schools
- substitution of other parish activities for church school
- rotation of class sessions with chapel or worship
- the yearly variations in the lectionary cycle that result in an "early" or "late" Easter, that affect the lengths of the periods after the Epiphany and after the Day of Pentecost.

Within any given Unit of nine sessions, some sessions should coordinate with the current Church Year calendar. Other sessions can be more flexibly scheduled. It is expected that users will rearrange the numerical order of sessions within a Unit to accomplish scheduling requirements. Referring to the session patterns in the chart above, consider the scheduling decisions to be made within each Unit.

Unit I—Old Testament Themes. Designed to be used during the period from September (start of church school) through November (but not into

Advent), Unit I coincides with the late Sundays after Pentecost. The nine sessions should be scheduled for use during this time period.

In those places where church school begins the first Sunday in September and meets weekly without interruption until Advent, the first Unit may need to be spread out over 13 or 14 weeks. Enough suggestions are provided in any session outline to make it possible to expand the activities over two class meetings. Teachers can choose which sessions to extend or, if need be, to combine as local needs demand.

Session 9 is always an All Saints' session. Depending on the local schedule, teachers could plan to use this session on the Sunday nearest to All Saints', the week before, or perhaps the week after if no classes are held on that principal feast day. The other eight sessions of the Unit can precede or follow the All Saints' session.

Unit II—New Testament Themes. Sessions 1-4 are for Advent/Christmas and Session 5 is an Epiphany session. Teachers should look at the focus statements for these sessions and match the most appropriate ones with the available dates for class meetings. Many congregations have traditions of plays, pageants, and other seasonal events that take precedence over focused class work at this time of year. Teachers may see a need to combine or compress material from Sessions 1-5.

Sessions 6–9 of Unit II are developed around the theme in the Unit title. These sessions likely will be used during the Epiphany season (January-February). Once again, the calendar can result in a long or short Epiphany season, requiring teachers to adjust sessions accordingly. Another option is to consider "borrowing" the first or second sessions from Unit III.

Unit III—Sacrament Themes. Schedule this Unit for use during Lent, Holy Week, Easter, and for one session into the Easter season. The sacramental focus of each year's material (Shell—Baptism; Chalice—Eucharist; Cross—Worship) is developed fully in Sessions 1-5. The material in Sessions 6–9 extends the year's specific sacramental focus, in connection to the liturgical events surrounding Easter.

Use the outlines related to sacraments in Sessions 1-7 before Easter Day, mainly during the weeks of Lent. Session 8 can be used for classes that meet on Easter Day or the next class meeting. Session 9 is for the early Easter season. Extend, combine, or compress session outlines to fit the calendar for your congregation.

Unit IV—Church Themes. Plan to begin this Unit during the latter weeks of the Easter season and into the weeks after Pentecost. Sessions 1-8 focus on church history and traditions. The themes for this Unit are: Shell Year—Bible; Chalice Year—*The Book of Common Prayer;* Cross Year—*The Hymnal 1982.* Session 9 is always about the Feast of Pentecost. Plan to use it on the most appropriate date for classes, even if it means interrupting the order of the other eight sessions.

The Intermediate Curriculum Materials

The Episcopal Children's Curriculum provides materials for both teachers and students. At each age level of the Curriculum, distinctive materials for students are designed to appeal particularly to that age group. Teachers' materials, while similar in format and function across age levels, reflect the changing characteristics of the classroom situation at each age level. At the Intermediate level, five different pieces of material are available.

For Directors
- Director's Guide

    Provides a comprehensive overview of all levels and years of the curriculum.

For Teachers
- Teacher's Guide (this volume)

    Contains 36 sessions of material organized into the four Units of the year. The Intermediate Shell Year Units are: Unit I. Covenant; Unit II. Miracles; Unit III. Baptism: New Life; and Unit IV. The Apostle Paul. The Teacher's Background includes helpful descriptive material and suggestions for additional resources.
- Supplemental Guide (Intermediate)

    Provides additional activities and alternative approaches for teaching at this age level.
- Teacher's Packet (posters and patterns)

    Offers 24 large sheets of color posters, black-and-white pictures, instructions, and patterns mentioned in the session outlines, this packet is intended as a classroom resource.
- Music Tapes

    Contains all the music for each year recorded by a children's choir.

The Guide, Supplemental Guide, Packet, and Music Tapes are sufficient for an entire year and can be reused. We recommend that congregations have one Teacher's Guide for each teacher along with one Supplemental Guide, one set of Music Tapes, and one Teacher's Packet for each class group.

For Students
- *Covenant Times* (student newspaper—36 issues, one for each session)

    Carries the content for every session. Numerous references are made to material from the newspaper throughout the activity suggestions in each session outline. We strongly recommend that a set of 36 newspapers be purchased for each teacher and made available for each student in the class group. In an attractive, colorful format, each newspaper has a mixture of feature stories, news articles, illustrations, puzzles, memory tasks, Scripture, maps, and more—all tailored to support a particular session. Feature stories are used in the "Introducing the Story" section.
- Symbol Cards (one to correspond to each of the 36 sessions)

    Appeal to students of this age and can be the beginning of a collection. These are small, full-color cards. Each has a symbol illustration, a Scripture verse, and an explanation on the back. They are designed to be collected, shared with parents, and even traded. Across the three years of the Intermediate level, students can accumulate 108 symbol cards.
- Shell Year Treasurebook (one book for the year)

    Serves as a student resource and reference book. Each year's Treasurebook has four parts that correspond to the four Unit themes of that year. Session outlines suggest ways to encourage student reading. The books will also be useful for teachers' preparation.

The student materials are intended to be distributed for personal use by students. As noted above, we consider it helpful for all students to have copies of the newspapers. The set of 36 symbol cards and the Shell Year Treasurebook have the potential to provide important bridges between classroom and family/home. If at all possible, congregations should plan to purchase cards and books to give to each student.

UNDERSTANDING INTERMEDIATE-AGE STUDENTS

Who are the children we teach? The key to understanding intermediate-age students—ages nine, ten, and eleven—lies in a respect for children as individuals. This respect, accompanied by the knowledge of the differences among us, shapes all our efforts as teachers.

Look closely at any group of intermediates, and it is apparent on physical appearances alone that there is considerable diversity in the group. Reflect on the impact of the different social and ethnic backgrounds, economic circumstances, educational opportunities, skills and interests, and it becomes clear that general descriptions do not reflect the variety of social and cultural diversity among children of the same age. Teaching children requires that we see them as individuals. There are, however, many sources of information to help us understand more about students in this age group.

Developmental theory offers insight for teaching. Educators look primarily to such theories for help in understanding the growth and development of children in the areas of physical, emotional, social, moral, and faith development. No single viewpoint is, however, adequate by itself.

Experience of teachers themselves can contribute reliable information, including memories of their own journeys as students and participants in the educational process.

Theory and experience contribute to a multi-dimensional perspective on the lives and learning experiences of children. This blend of insights will be especially helpful in church school settings.

Theory

Developmental theories help us see the expected patterns of change from birth through maturity. All theories of development hold that increasing maturity brings a general increase in the complexity of behavior. Children move from being centered on the self to social interaction with others. Whether or not a theory uses ages or stages, the emphasis is on general expectations. No theory will predict the behavior of an individual child.

Most of the mainstream theories were formulated without particular regard for gender. Today, we have a much greater sensitivity to the differences in development of boys and girls. (See Carol Gilligan, *In a Different Voice.*)

Ages and Stages. Ages are convenient ways of classifying behaviors that change as the student matures. A six-month-old can sit up, a six-year-old can skip, a nine-year-old can throw a ball accurately. With maturity, the range of different behaviors within an age group increases. Many two-year-olds can say a few words, but eleven-year-olds can vary from the ability to speak several languages to functional illiteracy. There are numerous books that describe the physical growth and behaviors of children in this manner.

Thinking. The Swiss psychologist Jean Piaget has helped us understand that children simply do not think in the same way adults think. Using cognitive stages, loosely associated with chronological ages, Piaget has identified the ways of knowing that we pass through from birth (sensory motor learning) through about age eleven (symbolic learning). According to Piaget, children ages nine to eleven are capable of increasingly complex thought processes and are no longer limited by what they can see, hear, or touch. They can think about situations from more than one perspective, deal with several ideas at once, and think across time—past, present, and future.

Around age eleven they begin to think abstractly; that is, they think about thoughts and ideas.

Understanding the ways in which children think is useful for teachers. Cognitive theories, however, do not specify about what we should have children think. Perhaps more importantly, Piaget's stages of knowing do not uniformly apply to children growing up in different socio-cultural environments. Many people feel that the variety of life experiences dramatically change the ages at which the various types of thinking abilities emerge. In relation to teaching in church schools, cognitive functioning has no direct relation to the development of faith. It only helps us understand how children think about the stories we teach.

Social context. During the intermediate years, children increase their social group of family, friends, and community. Personal interests dictate much of what children are likely to do and who they will encounter. Influence on the child moves from the parents to peers and others.

Erik Erikson's work suggests a view of development that interweaves the power of social interaction with ongoing biological maturity. According to Erikson, at each of eight stages of life a psychosocial crisis must be resolved in order for development to proceed normally. The dominant concern of intermediate-age children is that of industry versus inferiority. Children achieve competence as they focus on work that requires skill. It is a period of cooperation, competition, and learning information. All children have gifts to succeed and all have a sense of failure at some point in their development. Helping children to discover their gifts and deal with their struggles of inferiority is a major task of the teacher of this age student.

Lawrence Kohlberg and Carol Gilligan have given us ways to think about the moral development of children. With maturation, experience, and expanding ways of thinking, children and adults approach and resolve moral issues in more complex ways.

Each of these theorists has given us a broader view of the complicated process of development. While none of them specifically addresses the growth of religious thought, their work has been the basis for those theorists who have explored faith development.

New Ways of Approaching the Educational Process

In recent years, researchers have begun to explore the learning process within the classroom. How teachers teach and how students learn have come into a sharper focus.

Learning Styles. Some researchers have concentrated on the different ways individuals take in information and process it in order to learn. Auditory, visual, and kinesthetic learning styles are those most easily identified in classrooms. Auditory learners are those who listen carefully and are better able to retain what they hear. Since this is the dominant teaching style in many classrooms, auditory learners perform well. Visual learners must be able to connect what they are learning either with real pictures or ones they create in their imagination. Pictures and objects that students can see strengthen the educational experience for this type of learner. Kinesthetic learners need to be able to use their bodies to move, touch, or manipulate items related to ideas in order to fully remember what they learn.

All students use some form of all three styles in the early years of learning; later one style becomes more dominant based on school and other experiences. Teaching that incorporates a variety of opportunities to see, hear, and touch will be more successful and enjoyable for both teachers and students.

Multiple Intelligences is another approach to the classroom experience developed by Howard Gardner. Gardner has proposed that humans have eight different ability areas, or intelligences. Since most educational materials and experiences focus on only two, many students are left out of or are not using their potential for learning. Teachers who provide activities that enhance the different intelligences are able to engage more students in the learning process more of the time.

The eight intelligences are Linguistic (Word Smart), Logical-Mathematical (Number Smart), Musical, Visual-Spatial (Picture Smart), Bodily-Kinesthetic (Body Smart), Intrapersonal (Self-Smart), Interpersonal (People Smart), and Natural or (Nature Smart). Each of the intelligences can provide an entry way into the learning experience for different students. Using the biblical story of Noah, linguistic students would write poems; mathematical students could measure the ark and build a scale model; musical students could write a song, visual students would paint pictures, bodily-kinesthetic students would dance the story; interpersonal students would interview each other about the experience of being on the ark, intrapersonal students would reflect on their own feelings about the story and perhaps compose a prayer; and natural students would be concerned about the species of animals that were brought on board.

Using the multiple intelligences in the classroom provides all individuals with an entry point into a particular story. For most classrooms, time and space don't permit all eight intelligences to be in operation at one time. However, keeping the variety of experiences in mind as we plan for teaching and learning can help to make church school more exciting and meaningful for all involved.

Developmental Resources
Ames, Louise Bates & Carol Chase Haber. *Your eight-year-old.* New York: Delacorte Press, 1989.
Ames, Louise Bates & Carol Chase Haber. *Your nine-year-old.* New York: Delacorte Press, 1990.
Ames, Louise Bates, Ilg, Frances L., & Stanley M. Baker. *Your ten to fourteen-year-old.* New York: Delacorte Press, 1988.
Armstrong, Thomas. *Multiple intelligences in the classroom.* Alexandria, VA: Association for Supervision and Curriculum Development, 1994.
Coles, Robert. *The call of stories: Teaching and the moral imagination.* Boston: Houghton Mifflin, 1989.
Coles, Robert. *The moral life of children.* Boston: Atlantic Monthly Press, 1986.
Coles, Robert. *The spiritual life of children.* Boston: Houghton Mifflin, 1990.
Crain, William C. *Theories of development: Concepts and applications.* (3rd ed.) Englewood Cliffs: Prentice-Hall, 1992.
Elkind, David. *The hurried child.* Reading: Addison-Wesley, 1981.
Erikson, Erik H. *Childhood and society.* (2nd ed.) New York: W. W. Norton, 1963.
Gardner, Howard. *Multiple intelligences: the theory in practice.* New York: Basic Books, 1993.

Gilligan, Carol. *In a different voice.* Cambridge: Harvard University Press, 1982.

Hashway, Robert M. *Cognitive styles: a primer to the literature.* San Francisco: EM Text, 1992.

Kuhmerker, Lisa with Uwe Gielen & Richard L. Hayes. *The Kohlberg legacy for the helping professions.* Birmingham: R.E.P., 1991.

Lewis, Anne Chambers. *Learning styles: putting research and common sense into practice.* Arlington, VA: American Association of School Administrators, 1991.

Medrich, Elliott A. et al. *The serious business of growing up: Children's lives outside school.* Berkeley: University of California Press, 1982.

Singer, Dorothy G. & Tracey A. Revenson. *A Piaget primer: How a child thinks.* New York: Plume/New American Library, 1978.

FAITH IN THE CLASSROOM

Faith is a gift from God.
Children are people of faith.

These two premises underscore all that we say and do in church school classrooms. They are also basic to the Children's Charter. It is faith that gives church school its unique mission. We do not teach faith. We hope that our work as teachers will nurture faith in the hearts and minds of our students.

Structure of Faith

Knowing that faith is personal, understanding the structure of faith, and realizing that faith changes over time are important concepts for teachers. Knowledge of the faith process will help teachers interpret the actions and responses of their students.

According to James Fowler's formulation, intermediate-age students are literalists looking primarily to others for the concepts and beliefs of their faith. Another educator, John Westerhoff, uses the image of concentric rings to portray how faith grows and matures within the web of relationships in a faith community. In this model, the beginnings of faith come from meaningful experience and belonging to a faith community.

Content of Faith

Faith derives its content from the Holy Scriptures and the preserved traditions of the Church. Episcopalians also turn to The Baptismal Covenant for guidance on the content of our faith and practice. In this Covenant, the first three questions and responses (the "faith" questions) incorporate belief statements found in the Apostles' Creed. The second part of the Covenant (the five "practice" or "action" questions) lays out standards for a Christian life. At every age, people of faith—children included—share responses to the questions of the Covenant. We have a marvelous opportunity to nurture the faith of intermediate-age students and to strengthen their ties to the Church.

Intermediates and The Baptismal Covenant

By drawing on information from developmental and faith theories and observing children's lives, we can use the questions of The Baptismal Covenant as a structure for a composite description of the faith and practice of a "typical" intermediate-age student.

Faith: Threefold Affirmation

Do you believe in God the Father? Intermediates perceive God as the supreme being and creator. Generally confident in their relationships and competent with their daily tasks, they are more appreciative and less awestruck by God's power than they were in earlier childhood. They have a comfortable "I and Thou" relationship with God.

Do you believe in Jesus Christ, the Son of God? Jesus is known as a teacher, leader, and authority figure. Students of intermediate-age accept Jesus' relationship with God—Son and Father, child and parent—but do not yet fully appreciate the far-reaching theological implications of his divinity and humanity. They know that Jesus was loved and hated, and they can identify the actions and feelings of his friends and disciples. Most are quite interested in the details and facts of Jesus' life and have a sense of the sequence of events in his ministry.

Do you believe in God the Holy Spirit? Images of the dove and the wind are seen as plausible manifestations of the Holy Spirit. For students who are regular participants in a faith community, expressions of personal spirituality may begin through prayer or conversation with trusted adults.

Practice: Five Questions About Living

Will you continue in the apostles' teaching and fellowship, in the breaking of bread, and in the prayers? Regular and full inclusion in the sacramental life and worship of the congregation is essential for intermediate students. Faith is nurtured through interactive participation in the liturgical life of the Church. Their contributions as choir singers, acolytes, junior altar guild members, and ushers are genuinely helpful. To parents and friends they will readily acknowledge ties to their church and communicate a sense of satisfaction from taking part in group activities.

Will you persevere in resisting evil, and, whenever you fall into sin, repent and return to the Lord? Students at this age are aware of right and wrong, fairness and injustice, good and evil. They may be fiercely unyielding regarding the boundaries between any two sides of an issue. Firm judgments about where someone else stands are candidly advanced. Nine-, ten-, and eleven-year-olds are social creatures, engaged in many activities. Hence, the opportunities to offend others arise fairly often. Their words can be vicious, and their actions wounding. Trying something new, making mistakes along the way, and even failing, are a part of gaining new skills. Forgiving and forgiveness are practiced realities among friends and families.

Will you proclaim by word and example the Good News of God in Jesus Christ? Many students this age enjoy reading Bible stories. They are involved with Scripture and can be very active within their local church community. Within this sphere they may be aware of the Christian example of their words and actions.

Will you seek and serve Christ in all persons, loving your neighbor as yourself? Service to others is a feasible option for intermediate-age students. It can be a natural outgrowth of participating in community-wide activities. Their stamina, skills, and social ease combine to make them willing workers. A growing sense of responsibility to others stems from fulfilling commitments for chores, homework, and practicing with teams or performance groups. Best friends, strong group loyalties, and self-sorting into boys' groups and girls' groups characterize this age. These factors will at times set limits on intermediates' ability to embrace all persons with love, as the Covenant requires.

Will you strive for justice and peace among all people, and respect the dignity of every human being? Global awareness is a positive by-product of the television and Internet age. Knowing and seeing people all over the world is the first step. The daily images of people in all parts of the world, the ordinary and the not so ordinary, strengthen students' understanding that people everywhere are more alike than different.

Resources on Faith
Aleshire, Daniel O. *Faithcare.* Philadelphia: Westminster Press, 1988.
Berryman, Jerome W. *Godly play.* San Francisco: Harper & Row, 1991.
Coles, Robert. *The spiritual life of children.* Boston: Houghton Mifflin, 1990.
Dykstra, Craig & Sharon Parks, eds. *Faith development and Fowler.* Birmingham: Religious Education Press, 1986.
Fowler, James W. *Stages of faith.* New York: Harper & Row, 1981.
Hyde, Kenneth E. *Religion in childhood and adolescence.* Birmingham: Religious Education Press, 1990.
Sawyers, Lindell, ed. *Faith and families.* Philadelphia: Geneva Press, 1986.
Stokes, Kenneth. *Faith is a verb.* Mystic: Twenty-Third Publications, 1989.
Westerhoff, John H., III. *Will our children have faith?* New York: Seabury Press, 1976.

Episcopal Resources
The Book of Common Prayer. New York: The Church Hymnal Corporation, 1979.
The Book of Occasional Services. (2nd. ed.) New York: The Church Hymnal Corporation, 1988.
Booty, John E. *What makes us Episcopalians?* Wilton: Morehouse-Barlow, 1982.
Children in the Eucharist. New York: Episcopal Church Center, undated.
Called to teach and learn: A catechetical guide for the Episcopal Church. New York: The Episcopal Church Center, 1994.
The Hymnal 1982. New York: The Church Hymnal Corporation, 1985.
Lesser feasts and fasts. New York: The Church Hymnal Corporation, 1991.
Lift every voice and sing II: An African-American hymnal. New York: The Church Hymnal Corporation, 1993.
Molrine, Charlotte N. & Ronald C. Molrine. *Encountering Christ.* Harrisburg: Morehouse, 2000.
Prichard, Robert W. *History of the Episcopal Church.* Harrisburg: Morehouse, 1991.
Roth, Robert N., & Nancy L. Roth, eds. *We sing of God.* New York: The Church Hymnal Corporation, 1989.
Sydnor, William. *More than words.* San Francisco: Harper & Row, 1990.
The story of Anglicanism: Part 1-Ancient and medieval foundations; Part

2-*Reformation and its consequences; Part 3-Creating a global family.* Westlake Village, CA: Cathedral Films and Video, undated.

The story of the Episcopal Church: Part 1-From Jamestown to Revolution; Part 2-The call to mission. Westlake Village, CA: Cathedral Films and Video, undated.

Wall, John S. *A new dictionary for Episcopalians.* San Francisco: Harper & Row, 1985.

Westerhoff, John H. *A people called Episcopalians.* Atlanta: St Bartholomew's Episcopal Church, 1993.

Wonder, love, and praise: a supplement to The Hymnal, 1982. New York: Church Publishing, 1997.

USING THE CURRICULUM

The three age levels of the Episcopal Children's Curriculum correspond to traditional school groupings for children: Preschool/Kindergarten (ages 3-5); Primary (Grades 1-3); and Intermediate (Grades 4-6). The Curriculum supports both single-grade and broadly graded class groups.

Church schools with small numbers of children may wish to group students of similar ages together in broadly graded classes to correspond to the three levels of the Curriculum. Students could stay in each broadly graded group for three years, progressing through the Shell, Chalice, and Cross year materials for that group. When a student moves into the next age group, another set of Shell, Chalice, and Cross material is offered. While content themes are always a blend of the familiar and the new, no material is ever exactly repeated.

Where numbers and circumstances permit, church schools may be organized into nine single-grade groups (ages three years through Grade 6). In this situation, each class group can be assigned a different level and year of the Curriculum, beginning with Preschool Shell for three-year-old children and ending with Intermediate Cross for Grade 6. As students move through the grades, they will encounter new material each year.

Mixed-Age Groups

For many congregations, the decision about church school groupings cannot always be neatly handled. There may be only a few families with children of church school age. A growing parish or mission may find that the numbers of children are unevenly distributed across age levels, with many preschoolers and only two or three learners in Grades 4-6. Mixed-age groups are a practical necessity in these situations.

When a class group spans one or more age levels of the Curriculum, which level should be used? Consider both the teacher and learners in making the decision. Count and group the learners. The most desirable groupings for mixed ages combine children whose developmental capacities and learning styles are similar. If most are preschool-, primary-, or intermediate-age, purchase the ECC Level that matches the developmental/age level of the majority of the group. If this does not result in a clear-cut decision, consider choosing the Primary Level materials and adapting them for preschoolers and intermediates. Remember that most teachers will find it less complicated to simplify material for younger learners than to locate and design more sophisticated activities for older learners.

Mixed-age groups offer special opportunities as well as challenges for both teachers and learners. Two key concepts for teachers to consider when working with children of varied ages in the same group are:

- **the learners' emerging skills and capabilities**

Students themselves are aware of the varying levels of skill present among the groups to which they belong. Teachers can set the tone in a group by recognizing the value of every learner's effort and contribution. Teachers who praise learners truthfully affirm for children the value of their work. The message to be conveyed is simple: It is quite all right to be growing and trying and learning in different ways.

When teaching, think about how the youngest and oldest within the group handle various activities. Note the wide variations in the students' interests and gifts. With this range in mind, plan varied approaches to the class meetings. Ask: What is likely to have maximum appeal with this particular group?

For example, an art activity may appeal to all ages if there is latitude for process, product, and interpretation. Placemats can provide preschoolers with a canvas for fingerpainting; primary-age learners with a project/product they can take home and use at dinner with their families; and intermediates with a doodle page on which to add symbols, phrases, or pictures they have created.

- **the necessity for family-style social interaction**

Probably the most effective approach for handling group interaction for students of widely varying ages is to assist them in learning to be helpful to one another. At times, older children can assume leadership roles—sharing their skills with younger ones. At other times, they will work individually or rotate personal time with teachers. Give-and-take with siblings and parents provides a familiar and accessible model for managing group living in small, mixed-age groups.

Intergenerational Groups

Under the label Intergenerational Activities, church educators and program planners have rediscovered the virtues of "one-room" education. Potluck suppers, hymn-sings, Pentecost parties, storytimes, movie showings, greening the church, meal preparation for soup kitchens, house repairs, and outings for senior citizens can all invite the participation of people of all ages.

For small congregations, intergenerational activities offer a workable solution to the question of allocating leaders' time and resources, and the sometimes perplexing problems of meeting the needs of varied groups of learners. Large parishes, where age-group numbers dictate closely graded classes, may have to work hard to replicate the cross-age and cross-community linkages that occur naturally in small parishes. Meticulously planned intergenerational activities at regularly scheduled intervals can foster a very desirable sense of community in large parishes.

Celebrations of major feast days and special parish days are most successful when all ages are involved in the activities. The seasonal liturgical plan of the Episcopal Children's Curriculum is compatible with congregational plans for intergenerational celebrations. Within each Unit, the session outlines that are keyed to principal feast days and celebrations contain activity suggestions that can be adapted and incorporated easily into intergenerational programs. Each year's material, at all age levels of the Curriculum, includes one or more sessions targeted for use at particular points in the Church Year: All Saints (1), Advent/Christmas (4), Epiphany (1), Lent/Holy Week (3), Easter (2), and Pentecost (1). See the Intermediate Supplemental Guide for suggestions for intergenerational activities.

Intergenerational Resources
Carey, Diana & Judy Large. *Festivals, family and food*. Gloucestershire, England: Hawthorne Press, 1982.
Griggs, Donald, & Patricia Griggs. *Generations learning together*. Nashville: Abingdon, 1981.
Nelson, Gertrud Mueller. *To dance with God: Family ritual and community celebration*. New York: Paulist Press, 1986.
Westerhoff, John H., III. *A pilgrim people*. San Francisco: Harper & Row, 1984.
White, James W. *Intergenerational religious education*. Birmingham: Religious Education Press, 1988.
Williams, Mel, & Mary Ann Britain. *Christian education in family clusters*. Valley Forge: Judson, 1982.

PLANNING INTERMEDIATE CLASS SESSIONS

Planning sets the stage for teaching and learning. In preparation for meeting with students, teachers need to select a set of activities and then put these activities into an order for each class meeting. The session outlines of the Intermediate level of the Episcopal Children's Curriculum offer three sets of activity categories that can be used to compose a class session. These are:

Teacher Supports—five sections directed at helping teachers prepare

Essential Activities—Gathering, Introducing the Story, and Going Forth are the three core experiences for each session

Optional Activities—about ten different suggestions of activities teachers may choose to do in a given session. No teacher or class is expected to use every optional activity in any session outline. The emphasis is on choice.

The following illustration shows the overall relationship of the Intermediate activities. The three essential activities are shown in **bold** type. Flexibility and adaptability are evident. Time estimates are included to aid in choosing activities to fit class needs. (Teachers who have used either the Preschool/Kindergarten or Primary materials will notice certain similarities in the design of session outlines and specification of session categories.)

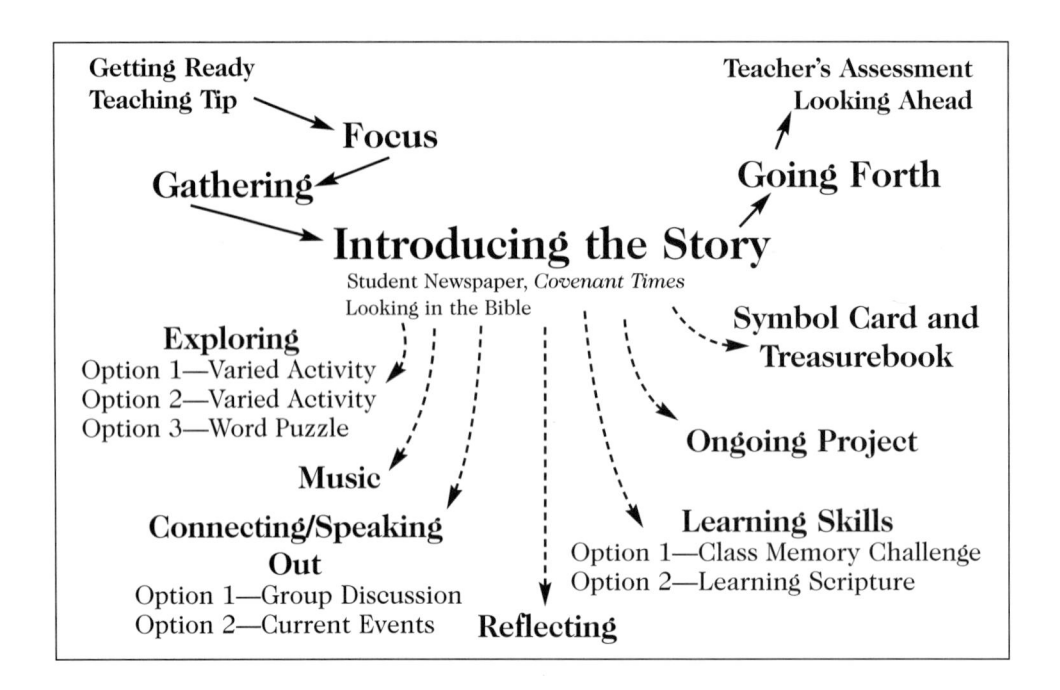

```
        Getting Ready                              Teacher's Assessment
        Teaching Tip                                    Looking Ahead
                        ↘ Focus                         ↗
             Gathering ↙                        Going Forth
                      ↘                             ↗
                        Introducing the Story
                        Student Newspaper, Covenant Times
                        Looking in the Bible
                                              ⋰      Symbol Card and
        Exploring                                    Treasurebook
   Option 1—Varied Activity
   Option 2—Varied Activity
   Option 3—Word Puzzle                              Ongoing Project

                       Music
                                               Learning Skills
       Connecting/Speaking                Option 1—Class Memory Challenge
              Out                         Option 2—Learning Scripture
   Option 1—Group Discussion
   Option 2—Current Events    Reflecting
```

Composing a Session

Church school sessions in congregations across the country vary greatly in length, typically ranging from 20 to 90 minutes or more. The ECC was designed with a "core" of just three essential activities to accommodate this time variation. At the Intermediate level, for example, the core steps are called Gathering, Introducing the Story, and Going Forth. Classes with 20-minute sessions can expect to accomplish these, but not much more. Teachers of classes with longer meeting times may choose from a variety of additional activities offered in each session outline.

The session categories function as the building blocks for planning. There is no single "right" way to plan a class session. Teachers can construct an activity/time schedule for each class session that fits the time available, builds on their own skills, and meets students' needs and interests. Activity blocks for the sessions can be selected and sequenced in a variety of ways. All the examples given below are based on use of the three essential categories.

Illustration 1. A way to proceed when session time is short and time schedules are tight. A different optional activity may be chosen for each session, thus providing a variety of ways over a period of time to examine the session themes.
   Gathering, Introducing the Story, Exploring (Option 1), and Going Forth

Illustration 2. This plan balances active and quiet activities and gives students both directed and imaginative ways to approach themes.
   Gathering, Music, Introducing the Story, Exploring (Option 2), Exploring (Option 3), Reflecting, and Going Forth.

Illustration 3. This is a full class session with a number of different types of activities and a comfortable flow for the session.

Gathering, Introducing the Story (incorporating questions from Connecting/Speaking Out), Exploring (Option 1), Exploring (Option 2), Music, Reflecting, Ongoing Project, Going Forth.

Illustration 4. This two-session plan illustrates how the material from one session outline can be extended over two class meetings. Fluctuations in the Church Year calendar may require teachers to expand or compress the nine sessions of a Unit in order to accommodate the current calendar.

First session. Gathering, Introducing the Story, Exploring (any option), Going Forth.

Second session. Connecting/Speaking Out, Exploring, Ongoing Project, Going Forth.

Centers

One approach to using the options in each session is to arrange the classroom into Learning Centers. Learning Centers are planned activities where all instructions and materials for a specific subject are provided for students to work independently or with others. Intermediate students particularly enjoy this opportunity to work with others and the change from traditional classroom activities. The advantage to Learning Centers is the chance to use more of the activities provided during one time period.

To begin, review the options in the session and choose the ones you think will interest the students with whom you work. Decide on the key concept for each option and ask what the student needs to find out. Design the learning task with clear directions and enticing titles. Choose the number of centers needed for the size of the group. Enough choices should be available to permit the last arriving student to choose among at least three options. Provide a list of the centers for the students to help them keep track of which ones they have completed.

Learning Centers have optimum impact when the class period begins and ends with a group time. Introducing the Story could be followed by time in the centers and a gathering for the Closing activity.

Supplies

The Episcopal Children's Curriculum assumes that teachers will have access to a reasonable variety of standard supplies, including pencils and markers, paper of various kinds, paints, tape and glue, modeling materials, "elegant junk," miscellaneous office supplies, and tools such as scissors and staplers.

Activity suggestions in the session outlines describe the materials needed and how they are to be used for a given activity. A list of materials is provided in the Director's Guide.

TEACHING STRATEGIES AND RESOURCES

Organized church school and other classroom-based activities are indispensable for students. The particular challenge for teachers working with intermediate-age students is to balance the pragmatic requirements of teaching preparation with the swiftly moving reality of classroom activity. Respecting the individuality of students, and honoring their genuine capabilities as leaders means sharing authority and tolerating flexibility. What does it mean to be a teacher in a church school classroom for intermediates?

Teacher and Student Roles

Five broad areas of competency characterize teachers in the Church. A summary of these universal functions follows, with descriptions tailored specifically to the nuances of classroom situations.

Teachers orchestrate learning. *Students are dependent on teachers for the provision of materials, sufficient opportunities for choices, and orderly management of learning situations.*

In the classroom, the teacher sets the stage. Teachers are responsible for preparing themselves, the room, the materials, and the session plans. Clearly, there is an element of control in this function of a teacher, but with preparation, planning, and structure comes the freedom to focus on students.

Teachers facilitate classroom activities through interactive planning with students. Intermediate-age students will be able to exercise leadership roles in choosing and implementing projects. Students' interests will strongly affect the direction of discussions.

Teachers understand their students. *Students deserve attention, affirming experiences, and reasonable challenges.* To nurture and guide the faith journey of another person demands a personal relationship. Bonds of trust, respect, and affection grow when caring and understanding prevail.

Appropriate sources of information for teachers of intermediate-age students include developmental theory, thoughtful observation of local community culture, sensitive appraisal of popular trends, and a sympathetic openness to each child.

Teachers are interpreters. *Students can expect honest answers to their questions— including the response, "I don't know."* In classroom situations, what students talk about, question, explore, and wonder about reflects their teachers' ability to mediate and interpret faith and heritage. Often the simplest of questions can evoke profound discussion.

Intermediate-age students can be intensely interested in wrestling with ethical issues. As teachers and students engage in conversations of faith, they are sharing feelings and values as well as words and facts. In a very real sense, teachers expose their beliefs when they engage in conversation with learners.

Intermediates' increasing skills enable them to be critical thinkers, although most still work best with concrete ideas. They are many-sided thinkers, able to handle dimensions, perspectives, possibilities, and conditions. Teachers have a responsibility to be equally open and flexible.

Teachers are links with the Christian community. *Students come to know and trust a community of adults.* Fourth, fifth, and sixth graders spend much of their time with peers who are a dominant force in their lives. Parents, other family members, and neighbors increasingly occupy a background role. Teachers function as a bridge between the familiar early childhood world of home and family and the allure of various church, school, and community groups.

Teaching in church school is an opportunity to make an enduring friendship with a group of boys and girls. It is a chance to cross generations in friendship and meet the friends of one's own children. Having taught a group of children, a teacher can continue to observe their growth and involvement in the church. Over the years, students can come to know and be known by an ever-increasing number of adult members of the congregation.

Teachers are part of a team of ministers. *Students' experiences will include many teachers in many different settings.* Teachers, especially volunteers in church schools, may work in teams to share time and talents. Teachers also work in partnership with parents, clergy, and church staff in helping to guide the faith journeys of students. The perspective of a teaching team is not confined to what happens in a particular classroom, but includes all the programs and events in the church. Teachers, therefore, do not work alone or in a vacuum.

Adults make church school happen. Critical decisions on time, schedule, budget, space, and program policy define the Christian education classroom-based program in a local congregation. When teachers work with students they are transmitting the particular vision of a particular congregation. Meaningful classroom experiences are most likely to occur when intermediate-age students are included in congregational worship and programs. They can serve as acolytes, ushers, choir members, bellringers, and in other capacities. Full participation in the congregation sets the stage for classroom-based explanations.

Teaching Resources

Bowman, Locke E., Jr. *Teaching for Christian hearts, souls, and minds.* San Francisco: Harper & Row, 1990.

Cohen, Elizabeth G. *Designing groupwork: Strategies for the heterogeneous classroom.* New York: Teachers College Press, 1986.

Furnish, Dorothy Jean. *Experiencing the Bible with children.* Nashville: Abingdon, 1990.

Gobbel, A. Roger & Gertrude G. Gobbel. *The Bible: A child's playground.* Philadelphia: Fortress, 1986.

Katz, Lilian G. & Sylvia C. Chard. *Engaging children's minds: The project approach.* Norwood: Ablex, 1989.

Harris, Maria. *Teaching and religious imagination.* San Francisco: Harper & Row, 1987.

Pritchard, Gretchen Wolff. *Offering the Gospel to children.* Boston: Cowley, 1992.

Ratcliff, Donald E., ed. *Handbook of children's religious education.* Birmingham: Religious Education Press, 1992.

STRATEGIES FOR ESSENTIAL CATEGORIES

Gathering Introducing the Story Going Forth

These three categories are the core experiences of the Episcopal Children's Curriculum at the Intermediate level. The conceptual integrity of the Curriculum is best preserved by consistent use of these core experiences.

Throughout all levels of the Curriculum, students are introduced to and given opportunities for practical rehearsal of the words and actions of the church. Teachers come to appreciate the combined power of *ritual* and *word* as they pursue the goals of awakening and nurturing faith in young students.

Gathering

Planned in two parts to provide a dependable structure to begin each session, the initial *Gathering* activities are orderly, brief, and designed to entice the interest of the group. When all students are present, the group deliberately shifts to a more formal mode for an opening ritual. The teacher leads the group in prayer using a designated Collect from *The Book of Common Prayer*. A student lector then introduces and reads a Scripture selection (NRSV) keyed to the session theme. This two-step process of *Gathering* follows our congregational pattern of coming together for worship and hearing the Word.

The goal of the *Gathering* activity is to make holy the coming together of teachers and students. We acknowledge that when Christians are together, it is a special time. Teachers will find that their confidence grows through the use of *Gathering* rituals and may be surprised at the energy with which students enter into such activities.

Hospitality and welcome. Teachers should view the *Gathering* activity as an occasion for offering hospitality and conversation. Words and gestures can communicate a sense of welcome and pleasure at being in this particular company. This opening informal time is prime time for "community-building." At every session, use students' names, introduce and re-introduce them, and inquire about activities and events in their lives. Try to connect students with one another just as a good host/hostess would do at a party. Do not assume that all students share the same neighborhoods and schools. Best friend pairs and tightly knit groups will be more inclusive of others when their teacher models hospitality.

Since all groups require time to gather slowly or quickly reaching the expected class size, the first part of the *Gathering* is an activity that anticipates in modest form the theme of the session. This activity helps students "settle in" and encourages students' interest and involvement.

Participation. Praying and hearing the Word are central components of our worship. The second, more formal part of the *Gathering* activity for intermediates provides for direct involvement of students. The teacher calls the group to prayer saying, "Let us pray." A relevant Collect from *The Book of Common Prayer,* or other appropriate prayer is used. (In time, older students may choose to take turns at calling the group to prayer and reading the selected Collect.) Next, a "student lector" reads from the Bible. The suggested Collect and the NRSV version of the suggested passage appear in the Teacher's Guide in every session outline.

Teachers can take some simple steps to enhance an attitude of reverence at the *Gathering.* Consider obtaining a special "class Bible" to be used for the readings. Mark the reading each week with a ribbon, direct the reader to a particular spot in the room, and post responses on large paper until all have memorized the words. Teachers should expect that fourth- through sixth- grade students will vary in their ability (or desire) to read aloud. Respect students' feelings. Ask for volunteers, or provide support with paired readings if necessary. In some situations it may be possible to schedule "student lectors" several sessions ahead, giving them ample time to practice. Encourage students to regard these class readings as a privilege. Perfection is not the only acceptable result; teachers should make it clear that all worthy efforts are to be praised.

Introducing the Story

This is the heart of the session for teachers and students. The goal is to engage the students' interest in the story. Students are asked to locate key passages in the Bible and respond critically to questions. This provides the group a communal base of information for subsequent session activities. The expectation is that both teachers and students will be mutually engaged with the material during this time. Each session outline proposes a creative strategy for teachers and students to employ. Practical suggestions are offered, including interactive storytelling, role plays and dramas, guided discussions, group interviews, reports, projects, and presentations. Articles and illustrations in the student newspaper, *Covenant Times,* are considered indispensable for this work. Wherever possible, all students and teachers should have their own copies of each session's issue. All subsequent, optional activity categories are keyed to both the Focus statement and the material explored in *Introducing the Story.*

Covenant Times, the Shell Year Intermediate student newspaper, helps students to examine the stories or concepts introduced in the sessions in a fresh way. The stories are written as if reporters had interviewed the participants directly. Issues or other significant information are presented for the student to think about and explore. Memory Challenges include the *Venite, Psalm 121,* the Summary of the Law, Saints and Seasons, and people and events from Church history. There are also opportunities for learning Scripture verses. A puzzle that reinforces the vocabulary for the theme is included. Original artwork, maps, and diagrams are used to enhance the students' understanding.

The colorful, attractive design of the paper is matched to students' interests and reading levels. The newspapers serve as an important bridge linking church school classroom and family activities. It is beneficial for all students working with the ECC to have copies of the newspaper. Activities frequently refer to material from the newspaper.

Activity suggestions for *Introducing the Story* assume that teachers and students will interact with one another. Consider each session's suggestion not as a fixed recipe for what to do but as a set of ingredients to prepare and set out. Prepare yourself, prepare your classroom, and expect the students to produce a dynamic, spirited exchange of views and roles.

Consider very carefully how to proceed. Either begin with the content or with students' experiences. This fundamental strategy decision will determine the shape of the learning experience for students and teachers. Use these two strategies as patterns of working.

Telling. The emphasis is on the content, or subject matter, of the session. The most familiar approach is for teachers to "tell" students about the subject, emphasizing the important details. Telling does not always mean the teacher lectures and students listen. Clever telling strategies might involve illustrations, dramas, and conversations. Teachers are responsible for identifying the scope of content. Students follow with questions. Projects and activities allow them to explore and create as they examine and apply the content to their daily experiences. This deductive strategy is efficient and precisely targeted. It begins at a specific point and ends by opening out to broader involvement.

Discovering. Students begin to approach the session's content through observation and investigation. Inquiry, speculation, and experimentation characterize these early activities. With guidelines and teacher support, the students look for ways to generalize and to form tentative conclusions. Together, students and teachers narrow their efforts to focus on the "key" discovery. This inductive strategy is free-formed and casts a wide net. It begins with an array of data and ends by clarifying a specific idea.

Teachers and students reinvent the learning process in every encounter. Teachers will find it helpful to visualize the shape of the process, selecting those "moves" and "resources" that seem best for their particular students.

STORYTELLING

Storytelling is a principal action in the teaching ministry. As part of the *Introducing the Story* activities at the Intermediate level, teachers will frequently employ storytelling techniques as a means of weaving together presentations and discussions. Indispensable ingredients for effective storytelling are:

- *Inviting your listeners.* Suspend ordinary time and enter a special place together. Consider the setting—the gathering place, the mood—the sights and smells, and the expectations—the invitation to open the imagination and join together on a story journey.
- *Knowing the facts and order of a story.* Storytellers shape their stories, pacing and punctuating to captivate their listeners. Imagine a shape for every story, and let that shape guide the telling. Listeners expect a beginning, a middle, and an end.
- *Describing people, places, and events from the "eye" of your imagination.* As the story unfolds, describe these details so that the listeners will "see" them just as you do: faces, ways of speaking, clothing, towns, roads, interiors of houses, and the like.
- *Capturing the climax or high point of an event in words that evoke a response from listeners.* Consider gestures and facial expressions that will best serve your intent. Convey reactions of joy, sorrow, surprise, or disappointment with specially chosen words and phrases.

Knowledge of the Bible. Session outlines give an orderly presentation of thematic material, noting highlights to emphasize. Teachers are urged to read the Bible. Storytellers share their personal beliefs and understandings in the process; this sharing is what makes stories such a powerful tool for transmitting the Christian heritage. Biblical stories last for a lifetime, and are truly multi-generational. The students in your class will hear them again and again, listening with new awareness and broader life experience each time.

Presentation/Storytelling Resources

Bausch, William J. *Storytelling: Imagination and faith.* Mystic: Twenty-Third Publications, 1984.
Griggs, Patricia. *Using storytelling in Christian education.* Nashville: Abingdon Press, 1981.
Maguire, Jack. *Creative storytelling.* New York: McGraw-Hill, 1985.
Mellon, Nancy. *Storytelling and the art of imagination.* Rockport: Element, 1992.
Moore, Robin. *Awakening the hidden storyteller.* Boston: Shambhala, 1991.
Russell, Joseph P. *Sharing our Biblical story.* Rev. Ed. Wilton: Morehouse-Barlow, 1988.
Ward, Elaine M. *The art of storytelling.* Brea: Educational Ministries, 1990.

Bible Study Resources for Adults

Bach, Alice & Cheryl J. Exum. *Miriam's well: Stories about women in the Bible.* New York: Delacorte, 1991.

Bach, Alice & Cheryl J. Exum. *Moses' ark.* New York: Delacorte, 1989
Brownrigg, Ronald. *Who's who in the New Testament.* New York: Oxford University Press, 1993.
Charpentier, Etienne. *How to read the New Testament.* New York: Crossroad, 1989.
Charpentier, Etienne. *How to read the Old Testament.* New York: Crossroad, 1989.
Comay, Joan. *Who's who in the Old Testament.* New York: Oxford University Press, 1993.
Donovan, John Britt. *The family book of Bible stories.* Wilton: Morehouse, 1986.
Heller, Marc. *Does God have a big toe?* New York: HarperCollins, 1989.
Jesus and His times. Pleasantville: Reader's Digest Association, 1987.
Roberts, Jenny. *Bible facts.* New York: Dorset Press, 1990.
Sayers, Dorothy L. *The man born to be king.* London: Victor Gollangz Ltd., 1969.
Teringo, J. Robert. *The land and people Jesus knew.* Minneapolis: Bethany House, 1985.
Williams, Michael E., series ed. *The storyteller's companion to the Bible (Multi-volume series).* Nashville: Abingdon, 1992-1995.
Woodrow, Martin & Sanders, E. P. *People from the Bible.* Wilton: Morehouse Publishing, 1987.

Going Forth

For each Unit, a selection from the Prayers of the People in *The Book of Common Prayer* is used for the closing. *Going Forth* is a ritual closing to mark the end of time teachers and students spend together. Students are given an opportunity to add their own prayers, petitions, or intercessions at this time. Occasionally, a prayer of intercession or thanksgiving from one of the activities may also be added. This simple dismissal models the conclusion of our Episcopal worship, signifying the fact that it is time to leave this place of explanation and exploration and re-enter the world as practicing Christians.

Without careful attention, class sessions usually end in a swirl of chaos as students and their parents race to get coats, find take-home items, and leave quickly for services or home. A concluding ritual will help to provide a transition away from the classroom activity. Be deliberate about taking time for *Going Forth,* if necessary scheduling the closing ritual slightly before the actual time for leave-taking. Strive to make the Closing unhurried and reverent in tone.

Following the prayer suggested for the Unit, the dismissal is the familiar "Let us go forth in the name of Christ," to which the learners respond, "Thanks be to God."

OPTIONAL SESSION CATEGORIES: ACTIVITIES AND RESOURCES

Exploring

This category offers three distinct options for students to become actively involved with the content presented in *Introducing the Story.* Suggested activities include art, drama, projects, and games for full group activities, individual projects, and word puzzles for independent or group use. All the activity options are self-contained, with no expectation of carryover into the next session. Access to standard supplies is assumed. Some patterns, diagrams, or instructions are included in the Teacher's Packet. The time estimates given in the Curriculum may need to be adjusted to reflect the work habits of particular classes.

These are guided opportunities to "do" something with the session content. The wide range of options is intended to help students experience the ideas and facts of the session in a variety of ways. Some of us learn best by looking, some of us by hearing, and some of us by doing. Play—the serious, yet magical business of making experiences our very own—is a necessary ingredient for learning at every age. We play with ideas, we role play feelings, and we can display responses. Still able to be captivated by the sensory pleasures of play, intermediates are readily engaged by art materials, costumes, and games.

What distinguishes activities for intermediates is the critical role language plays. Speaking, reading, and writing are genuine tools for exploring. This age group will take great satisfaction from group efforts as well as individual work.

Group Activities. The group is of utmost importance to intermediates. Belonging, being recognized as a group member, and knowing others are highly desirable social achievements. Teachers should recognize that group activity suggestions, for some students, may simply provide a common purpose, a good excuse for a group to form and work together. The activity needs to be relevant, but an equally compelling goal is building community among class members. Seek ways for students to assume responsibility for setting up, choosing alternatives or devising adaptations of an idea, supporting the ongoing work, and cleaning up after activities. Teachers can invite intermediates to be part of the planning and preparation in very real ways. Facilitate conversation during the activity. (Consider incorporating the conversation suggestions in *Connecting/Speaking Out.*) Observe how comfortably students relate to and work with one another. Use smaller groupings to ease shyness or defuse negative behaviors.

Individual Activities. Art projects and impressionistic activities are offered in many sessions. While the description presumes that students will work singly, teachers could adapt the suggestions for group work. Needed supplies are described; teachers are encouraged to substitute whatever available materials they deem suitable.

Every suggested activity has a purpose and an explicit link to the themes presented earlier in the session. Encourage students to explore these connections through conversation and reflection at the start of the activity. Invite students to offer comments and thoughts as they work. When appropriate, provide a way for students to share their work.

Teachers can expect a very wide range of artistic ability among intermediate-age students. Meticulously detailed work will co-exist with passionate strokes of line and color. Students may be eager to speak about their efforts, or quite willing to write explanations about their work. For intermediates, thinking and talking about what has been expressed is an integral part of the act of creating.

Word Puzzles. The vocabulary of our faith can be encountered in print as well as in speaking. Many intermediate-age students enjoy working with words and ideas. They have the opportunity to think about concepts such as prophecy, justice, teaching, community, thanksgiving, names such as Isaiah, John the Baptist, Mary Magdalene, places such as Bethlehem and Jerusalem, and key events of Jesus' life: baptism, the Last Supper, footwashing, crucifixion, resurrection, ascension, or words such as these from *The Book of Common Prayer:* Liturgy, Morning Prayer, and Eucharist.

The student newspaper, *Covenant Times,* includes a word puzzle in every issue (typically appearing on the back page). The puzzles may be crosswords, word searches, word scrambles, acrostics, fill-in-the-blank, etc. Each puzzle has been created to highlight words representing key concepts or facts of the session.

Puzzles can be done in class independently, in pairs, or as a total group activity, another option is to allow students to do the puzzles at home with family members. Teachers may establish a routine method for inserting the puzzle activity into class sessions or vary its use session by session.

> **Music**
>
> The Episcopal Children's Curriculum introduces students to music that is part of our Episcopal heritage. The chosen hymns are consistent with session themes and/or the Church calendar. Hymns selected for emphasis in the Curriculum are ones students are likely to hear and sing in their corporate worship with their congregations. All appear in *The Hymnal 1982* and on the tape *Children Sing!* for the Intermediate Shell Year. (Many can also be found in *We Sing of God*, a children's hymnal with Teacher's Guide available from Church Publishing.) In each session outline, brief suggestions are offered for introducing and singing the hymns or exploring aspects of the hymns' texts through projects and discussion.

Music is an elemental part of the language of faith. Consider the full meaning of the oft-quoted phrase, "Those who sing, pray twice."

We are blessed in the Episcopal Church with a wealth of great music as part of our liturgical tradition. *The Hymnal 1982* includes service music and hymns for congregational singing. The texts and settings are drawn from ancient and contemporary sources from around the world.

Appreciation and familiarity with this music is an uncomplicated, worthwhile goal for Christian education.

Intermediates and music. At this age level, it is likely that students will have had prior exposure to music in schools. They are capable of learning the words, the rhythmic structure, and the melody of a hymn or song. As singers, they can imitate and echo what they hear. In addition, many intermediates will be interested in reading music. Many will be highly motivated, enjoy performing, and achieve remarkable success during these years of musical study.

Pre-adolescents are big consumers of cassettes, compact discs, and music videos. These are also the years of judgments about personal musical abilities, exemplified by comments such as "I'm not a good singer." Even those who enjoy music may not fully participate because of peer pressure.

Music at church. Suggest to those who plan the liturgy that they include one or more of the hymns selected for emphasis during a Unit in worship services that the students attend. This may be easier with the seasonal hymn selections. (See the session plans for selected hymns.)

How can a "non-singing" teacher incorporate music in a group's classroom activities? The answer is two parts attitude and one part strategy. For attitude: Express your feelings in words and actions about the value of music, along with your pleasure in making music. For strategy: Get help from your students and musicians in the congregation. A few specific tips:

- Remember that the line can be very blurred between singing, chanting, and saying the words of a hymn. It is not necessary to "sing a solo" to introduce a hymn in class. Saying words with feeling also communicates powerfully.
- If a hymn tune is unfamiliar, ask for help from a musician. Listen to the

tape available for the Cross Intermediate Year entitled *Children Sing!* Play it at home or in the car as you go about your daily activities. Let the tune creep into your memory. Share this recording with the class.

• Use some kind of "body language" to help you memorize words and rhythm. Working phrase by phrase, clap or tap the beat, or swing and sway with the words. Even with familiar hymns, this technique will entice you more fully into the music.

• Solicit help from your students. Maybe you have a "song leader"—someone who can start on pitch and carry a tune. Do you have anyone who plays an instrument? Affirm these skills and nurture student leadership.

• Pay close attention to the social interaction within your class, and the general atmosphere. With music activities, initially, try to match the emotional dynamic. For example, in a class of socially cohesive, eager talkers invite everyone to chant the words and clap the rhythm. Solicit discussion about the text. If yours is a quiet class, hesitant and wary, let the music surround them first. Play recordings, read the text silently, softly whisper the words or tap the rhythm.

Music Resources. If at all possible, arrange to have a sufficient number of copies of *The Hymnal 1982* available for class use as well as one music cassette of *Children Sing!* for the Intermediate Shell Year. The Church Hymnal Corporation has published a set of companion volumes to the hymnal that are designed for children's worship. The paperback hymnal, *We Sing of God: A Hymnal for Children* contains selected stanzas and refrains of hymns. A separate volume, *We Sing of God: Teacher's Guide* is a compendium of creative activity suggestions keyed to each hymn. Editors Robert and Nancy Roth share insight gained from their many years of singing with children.

Connecting/Speaking Out

Conversation is sparked by good questions. Two approaches to conversation are included in this category. **Option 1, Group Discussion,** proposes questions intended to elicit students' opinions about the session's theme, the people, events, symbols, and concepts. **Option 2, Current Events,** proposes questions aimed at helping students make connections between the themes of the session and their daily lives. Teachers may use either option singly or combined with another selected activity.

One insightful definition of teaching states that it is purposeful conversation. Throughout any classroom encounter, teachers and students should trade turns talking and listening. Within this framework, students may come to understand prayer itself as a conversation with God.

We need not hesitate to use the words of our faith with students. "Teachers in the church are aware that they must provide bridges between the Word of God (known to us in Jesus Christ, the Bible, and the Church) and the everyday life of learners." (The ECC Foundation Paper, 1990.) Throughout this Teacher's Guide, stress is laid on the importance of language and the need for language to be part of the transaction between teacher and learner.

Embedded in Scripture and liturgy, history, and tradition, the language and vocabulary of faith become part of our common experience.

Teachers use language to label, interpret, and convey meaning. The vocabulary of faith, the words students have available with which to talk about their faith, grows in direct relationship to exposure and practice. To teach the stories of our faith requires language.

Teachers can ask themselves, "Do we have an adequate command of the vocabulary of our faith tradition? Are we comfortable in using the language of Scripture and the Church in our teaching ministry?"

Intermediate-age students can be good conversationalists. Conversation is an elemental part of the nurture of faith for young students. The lively dynamic of conversation includes both speaking and listening. Through speaking and listening, the participants in a conversation use language to create a relationship within which one's thoughts, feelings, and values can be shared.

Some observations on conversation for intermediate-age students:

- The pattern of moves in intermediates' conversation is almost always a mutual duet; I talk and you listen, you talk and I listen; I talk and you listen, etc.
- The "pregnant pause" as someone gets ready to speak, and the silence of an active "inner conversation," are respected and occur routinely.
- Conversations are multi-directional. Students will talk directly to each other (listening to and commenting on each other's thoughts), perhaps temporarily bypassing any adults.
- Students expect conversation to be interactive. Good conversationalists talk *with* others, not *at* them.
- Conversation is purposeful.

Schedule class conversation time to minimize interruptions. For example, it is tough to start a discussion if class is over in five minutes and students are starting to get itchy about getting their things, meeting their families, and leaving. Plan sufficient time to allow the group to wait comfortably. Avoid pressing for pauses and silences to flow into words. Plan to "talk" in a location where all members of the group can easily make eye contact with and hear one another. Sitting in a circle or dividing a large group into several smaller groups are good strategies.

Intermediates need more than props or pictures to provide a sense of purpose for their conversations (although these can be helpful at times). Express through your voice a sense of invitation and welcome as you request students to join the conversation. Then invite student contributions almost immediately. Weave the purpose of the conversation into the early questions rather than announcing it like a master of ceremonies.

Another strategy for conversation is to tuck in the talking around activities. Working together on a project creates an encouraging mood for spontaneous conversation. Moments of cooperation are ripe for starting conversations.

Reflecting

Activity suggestions are fashioned to furnish a quiet time for students to make a personal, and perhaps private, response to material presented in the session. Students' responses may take the form of a journal entry, a prayer, an artistic response, or meditative thoughts. Each Unit follows a particular approach through its nine sessions. Sturdy envelopes, called, "Reflection Collections," are suggested to preserve students' work. Reflecting could be a regularly planned activity or an occasional exercise.

Without imagination, learning may be reduced to sets of facts and fixed meanings. Students gain immeasurably from the opportunity

> to wonder and to wish . . .
>   to muse and to mull . . .
>   to puzzle and to probe . . .
>   to contemplate and to cogitate . . .
>   to speculate and to surmise . . .

Through private and personal reflection, students can "move into" a scene or "play with" an idea, engaging in quiet, inner conversation.

Reflecting suggestions provide guidance for teachers to kindle students' thoughts through absorbing descriptions, intriguing questions, conditional statements, or soothing, sensory-based meditations.

Teachers can consider following a three-stage process: a peaceful beginning, an engrossing reflection, and a gently guided closure.

In each Unit, various types of responses are suggested—writing, drawing, just thinking. Materials needed for students' responses should be set out *before* the guided portion of the reflection activity.

Pay careful attention to preserving and protecting the privacy of students' responses. This will communicate the intimate, absorbing possibilities of reflecting activities. Use large sturdy envelopes with clasps, accordion file folders, boxes, portfolio folders, and the like. The idea is to have something for each student that can be easily stored between sessions, and that offers some type of secure fastening for privacy. These "Reflection Collections" can be sent home at the end of each Unit or the year.

Learning Skills

The Bible, *The Book of Common Prayer*, and *The Hymnal 1982* are important books for Episcopalians. Bible study is integrated into session activities throughout the Curriculum. The options in this category are designed to focus on particular skills and understandings which will be most beneficial for students using these great books. *Option 1, Class Memory Challenge*, presents suggestions for memorizing material suitable for a lifetime of practical use. *Option 2, Learning Scripture*, presents selected verses related to the session themes for individual students to commit to memory over the course of the Unit.

In Proper 28, we pray: "Blessed Lord, who has caused all holy Scriptures to be written for our learning: Grant us . . . to hear them, read them, mark, learn, and inwardly digest them . . . ." (BCP, p. 236)

Intermediate-age students need some sense of how the Bible came to be. They are now able to grasp the historical time-frame for the events in the Old and New Testaments. Teachers need to speak aloud of their love of the Bible, articulating clearly that it is a treasure for us. Similarly, students can be expected to explain in their own words what the Bible and other books of our faith mean to them personally. The *Treasurebooks*, which accompany each year of the ECC Intermediate level, are written to convey a sense of the value Episcopalians place on the Bible, the Prayer Book, and the Hymnal.

Bible study is integrated into the essential activities of every session. Reading from the Bible, locating Scriptures, and interpreting passages are part of virtually every session's *Gathering* (a student lector reads a passage) and *Introducing the Story* (students locate passages and respond to questions). Throughout the Curriculum, material from *The Book of Common Prayer* and *The Hymnal 1982* is incorporated into the optional activities within each session, or in some cases, may be used at *Gathering* or as part of *Introducing the Story*.

The category Learning Skills focuses explicitly on memory skills. Skill expectations include:
- Bible—names and order of the 66 books, how to use appendices, and maps
- Prayer Book—names and location of the various offices, collects, sacramental liturgies, other services, prayers and thanksgivings, psalter, and other material
- Hymnal—location and types of service music, the sequence in which hymns appear, and the several indices for the book

At the Intermediate level of the Curriculum, Scripture passages have been taken from the New Revised Standard Version (NRSV) of the Bible. This translation offers the most contemporary language of any, and is likely to be what many students will hear as part of their congregational worship. Teachers should feel free to substitute other approved versions.

Memory Work

Now is a great time for memory work. Intermediate-age students are capable learners, eager to acquire skills that will extend their competence. Many are beginning to participate fully in the worship and community life of their local congregation. Many are enthusiastic attenders of various organized Christian education programs. Students are hearing and saying the texts of our faith from the Bible, *The Book of Common Prayer*, and *The Hymnal 1982* in worship and the classroom. Memorizing some of these texts is a natural next step.

The Episcopal Children's Curriculum, at the Intermediate level, introduces two types of memory tasks for students. In the category *Learning Skills: Option 1. Class Memory Challenge* students are offered four memory tasks—one for each Unit. For the Shell Year these are: Unit I—books of the Old Testament, Unit II—outline of the Gospels' content and the location of key passages, Unit III—Baptismal Covenant, and Unit IV—books of the New Testament. These are all items that will be useful now and in the future. Suggestions in each session include tips for helping students learn the material and ways to recognize those who have done so. This is a Class Memory Challenge, designed to be used as a total group activity.

A second, individual memory option is provided in *Option 2. Learning Scripture*. Inspirational Scripture verses were selected from each session's theme for students to memorize. One of these appears on the session symbol card. Instructions are provided in the session outlines to guide teachers in managing this project. Support material for both the *Class Memory Challenge* and *Learning Scripture* appears in each issue of the student newspaper, *Covenant Times*.

Ongoing Project

Explicitly intended to carry over from session to session, a cumulative class project offers students and teachers the opportunity for continuity and review across the Unit sessions. Typically, these continuing projects lend themselves to display or sharing with the entire congregation.

Each session in the Episcopal Children's Curriculum is designed to be discrete and self-contained.

Yet for intermediate-age students in particular, there are excellent reasons for entertaining the possibility of an *Ongoing Project*. Students can become interested in a theme and handle complex projects. Cooperation among class members heightens the possibility that those who may have

Background

missed a session will still know what happened. Also, during some Units, or some seasons of the Church Year, students' attendance may be predictably steady. Of greatest significance, however, is the potential of substantial ongoing projects to tap the talent of intermediates. They can organize, plan, and carry out these projects. Let the group help to solve any problems of space, storage, or participation.

An ongoing project can also be used at the *Gathering* in each session. A classroom display of the previous pieces of the project can provide a quick review of previous sessions' themes.

Projects of the scope and scale suggested in this category offer an opportunity to reach out to the congregation. In the Shell Year of the Intermediate level, suggested projects include a biblical time line (Unit I), a series of billboards designed around a spiritual theme (Unit II, Sessions 1–5), pictures of Jesus' deeds of power (Unit II, Sessions 6–9), an exhibit of items connected to Holy Baptism (Unit III), and a series of travel posters for cities connected with the apostle Paul (Unit IV).

Teachers interested in using an ongoing project are advised to read through the descriptions for all nine sessions of the Unit. After the first, fully detailed description, each session's outline suggests a small piece of the project that teachers could reasonably be expected to accomplish in one session. If circumstances do not permit work on the ongoing project at every session, teachers could combine one or two of the small steps later. Similarly, the ongoing project can be started or stopped at several points.

Symbol Cards

One of the developmental milestones for intermediate-age students is their ability to understand symbols. Symbols are included in sessions throughout the Intermediate level of the Curriculum. Each session of the ECC is accompanied by a small, collectible card that includes an illustration of a Christian symbol, an explanation, and a Scripture passage.

Teachers are encouraged to devise appropriate ways to include the cards as part of their class activities. Cards can be used to conclude the session, handed out as part of the Going Forth activities. Cards can be used to stimulate conversation, as references for art projects, or simply cherished as a gift from the church to each student. Symbol Cards, the *Treasurebook*, and *Covenant Times* are concrete and desirable links between home and church.

Treasurebook

Intended for guided, independent reading, the *Treasurebook* provides support for the four Units. Intermediate students can read on their own to learn more about their faith.

In the *Shell Year Treasurebook*, students can examine the treasures of God's covenant with God's people (Unit I), investigate the miracles of Jesus (Unit II), explore aspects of the service of Holy Baptism (Unit III), and learn about the conversion of apostle Paul and his missionary journeys (Unit IV).

At the end of the session, along with the symbol card description, a suggestion is given to guide students' independent reading, along with a question for students to think about. Teachers are encouraged to read appropriate *Treasurebook* sections as part of their personal preparation in *Getting Ready*.

Resource and Reference Books

A book about Jesus. New York: American Bible Society, 1991.

A few who dared to trust God. New York: American Bible Society, 1990.

Aaseng, Rolf E. (Annegert Fuchshuber, illus.) *Augsburg story Bible.* Minneapolis: Augsburg, 1992.

An illustrated history of the Church. (Ten volume series). Minneapolis: Winston Press, 1980.

Batchelor, Mary. *The children's Bible in 365 stories.* Batavia: Lion Publishing, 1985.

Beguerie, Philippe, & Claude Duchesneau. *How to understand the sacraments.* New York: Crossroad, 1991.

Bible for today's family: New Testament. New York: American Bible Society, 1991.

Billington, Rachel, & Barbara Brown. *The first miracles.* Grand Rapids: Eerdman, 1990.

DePaola, Tomie. *The miracles of Jesus.* New York: Holiday House, 1987.

DePaola, Tomie. *The parables of Jesus.* New York: Holiday House, 1987.

Dickinson, Peter. (Michael Foreman, illus.) *City of gold and other stories from the Old Testament.* Boston: Otter Books, 1992.

Dillenberger, Jane. I*mage & spirit in sacred and secular art.* New York: Crossroad, 1990.

Dillenberger, Jane. *Style & content in Christian art.* New York: Crossroad, 1986.

Fluegelman, Andrew, ed. *The new games book.* Garden City: Dolphin Books, 1976.

Good news travels fast: The Acts of the Apostles. New York: American Bible Society, 1988.

Gregson, Bob. *The incredible indoor games book.* Carthage: Fearon Teacher Aids, 1982.

Griggs, Patricia. *Beginning Bible skills: Opening the Bible with children.* Nashville: Abingdon, 1986.

Halverson, Delia. *Teaching prayer in the classroom.* Nashville: Abingdon, 1989.

Hebblethwaite, Margaret. *My secret life: A friendship with God.* Harrisburg: Morehouse, 1991.

Keithahn, Mary Nelson. *Creative ideas for teaching: Learning through writing.* Brea: Educational Ministries, 1987.

L'Engle, Madeleine. *Ladder of angels.* New York: Seabury, 1979.

Luke tells the good news about Jesus. New York: American Bible Society, 1987.

Marchon, Blandine. (Claude & Denise Millet, illus.) *The Bible: The greatest stories.* Nashville: Abingdon, 1992.

Milord, Susan. *Hands around the world.* Charlotte: Williamson Publishing, 1992.

Prichard, Robert W. *The bat and the bishop.* Harrisburg: Morehouse, 1989.

Roth, Nancy L. *Praying: A book for children.* New York: The Church Hymnal Corp., 1991

Smith, Judy Gattis. *Teaching to wonder: Spiritual growth through imagination and movement.* Nashville: Abingdon, 1989.

Smith, Judy Gattis. *Teaching with music through the church year.* Nashville: Abingdon, 1979.

Sparks, Lee, ed. *Fun group games for children's ministry.* Loveland: Group Publishing, 1990.

Staeheli, Alice M. *Costuming the Christmas and Easter play: With ideas for other Biblical dramas.* Colorado Springs: Meriwether, 1988.

Stewig, John Warren. *Informal drama in the elementary language arts program.* New York: Teachers College, 1983.

Stoddard, Sandol. (Tony Chen, illus.) *The Doubleday illustrated children's Bible.* New York: Doubleday, 1983.

Stoddard, Sandol. (Rachel Isadora, illus.) *Prayers, praises, and thanksgivings.* New York: Dial, 1992.

The Taizé picture Bible. Philadelphia: Fortress, 1968.

Turner, Philip. (Brian Wildsmith, illus.) *The Bible story.* Oxford: Oxford University Press, 1968.

Wiseman, Ann. *Making things: The handbook of creative discovery.* Boston: Little, Brown, 1973.

Note: The following letter is for teachers and parents of children in the Intermediate level of church school. These two pages can be reproduced or used as a model for a personalized letter.

EPISCOPAL CHILDREN'S CURRICULUM
Unit I: COVENANT

Dear Parents and Guardians,

In the upcoming weeks Intermediate students will be exploring the Bible to learn about the Hebrews' journey over hundreds of years. Scripture and activities will give them an account of Old Testament history in this Unit on covenants.

The theme that holds the Old Testament together is "covenant." Testament and covenant are actually synonyms. The fortunes of God's people are in large measure determined by the degree of their obedience to God's covenant.

The chosen people of God, whose story unfolds in the Hebrew Scriptures (the Old Testament), were continually reminded that God had reached out to their ancestors again and again in covenant relationships. To be obedient to God meant remembering and keeping the covenant into which God had called them.

When Jesus took the wine and gave thanks at the Last Supper, he said, "This is my blood of the covenant, which is poured out for many" (*Mark 14:24b*). Christians have always understood that Jesus was establishing a new covenant—not to replace earlier covenants but to fulfill them.

In the Baptismal Covenant (*The Book of Common Prayer*, pp. 303-304), we reaffirm our faith in the words of the Apostles' Creed. We promise to live as responsible members of the Church, the Body of Christ. We acknowledge that we are bound to God and to one another in a covenant relationship.

The sessions of the Covenant Unit focus on sequential segments of the story of God's covenant people. For many people, the tales of well-known figures like Noah, Abraham and Sarah, Jacob and Rachel, Moses, Deborah, Gideon, Samson, and David tend to take on a life of their own. Often they are not fitted into a chronology or seen as parts of one long story that leads to the life of Jesus Christ and the formation of the Church.

Spend some time talking to your student about what he or she is learning. You can do this by reading the Scripture cited below, discussing the **Symbol Cards** and *Covenant Times* sent home each week, and by reading together Part I of the Shell Year Treasurebook, which includes information about covenants.

Below is a brief summary of the sessions in the Covenant Unit. The Scripture passage the students will read for each session is included.

Session 1: "God Preserves Creation" introduces the concept of covenant through the story of Noah. This ancient narrative underscores God's reaching out to humanity. After the great Flood, which was an act of judgment upon a wicked world, God promised the obedient Noah that there would never again be such a wholesale destruction. The rainbow is a sign of God's promise. (*Genesis 9:8-13*)

Session 2: "God Calls a People into Covenant" describes the covenant God made with Abraham and renewed with Isaac, Jacob, and Joseph. We still think of Abraham as the great parent figure of biblical faith. He was told that his descendants would be as numerous as the stars and the grains of sand. (*Genesis 17:1-5*)

Session 3: "Moses Receives the Commandments" focuses on the time of Moses' leadership of the people of Israel. God has delivered the chosen people out of bondage in Egypt and formed a new covenant with them. It is marked by the giving of the Law or the Ten Commandments. These Commandments form the basis for all the laws governing the life of Israel. (The Decalogue in *The Book of Common Prayer*, p. 350, or *Exodus 20:1-17*)

Session 4: "God Provides Leaders" surveys the long succession of heroes who appear in the history of the chosen people after the death of Moses. First of these is Joshua, who had been Moses' assistant. The "judges" or leaders—both male and female—follow. These stories are found in the Book of Judges. (*Joshua 1:1-3, 5-7*)

Session 5: "A Place for the Ark of the Covenant" reviews a new phase when God hears and responds to the Israelis' desire to have kings like those of other nations. Anointed to keep the covenant during their rule, Saul, David, and Solomon serve the united people. Under their leadership, the kingdom is well established. The reign of Solomon includes the building of a great temple for God in Jerusalem. (*I Samuel 8:1-9*)

Session 6: "Covenant People Divided" offers a survey of the division of God's people, with the kingdom of Israel in the north and the kingdom of Judah to the south. Shifts in leadership during this period are too numerous to detail. However, during this time, the various Old Testament prophets began to warn the people that they were not keeping faith with God's covenant. Disobedience would ultimately lead to disaster. (*I Kings 12:16-20*)

Session 7: "Covenant People in Exile" treats the sad period following the capture of the people by the king of Babylon. They were sent to a strange land, and their cherished temple and treasures destroyed. But the people were never left without hope; the prophets Jeremiah and Ezekiel spoke words of comfort and reassurance. (*II Kings 12:16-20*)

Session 8: "Covenant People Return" tells the story of the people's return to their land with the permission of Cyrus, king of Persia. Those returning first began rebuilding the temple. Jerusalem was far from safe, however. Frequent attacks from enemies discouraged people from settling there again. Finally Nehemiah and Ezra completed the restoration of the city's walls and reestablished the laws of Moses. (*Ezra 1:2-4*)

Session 9: "All Saints" is designed for use in the week nearest the Feast of All Saints (November 1). (This session may be taught out of sequence.) This session focuses partly on the inclusion of the Hebrew saints of God in our Church's celebration of All Saints' Day. (*Psalm 145:8-21*)

Yours in Christ,

Church School Teachers

COVENANT
SESSION 1
GOD PRESERVES CREATION

FOCUS

The covenant made with Noah affirms that God, the Creator, cares about all creation and desires its preservation. The students should be able to define the word "covenant," explain the symbol of the rainbow, and state in their own words how God's covenant with Noah relates to us today.

GETTING READY

This Unit traces the theme of *covenant* through the Hebrew Scriptures. Refer to the Unit I letter for an overview of the sessions. Session 1, on the covenant with Noah, is intended to highlight these themes:

a. God the Creator cares about all creatures and desires their preservation.

b. We have life because of God's gracious act of saving us from destruction.

c. We give thanks for God's covenant with Noah as a sign of the Creator's love and care.

d. As teachers, we can encourage the students in taking on responsibility for the environment—physically, morally, and spiritually.

Intermediate-age students who have grown up in the Church will have heard the story of Noah and the great Flood many times. Because of the story's familiarity, and the somewhat lighthearted treatment it receives in many popular tellings (particularly in illustrated children's books), young people may have concluded there is little to be learned from it. Modern readers can too easily discard Noah's tale as no more than a primitive, unscientific account.

It is important, therefore, to look more closely at the story and its purpose (*Genesis*, chapters 6-9). Young people who are sensitized to the issue of preserving the Earth and its environment—and who care deeply about the preservation of the natural world and humanity—can find new meaning in what happened to Noah and his family. One thrust of the story is that God, who created everything, desires to preserve the world. When corrupt and degrading behavior contaminated Creation, God washed everything clean in order to make a new beginning.

Following the Flood, God made a covenant with Noah: Such destruction would not occur again, and the rainbow would be a sign of God's promise. This is the first of the covenants in the *Book of Genesis*.

Almighty God, in giving us dominion over things on earth, you made us fellow workers in your creation: Give us wisdom and reverence so to use the resources of nature, that no one may suffer from our abuse of them, and that generations yet to come may continue to praise you for your bounty; through Jesus Christ our Lord. *Amen*.

For the Conservation of Natural Resources
The Book of Common Prayer, p. 827

TEACHING TIP

In the Episcopal Church, members of the congregation serve as readers of Scripture (lectors) at services of worship. Intermediate students can fill a similar role in their own classroom. All class members should be given the opportunity to prepare for this important task. At the same time, respect a student's decision not to be a part of this activity. (See the suggestions given for Gathering in the strategies section of the Teacher's Background at the front of this Guide.)

GATHERING

Display Poster No. 1 from the Teacher's Packet showing a rainbow, ark, and a rain forest. Display other posters of the environment that may be available. As the students gather, invite them to talk with one another about any experiences they have had with environmental issues (Earth Day observances, community recycling programs, or school projects on ecology or conservation).

When everyone is present, say:

Let us pray. (Use the prayer "For the Conservation of Natural Resources," above, or a prayer of your own choosing.)

The chosen student lector reads from the class Bible:

A Reading from the Book of Genesis, chapter 9, verses 8 through 13.

Then God said to Noah and to his sons with him, "As for me, I am establishing my covenant with you and your descendants after you, and with every living creature that is with you, the birds, the domestic animals, and every animal of the earth with you, as many as came out of the ark. I establish my covenant with you, that never again shall all flesh be cut off by the waters of a flood, and never again shall there be a flood to destroy the earth." God said, "This is the sign of the covenant that I make between me and you and every living creature that is with you, for all future generations: I have set my bow in the clouds, and it shall be a sign of the covenant between me and the earth."

Reader: The Word of the Lord.
Response: Thanks be to God.

INTRODUCING THE STORY
(Time: 10–20 minutes)

Ask students to turn in their Bibles to *Genesis 9:13*. Ask: what does God tell Noah? Discuss God's covenant with "the Earth." What do you think this means for us now?

In the student newspaper, **Covenant Times** (Unit I, Issue 1), an imaginary interview with Noah begins on page 1. At his 900th birthday, he reminisces about the Flood. Invite the students to join in reviewing this story of Noah or by telling Noah's story in your own words. Include the following: God instructed Noah to build an ark and to take aboard his own family and pairs of every kind of living creature. A great Flood washed the earth clean. The ark came to rest on Mt. Ararat.

After the Flood, God promised never again to use such a catastrophe as punishment. God's promise to Noah is called a covenant—the theme of this Unit. Covenants in the Bible are usually like a formal agreement between two parties. Each promises to do something.

The first covenant in the *Book of Genesis* that God makes with Noah is different. God alone does the promising. Discuss the rainbow as a symbol of God's promise never to destroy all of creation by flooding.

EXPLORING
(Time: 15–20 minutes)

Option 1. Covenant with God

As a class, write your own covenant on a large sheet of newsprint or a chalkboard. Begin the covenant with the statement, "We promise to do our best to serve God in the following ways: . . ." Decide together on some specific commitments the students are willing to make. Examples might be: prayer, caring for others, helping around the house without being asked, calling a grandparent, or helping a friend.

You may want to provide copies of the finished covenant for each student.

Option 2. Class Rainbow

Using large sheets of construction paper or poster board, cut strips of red, orange, yellow, green, blue, indigo, and violet to make the bands of a rainbow. (You may wish to make it large enough to go above the entrance to the classroom.) Ask the students to write words and phrases or draw pictures on each color to represent aspects of nature represented by that color or that begin with the first letter of each color. Examples: blue—water, sky, bluebirds, baby animals, bushes; red—sunsets, cardinals, recycling, river.

As students work on the project, ask them to describe rainbows they have seen. Ask: What did the rainbow mean to Noah? What does it mean to you? If possible, leave the rainbow on display during this Unit.

Option 3. Search and Unscramble

Turn in the student newspaper, *Covenant Times*, Unit I, Issue 1, to the word scramble titled "Covenant with Noah." Students may work individually, in pairs, or as a total group.

MUSIC
(Time: 10 minutes)

Listen to "Canticle 1, A Song of Creation" (*The Hymnal 1982*, S177; *We Sing of God*, S3) on the *Children Sing!* tape. "Canticle" means a song based in Scripture.

Help the students find this Canticle in both the Hymnal and the Prayer Book (Morning Prayer II, p. 88). Replay the tape, joining in the singing as a group.

CONNECTING/SPEAKING OUT
(Time: 15–20 minutes)

Option 1. Group Discussion

The preserving of creation (in the story of Noah) marked a new beginning in human history—a beginning based solely on God's grace. As a sign of God's faithful covenant, life on Earth would continue.

Discuss with the students:

What can we do as "people of the covenant" to preserve and support all that God has created? In what ways do people and all the other creatures of the Earth need each other? How can we show our respect to other people and to everything that God has created? What are our responsibilities to God, to other people, and to our environment?

Option 2. Current Events

Bring in newspapers and news magazines. Ask students to look for stories or pictures about environmental issues.

Invite students to point out places and ways in which the Earth's environment is being abused. Encourage them to share information they have learned in school or the media. (Examples: air pollution, acid rain, destruction of rain forests, damage to the ozone layer.)

Cite governmental and private groups that are concerned about ecology and work to protect the environment. For example, local organizations may schedule work days to clean rivers and streams. Civic groups and churches in some communities have volunteered to pick up trash along roadways. Ask: What are some ways in which Christians can share in these concerns?

REFLECTING
(Time: 10 minutes)

Provide each student with a sturdy envelope approximately 9 x 12 inches in size. Label each one "Reflection Collection." Ask students to add their names and decorate the envelopes. These will be used for storing and saving the personal reflections of students during the course of the Unit. It is important to preserve what the class members have created. Store envelopes between sessions, assuring class members that the contents are private. They are taken home at the end of the Unit.

Either orally or in writing, offer direction on what could be written for the reflection collections. Use something like the following for this session:

Think of a beautiful place you have visited, or where you enjoy going—a park, playground, public garden, or a quiet spot near your home. Why do you enjoy going there? What is special about this place?

Now imagine how you would feel if this place were suddenly destroyed. What would you miss most?

Think of ways you could protect this place. Is there anything you could do to preserve it? Write down your responses to these questions. At the end of your reflection, you may write a brief prayer in your own words.

LEARNING SKILLS
(Time: 10–15 minutes)

Option 1. Class Memory Challenge

Introduce the skill of locating sections and passages of the Bible. Ask the students to open their Bibles to the Table of Contents. Notice the arrangement of the books into Testaments. (Some student Bibles may include the Apocrypha in addition to the Old Testament.)

You can introduce a simple way of finding one's way through the Bible by opening the book at the center, which is likely to fall within the *Psalms*. Dividing the second half helps to locate the New Testament more easily.

Begin to memorize the books of the Old Testament, in order. The first five books are called the Torah ("teachings"), especially by Jewish readers. Another name for these books, in Greek, is Pentateuch.

Note the chart that appears in the student newspaper, *Covenant Times*, Unit I, Issues 1-8.

The books are *Genesis, Exodus, Leviticus, Numbers,* and *Deuteronomy*. Say the names over together several times in unison. (Some persons remember the order by recalling the first letters of each one: GELND, which can be formed into a nonsense word, Gel'n'deu—the final syllable standing for Deuteronomy.)

Option 2. Learning Scripture

Invite the students to choose either of the following to learn before the next class session: *Genesis 9:13* or *9:16* (in any version or translation). See "Learning Scripture" in the student newspaper, *Covenant Times*. Encourage the students to use their Bibles at home and work with friends or parents.

Prepare and display a colorful blank Scripture Banner (or poster) to encourage the students to accomplish this memory task. Explain that a card with each verse written on it will be added to the banner as soon as a class member has memorized it.

Add a sticker or draw a symbol (such as a star) for each student who memorizes the verse. Additional verses or passages will be suggested at each session.

ONGOING PROJECT
(Time: 5–10 minutes)

Encourage students to collaborate in making a biblical timeline to display in the classroom. The timeline may be formed with large index cards. Tape these in order to a wall or clip them to a clothesline strung somewhere in the room.

Include on the card for this session a picture of a rainbow with "Noah" written beneath it, and a Scripture verse chosen from *Genesis 9:8-17*. (Noah's card will be the first one on the left as the timeline begins. Note that we cannot assign a date to Noah's story because it comes from the early part of Genesis that we call prehistorical.)

SYMBOL CARD and TREASUREBOOK

Card 1 contains a rainbow symbol, a verse of Scripture, and an explanation on the back.

Invite the students to explore Part I of the *Shell Year Treasurebook*, which surveys the history of the Bible and Hebrew people. How does God relate to the people?

GOING FORTH

Gather the group for the dismissal. The teacher or a student will say:

I ask your prayers for all who seek God, or a deeper knowledge of him.
Pray that they may find and be found by him.
Silence

[Learners may add their petitions.]

Praise God for those in every generation in whom Christ has been honored especially those whom we remember today.
Pray that we may have grace to glorify Christ in our own day.

From The Prayers of the People
The Book of Common Prayer, p. 386

Teacher: Let us go forth in the name of Christ.
Students: Thanks be to God.

TEACHER'S ASSESSMENT

In the Hebrew Scriptures as well as in today's society, covenants (agreements) play an important role in human relationships. Did students understand the meaning of the word "covenant"? Were they aware of God's covenant in the story of Noah, and of the rainbow symbol?

LOOKING AHEAD

In the next session, the students will be exploring the covenant between God and Abraham. Think about the covenants or commitments you have made in your own life. How are these affected by your understanding of biblical covenant-making? Consider the promises you live by. Can they be expressed in simple sentences? In more complex ways? Are the promises alive?

COVENANT
SESSION 2
GOD CALLS A PEOPLE INTO COVENANT

FOCUS

The covenant God made with Abraham established the people of God through whom God would bless all the world. The students should be able to describe the covenant with Abraham as the beginning of the story of God's people, explain the symbol of the field of stars, and state that we are all spiritual descendants of Abraham.

GETTING READY

The historical portion of the *Book of Genesis* begins with the story of Abram and Sarai, chapters 12-25:11. God made a covenant with Abram and changed their names to Abraham and Sarah. In this session, the highlighted themes are:

a. We trace our spiritual identity as God's people from the story of Abraham and Sarah.

b. Abraham heard and obeyed God's call into a special covenant relationship.

c. We take part in a faith that comes from Abraham's act of trust long ago.

Most students of the intermediate-age level have a growing interest in history—not just the "olden days" (a term used for events preceding our own memories). They have a need to understand more about from where they (and their ancestors) came. Stories of families, communities, and nations take on new importance.

This is an important time to introduce the beginnings of our religious history—in God's covenant with Abraham. Jews, Christians, and Muslims trace their spiritual roots to this account.

Almighty and eternal God, so draw our hearts to you, so guide our minds, so fill our imaginations, so control our wills, that we may be wholly yours, utterly dedicated to you; and then use us, we pray, as you will, and always to your glory and the welfare of your people; through our Lord and Savior Jesus Christ. *Amen*.

A Prayer of Self-Dedication
The Book of Common Prayer, p. 832

TEACHING TIP

Intermediate students are beginning to use analogies and metaphors. For example, comparing the number of Abraham's descendants to the infinite number of stars, or grains of sand, can be understood at this age level. Some students will be able to move beyond the concrete images of such comparisons and begin to discuss concepts in abstract ways, but most need concrete examples.

GATHERING

Display Poster No. 2 of stars found in the Teacher's Packet or use a picture of a starry night sky. Place a small jar of sand where everyone can see. Invite the students to look at the picture and the sand. Talk about how many stars or grains of sand there may be. You may want to introduce the concept of "infinity."

When everyone is present, say:

Let us pray. (Use "A Prayer of Self-Dedication," above, or a prayer of your own choosing.)

The chosen student lector reads from the class Bible:

A Reading from the Book of Genesis, chapter 17, verses 1 through 5.

When Abram was ninety-nine years old, the Lord appeared to Abram, and said to him, "I am God

Almighty; walk before me, and be blameless. And I will make my covenant between me and you, and will make you exceedingly numerous." Then Abram fell on his face; and God said to him, "As for me, this is my covenant with you: You shall be the ancestor of a multitude of nations. No longer shall your name be Abram, but your name shall be Abraham; for I have made you the ancestor of a multitude of nations."

Reader: The Word of the Lord.
Response: Thanks be to God.

INTRODUCING THE STORY
(Time: 10–20 minutes)

Review the story of Abraham as it appears in *Genesis 12:1-7*, and chapter 15 and read the imaginary interview with Abraham and Sarah in the student newspaper, ***Covenant Times*** (Unit I, Issue 2). The story describes how God kept the promise that they would have descendants.

Tell the story of Abraham and Sarah in your own words. Emphasize Abraham's faith in God: an act of trust in a promise from God. To be the father of many nations, Abraham needed descendants and land. The promise must have seemed impossible. How could a couple so old have a child?

Explain Sarah's barrenness and God's promise of Isaac's birth as evidence of God's great power to make the impossible a reality.

Describe the changing of the name Abram, "exalted father," to Abraham, "father of many nations," to signify the new covenant relationship. Sarai's name was changed to Sarah; both mean "princess, or noble woman."

The stars and the sand of the seashore have been created by God; there are so many, no one can count them. God promised that Abraham's descendants would be as numerous as the stars or as the grains of sand (*Genesis 15:5; 22:17*).

Review the meaning of the word "covenant." Just as God entered into a covenant with Noah to preserve creation, God now enters into a covenant with Abraham to establish a people through whom the whole world would be blessed.

Invite the students to turn in their Bibles to *Genesis 17:1-9, 15-21*. Note that God's covenant is not only with Abraham but also with his descendants. Ask: Are we a part of God's covenant with Abraham?

Use the map on Poster No. 3 to locate the land (Canaan) that was promised to Abraham and his descendants. Identify the route from Ur (Babylon) up the Tigris/Euphrates river basin, through Syria to Israel. Identify modern countries there today. Note that Islam, not Christianity or Judaism, is the dominant religion in the land of Abraham's beginning and also claims him as spiritual founder.

EXPLORING
(Time: 15–20 minutes)

Option 1. Making a Matrix

As a group, create a matrix with words radiating from the word covenant. Write the word "COVENANT" in the center of a chalk board or piece of newsprint. See how many words relating to covenant the group can place in a matrix. For example:

```
        P
        R
    C O V E N A N T
        M   O
C O M M I T       A G R E E M E N T
        S   H
    O B E Y I N G
```

As the groups works, be sure to define words if meanings are unclear.

Option 2. Sand Relay

Bring in soup spoons, sand, and several empty containers for a relay game. Divide into two or more teams, depending on the size of the group. Ask the teams to line up, one person behind another. Set an empty container and a spoon at the front of each team line. At the opposite end of the room, put a container of sand for each team.

At your signal, the first person for each team will run to the assigned container and scoop up a spoonful of sand. Then, without spilling any sand, run back to the head of the line, dump the sand, and give the spoon to the next person in line. If any sand is spilled, the person must run to the side, get a broom and sweep it up before continuing. The game ends when everyone has had a chance to play.

Announce to each team that the winner will be determined by how many grains of sand each team managed to transport. Talk about the best way to do this. Compare the amount of sand in each container with those at one beach. Discuss God's promises to Abraham and Sarah.

Option 3. Dot-to-Dot Puzzle

Turn in the student newspaper, *Covenant Times*, Unit I, Issue 2, to the dot-to-dot activity titled "Symbol for Abraham."

Students may work individually, in pairs, or as a group to identify the ten words used in this Session. The words are connected in *alphabetical order* to form the symbol of a five-pointed star.

MUSIC
(Time: 10 minutes)

Sing "Canticle 1, A Song of Creation" (*The Hymnal 1982*, S177; *We Sing of God*, S3) with the *Children Sing!* tape.

Spend some time becoming familiar with the musical setting for this Canticle. Note that it may be shortened by omitting either section II or III.

CONNECTING/SPEAKING OUT
(Time: 15–20 minutes)

Option 1. Group Discussion

Supply an assortment of old magazines and newspapers. Ask the students to cut out pictures of people of all races, cultures, and nationalities. Together, assemble these on poster board with the caption: "Spiritual Descendants of Abraham."

Talk about the different kinds of people that are depicted. Ask: Why are these people descendants of Abraham? What does the phrase "spiritual descendants" mean? God promised Abraham that he and his descendants would be a blessing to others. How has that promise been kept?

As a class, compose a prayer for all of God's people, and attach a copy of it to the poster. (You may want to consult the "Prayers and Thanksgivings" that begin on page 814 in *The Book of Common Prayer*.)

Option 2. Current Events

Using recent newspapers, ask students to find stories or pictures that suggest solemn promises (covenants) that have been kept or broken. Look for disagreements among nations, political parties, or individuals in places of trust. Other examples may involve families or local neighborhoods in which promises were made. What is the evidence that the covenants have been respected? disregarded?

Talk to the students about the universal nature of covenant-making and covenant disobedience. Ask: What kind of promises do we make to each other? How seriously do we take them?

REFLECTING
(Time: 10 minutes)

Either orally or in writing, share the following possibilities for the students' personal reflection time:

Think about Abraham's laughter when God said that Sarah would have a son. This seemed totally impossible to him because they were both almost 100 years old.

What if someone told you that you would be the next President of the United States? Would you laugh at the idea? How would you react if God told you that it would come true?

Put your thoughts on paper in words or by drawing. At the end of your reflection, you may write a short prayer.

If the students have prepared "Reflection Collection" envelopes (see the previous session), add the sheets from this session. Envelopes can be started at any time.

LEARNING SKILLS
(Time: 10–15 minutes)

Option 1. Class Memory Challenge

Practice the skill of "decoding" printed citations in the Bible by book, chapter, and verse. Write some typical biblical citations on a chalkboard or newsprint, and ask students to read the citations aloud. For example, *Genesis 17:1-9, 15-21* is read: "The *Book of Genesis*, chapter 17, verses one through nine, and verses fifteen through twenty-one." Offer the students an opportunity to read other citations aloud.

Review the students' task of memorizing the first five books of the Bible (*Genesis, Exodus, Leviticus, Numbers*, and *Deuteronomy*).

Begin to learn the list of twelve historical books. Concentrate in this session on learning to recite the first nine.

A way to make this task easy is to think of two triplets of initial letters, JJR and SKC. The two J's and R are: *Joshua, Judges, Ruth*. The S, K, and C stand for books that come in pairs, *I and II Samuel, I and II Kings,* and *I and II Chronicles*.

Refer to the chart in the student newspaper, *Covenant Times*, Unit I, Issue 2.

Option 2. Learning Scripture

If class members have memorized verses given in the previous session, add cards and symbols to the

Unit I. Covenant—Session 2
Shell Year Intermediate—Copyright © 2000 Virginia Theological Seminary and Morehouse Publishing

Scripture Banner (or poster) described in Session 1.

Invite the students to memorize *Genesis 15:5b,c* or *17:9* before the next class session. See "Learning Scripture" in the student newspaper, *Covenant Times*.

ONGOING PROJECT
(Time: 5–10 minutes)

Continue the biblical timeline (see Session 1). Add a symbol for Abraham and his descendants—a large star surrounded by a field of smaller ones. Print "Abraham" on the large index card containing the symbol, and a Scripture verse chosen from *Genesis 17:1-9, 15-21*. (It is not possible to date Abraham exactly, but we know he lived in the period around 2100-1800 BCE.)

Place Abraham's card to the right of Noah's.

SYMBOL CARD and TREASUREBOOK

Card 2 has a symbol for Abraham and his descendants, a Scripture verse, and an explanation on the back.

Suggest that students look over Part I, Section 2, in the *Shell Year Treasurebook*, titled "One Bible in Many Languages." Why would we want different versions of the Bible?

GOING FORTH

Gather the group for the dismissal. The teacher or a student will say:

I ask your prayers for all who seek God, or a deeper knowledge of him.

Pray that they may find and be found by him.
Silence

[Learners may add their petitions.]

Praise God for those in every generation in whom Christ has been honored especially those whom we remember today.

Pray that we may have grace to glorify Christ in our own day.

From The Prayers of the People
The Book of Common Prayer, p. 386

Teacher: Let us go forth in the name of Christ.
Students: Thanks be to God.

TEACHER'S ASSESSMENT

What are some of the ideas about promise or commitment emerging from the class? As the students continue to explore the biblical concept of covenant, what kinds of questions do they have? What are they wondering about?

LOOKING AHEAD

In the next session, the class members will consider God's covenant with Moses and the giving of the Ten Commandments. When did you first learn the Commandments? Does your knowledge of the Commandments affect your daily life?

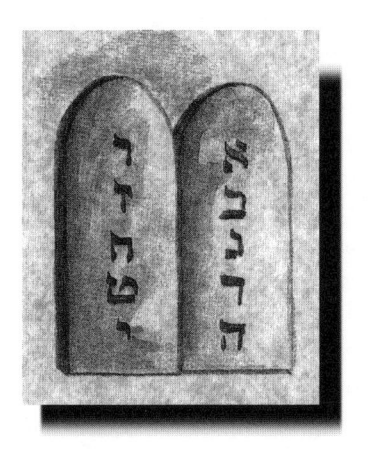

COVENANT
SESSION 3
MOSES RECEIVES THE COMMANDMENTS

FOCUS

In the covenant made with Moses, God provided the Ten Commandments as a way of life in obedience to God. The students should be able to tell the story of how Moses received the Commandments on Mt. Sinai, explain the symbol of the tablets of the Law, and describe the Ten Commandments.

GETTING READY

God's covenant with Moses was different from the earlier ones with Noah and Abraham. This session underscores the following:

a. Through Moses, God gave the Hebrews the Ten Commandments.

b. God placed a new and serious obligation on the people—to obey the Commandments.

c. These Commandments became the basis for all the other laws found in the Torah (the first five books of the Hebrew Scriptures).

It would not be possible for us to tell our faith history as Christians without stressing the importance of the Ten Commandments. They remind us of what it means to love and serve God and our neighbors. Achieving justice and peace among people requires that we return again and again to the words of the Ten Commandments.

Intermediate-age students may recall the story of Moses' life and his call to be the leader of God's people: He heard the voice of God in a bush that burned but was not consumed. He led the people out of slavery in Egypt, directed their life in the wilderness, and kept alive the vision of the promised land. The students can now consider the story of God's covenant with Moses, found in *Exodus*, chapter 20. Note especially God's promise in verse 24: ". . . in every place where I cause my name to be remembered I will come to you and bless you."

O God, by whom the meek are guided in judgment, and light rises up in darkness for the godly: Grant us, in all our doubts and uncertainties, the grace to ask what you would have us to do, that the Spirit of wisdom may save us from all false choices, and that in your light we may see light, and in your straight path may not stumble; through Jesus Christ our Lord. *Amen*.

For Guidance
The Book of Common Prayer, p. 832

TEACHING TIP

Students at the intermediate-age level face many "do's" and "don'ts" at home, at school, and in the community. While complaining about rules, however, they are likely to form groups and clubs in which they make up their own regulations. Help class members understand that God's Commandments are more than just a list of "don'ts." They are a gift from God to provide a pattern for obedient living.

GATHERING

Ahead of time, collect examples of promises made by individuals and groups, such as Scout promises and vows made in baptism, marriage, and ordination (from *The Book of Common Prayer*). As students arrive, invite them to look at the display and to discuss who makes the promises. Ask: What do the promises have in common? What are some promises you have made?

When everyone is present, say:

Let us pray. (Use the prayer "For Guidance," above, or a prayer of your own choosing.)

The chosen student lector reads The Decalogue: Contemporary, from *The Book of Common Prayer*. The students are invited to join in the response,

"Amen. Lord have mercy." The text, with responses, appears on Poster No. 4 in the Teacher's Packet. (Decalogue is the Greek word meaning Ten Commandments.)

A Reading from The Book of Common Prayer, page 350.

> Hear the commandments of God to his people:
> I am the Lord your God who brought you out of bondage.
> You shall have no other gods but me.
> *Amen. Lord have mercy.*
>
> You shall not make for yourself any idol.
> *Amen. Lord have mercy.*
>
> You shall not invoke with malice the Name of the Lord your God.
> *Amen. Lord have mercy.*
>
> Remember the Sabbath day and keep it holy.
> *Amen. Lord have mercy.*
>
> Honor your father and your mother.
> *Amen. Lord have mercy.*
>
> You shall not commit murder.
> *Amen. Lord have mercy.*
>
> You shall not commit adultery.
> *Amen. Lord have mercy.*
>
> You shall not steal.
> *Amen. Lord have mercy.*
>
> You shall not be a false witness.
> *Amen. Lord have mercy.*
>
> You shall not covet anything that belongs to your neighbor.
> *Amen. Lord have mercy.*

INTRODUCING THE STORY
(Time: 10–20 minutes)

Briefly, tell the story of how Moses led the people of God out of slavery in Egypt. For background information, read the fictional account of the death of Moses at the age of 120 in the student newspaper, *Covenant Times* (Unit I, Issue 3). The article includes a survey of his life.

Emphasize the importance of the Exodus—the "going out" of the people. Use the map provided in the Teacher's Packet on Poster No. 3 (also found in the student newspaper, *Covenant Times*, Unit I, Issue 3) in your discussion.

Soon after the departure from Egypt, the people were in the wilderness at the foot of Mt. Sinai. Describe, in your own words, the scene as it unfolds in *Exodus 19*. The people were encamped in the wilderness in front of the mountain. They were warned not to go up the mountain until the trumpet sounded a long blast. As they waited, the mountain became engulfed in a thick cloud.

As Moses reached the top of the mountain, God spoke with him and gave him the Ten Commandments.

Ask the students to turn in their Bibles to *Exodus 20:1-17*. (Assist the group in locating the passage, noting that Exodus is the second book of the Hebrew Scriptures.) Compare the biblical text with the contemporary version that was read at the Gathering.

Discuss some of the different expressions for the same ideas. For example, the traditional way of reciting the third Commandment is, "Thou shalt not take the Name of the Lord thy God in vain." (See the King James Version of the Bible and the BCP, p. 318.) In the New Revised Standard Version, the words are "You shall not make wrongful use of the Name of the Lord your God." Talk about the differences the group finds.

EXPLORING
(Time: 15–20 minutes)

Option 1. Going Up the Mountain

Bring in old clothes and shoes, empty containers for water, towels, soap, and a toy horn for a relay race. Before describing the rules of the game, set the stage by describing preparations the people made at the foot of Mt. Sinai as they waited for God to give them the Ten Commandments.

Exodus 19 describes the scene. God told Moses to tell the people to spend two days getting ready for the event. They were to wash their clothes and consecrate themselves. If anyone even touched the mountain until the appointed time, he or she would be put to death.

Divide the group into teams. At the end of the room, make circles using masking tape for each team and put in it a set of clothes, a basin filled with water, soap, and a towel. When you give the signal, the first person for each team will run to the team's circle, wash their hands, put on the clothes, then blow the horn (or ring a bell or whistle). Then they take off the clothes, and run back and tag the next person in line. If students step on or out of the circle before blowing the horn, they are disqualified and must repeat a turn.

The game is over when everyone has had a turn.

Option 2. Paraphrasing

Provide each student with a sheet of light-colored construction paper that has been folded in half and trimmed into the traditional two-tablet shape (see Symbol Card 3).

Ask each student to choose one Commandment and copy it on the left tablet. On the right tablet, each student can write the meaning of the chosen Commandment in his/her own words. On the backs of their tablets, the students can list ways in which they themselves follow that particular Commandment in their everyday lives. For example, not stealing might include not copying another person's homework or taking a sibling's possessions without asking.

Option 3. Crossword

Ask the students to work individually, in pairs, or as a group to complete the "Commandments Crossword," found in the student newspaper, *Covenant Times*, Unit I, Issue 3.

MUSIC
(Time: 10 minutes)

Sing again "Canticle 1, A Song of Creation" (*The Hymnal 1982*, S177; *We Sing of God*, S3) with the *Children Sing!* tape.

Students could be assigned individual portions of the Canticle to illustrate on a poster, using any medium (crayons, fingerpaint, markers, watercolors, collage items). Posters can be used to accompany the singing of the Canticle.

CONNECTING/SPEAKING OUT
(Time: 15–20 minutes)

Option 1. Group Discussion

The giving of the Commandments marked the covenant people of Israel; they were different from others. They were called to obey God, their Creator. The Commandments belong to us today as we take our places in the story of God's people.

Lead the students in discussing questions like the following:

What is our covenant with God? When did it begin?

In what ways do we show that we consider ourselves to be "people of the covenant" (children of God)?

How does it feel to have rules (laws) that are different from those of your friends? (Consider examples of different rules for curfew, codes of dress, church attendance, and degree of adult supervision.)

Option 2. Current Events

Pass out current newspapers and magazines and invite the students to look for examples of disobedience to the Commandments. Consider taping portions of a news program during the week for students to view. (This would be especially appropriate if something has happened recently in the community or world in which young people are interested.)

Ask: Why do people and groups break the Commandments? When is it most difficult to obey them? How do you feel when the Commandments are broken by others? by yourself?

REFLECTING
(Time: 10 minutes)

Share the following possibilities for the students' personal reflection:

A personal "rule of life" is a guide for individuals to help them live as Christians each day. What is your personal "rule of life"? What are some of the daily or weekly activities that could be included in a rule? (Examples: Reading the Bible, praying at a regular time every day, saying a blessing before each meal, doing at least one good deed each day, exercising several times each week, or practicing a skill.)

At the end of your reflection, write a one-line prayer.

Unit I. Covenant—Session 3
Shell Year Intermediate—Copyright © 2000 Virginia Theological Seminary and Morehouse Publishing

Add the sheets from this session to the "Reflection Collection" envelopes (see Session 1). Envelopes can be started at any time.

LEARNING SKILLS
(Time: 10–15 minutes)

Option 1. Class Memory Challenge

Continue working on the memorization of the books of the Old Testament. Ask the students to assemble in groups or teams to recite what has been learned thus far: the books of the Pentateuch (Torah), and the first nine of the historical books. Refer to the chart in the student newspaper, *Covenant Times*, Unit I, Issue 3.

For this session, add only the three remaining historical books: Ezra, Nehemiah, and Esther. Note that an easy way to remember these is to think of the initial letters ENE. (You might want to put on a board these patterns of letters: GELND, JJR, SKC—I's and II's, and ENE. Ask the students to name the books as you point to the cue letters.)

Option 2. Learning Scripture

If class members have memorized verses from the previous sessions, add cards and symbols to the Scripture Banner (or poster) described in Session 1. Remind the students that any verse from this Unit may be memorized at any time; the complete list of passages for the Unit appears in the student newspaper, *Covenant Times*.

Invite the students to memorize any or all of the Commandments (*Exodus 20:3, 4a, 7a, 8, 12a, 13, 14, 15, 16, 17a; 24:12*) before the next class session.

ONGOING PROJECT
(Time: 5–10 minutes)

Add to the biblical timeline the symbol of the Tablets of the Law (Ten Commandments), with the name of Moses and a Scripture verse chosen from *Exodus 20*. (Place the card for Moses an appropriate distance to the right of Abraham's. The estimated dates for receiving the Commandments are from 1330-1250 BCE. Scripture records that Moses lived 120 years.

SYMBOL CARD and TREASUREBOOK

Card 3 has tablets as a symbol for the Ten Commandments, a Scripture verse, and an explanation on the back.

Encourage the students to read Part I, Section 4, of the *Shell Year Treasurebook* about the Pentateuch. What Scripture is on the Liberty Bell?

GOING FORTH

Gather the group. The teacher or a student will say: I ask your prayers for all who seek God, or a deeper knowledge of him.
Pray that they may find and be found by him.
Silence

[Learners may add their petitions.]

Praise God for those in every generation in whom Christ has been honored especially those whom we remember today.
Pray that we may have grace to glorify Christ in our own day.

From The Prayers of the People
The Book of Common Prayer, p. 386

Teacher: Let us go forth in the name of Christ.
Students: Thanks be to God.

TEACHER'S ASSESSMENT

As the students explored God's covenant with Moses, and the giving of the Commandments, what feelings did they express? In what ways are they making connections between the biblical covenants and their own lives? What can you discern about the students' perceptions of authority and obedience?

LOOKING AHEAD

The next session is on Joshua, chosen to succeed Moses as the leader of the covenant people. The advent of judges, after Joshua, represents a new system of government for God's people. Think about our present-day understanding of the differences between judicial, legislative, and executive responsibilities. Why do we have all three? What are the special contributions of judges?

COVENANT
SESSION 4
GOD PROVIDES LEADERS

FOCUS

After the death of Moses, the people of God were led by Joshua into the land God had promised them. Following Joshua's death, the people had a succession of leaders called judges. Throughout these years, the people were continually tempted to break the covenant and follow false gods. The students should be able to tell who Joshua was, define the role of the judges of Israel, and explain the symbol of the Ark of the Covenant.

GETTING READY

In the previous three sessions, the focus has been on God's covenants with chosen figures: Noah, Abraham, and Moses. Under Moses, the people of Israel were set free to seek the promised land beyond the Jordan River.

This session sweeps across several centuries, highlighting the following:

a. Joshua took over the leadership of the people after the death of Moses.

b. A long series of "judges" came next.

c. At every point in their history, the Israelites were tempted to be unfaithful to their God.

As successor to Moses, Joshua enabled the covenant people to fulfill their historical destiny, occupying the promised land. He led the people into Canaan, and we remember especially his dramatic conquering of the city of Jericho (*Joshua*, chapter 6). He took great care to preserve The Ark of the Covenant, which went with the people into the promised land. This ark may have contained the tablets with the Ten Commandments. It was a significant symbol of divine power and strength for God's people.

The period that followed Joshua's lifetime, called the time of judges, covered more than two centuries. Stories of fourteen leaders are told in the *Book of Judges*. The heroic figures we remember are Deborah (chapters 4 and 5), Gideon (chapters 6 to 8), and Samson (chapters 13 to 16). The Song of Deborah is one of the oldest poems in the Old Testament, dating from around 1125 BCE.

We can piece together a picture of what life was like for the people of Israel in this era. It was the beginning of the Iron Age; the enemies of Israel had iron weapons. The people were nomads, and their chief livelihood was agriculture. A sort of anarchy prevailed.

The people sometimes forgot their covenant responsibilities to God, and they joined in the pagan worship of Baal, an agricultural deity.

Almighty God, who sits in the throne judging right: We humbly beseech you to bless the courts of justice and the magistrates in all this land; and give to them the spirit of wisdom and understanding, that they may discern the truth, and impartially administer the law in the fear of you alone; through him who shall come to be our Judge, your Son our Savior Jesus Christ. *Amen.*

For Courts of Justice
The Book of Common Prayer, p. 821

TEACHING TIP

This session offers an opportunity to look at the men and women chosen by God to govern and lead the people of Israel over centuries. Encourage students to name the people they admire in society. Be attentive to the students' awareness of contemporary leaders, and name some of the people who are leaders in the Church today.

GATHERING

Display a gavel or a picture of one. As the students arrive, talk with them about who uses a gavel. Ask: What does a gavel stand for? How do judges go about their work? What kinds of decisions do leaders and judges make?

When everyone is present, say:

Let us pray. (Use the prayer "For Courts of Justice," above, or a prayer of your own choosing.)

The chosen student lector reads from the class Bible:

A Reading from the Book of Joshua, chapter 1, verses 1 through 3 and 5 through 7.

After the death of Moses the servant of the Lord, the Lord spoke to Joshua son of Nun, Moses' assistant, saying, "My servant Moses is dead. Now proceed to cross the Jordan, you and all this people, into the land that I am giving to them, to the Israelites. Every place that the sole of your foot will tread upon I have given to you, as I promised to Moses. No one shall be able to stand against you all the days of your life. As I was with Moses, so I will be with you; I will not fail you or forsake you. Be strong and courageous; for you shall put this people in possession of the land that I swore to their ancestors to give them. Only be strong and very courageous, being careful to act in accordance with all the law that my servant Moses commanded you; do not turn from it to the right hand or to the left, so that you may be successful wherever you go."

Reader: The Word of the Lord.
Response: Thanks be to God.

INTRODUCING THE STORY
(Time: 10–20 minutes)

Explain that the history of the covenant people, following Moses, covers hundreds of years. In this session, two periods are surveyed—Joshua's leadership and the group of judges who followed him.

Briefly, tell the story of Joshua's leadership of the people of God from the plains of Moab to the land of Canaan. Emphasize the importance of taking possession of the "promised land." Joshua was leader for twenty-six years.

In your story, use information from the student newspaper, *Covenant Times* (Unit I, Issue 4). This issue includes background information on both Joshua and the period of the judges: a story on the fall of Jericho, an account of the crossing over the Jordan River, and a listing of all the judges who followed Joshua.

Describe the Ark of the Covenant. Joshua saw to it that the Ark was protected. The people took it with them over the River Jordan and into the land of Canaan. (Use Poster No. 5 provided in the Teacher's Packet to explain the construction and contents of the Ark.)

Invite the students to turn in their Bibles to *Joshua 3:1-6*. Read the passage aloud. Ask: What did the officers tell the people? How was the Ark treated?

After the death of Joshua, God called a series of leaders (judges) who governed the people in their time of oppression. Suggest that students find *Judges 2:16-18* and read the verses aloud. Ask: Why did God appoint judges over the people? How well did the people listen to the judges? Note that time of the judges was more than two centuries altogether.

Point out that the people during this time were tempted to worship the gods of Canaan and to turn away from the covenant God had made with Moses. Disobeying God's commandments led to struggle and troubles.

EXPLORING
(Time: 15–20 minutes)

Option 1. Crossing the Jordan River

Beforehand, make two parallel lines on the floor with masking tape about six to eight feet apart. Bring in one or two shoe boxes, and at least two, 2 x 4 inch boards that are about two feet long. Divide into groups of four or six.

Read or tell the story of the crossing of the Jordan River in *Joshua 3:14-17*. Announce that each group must find a way to cross the river (the space between the parallel lines) with a "sacred" shoe box. The only thing that can touch the "water" are the two boards. Everyone on the team must reach the other side along with the team box.

Talk about the activity after each team has had a turn. Ask: What was the most difficult part of the "crossing"? Did each team do it the same or differently? How do you think the Hebrew people felt when they reached the swollen banks of the Jordan River? How would you have felt if you had been there?

Option 2. Making an Ark

Use the pattern provided in the Teacher's Packet on Poster No. 4 for cutting and folding an Ark of the Covenant from construction paper. Follow the directions for assembly. Insert straws or lightweight dowels for carrying each completed Ark. As the students work, discuss the significance of this Ark in the life of the people of Israel.

Option 3. Word Search

Invite the students to work individually, in pairs, or as a group to complete "Words from Joshua and Judges," found in the student newspaper, *Covenant Times*, Unit I, Issue 4. Review the words' relationship to the historical period surveyed in this session.

MUSIC
(Time: 10 minutes)

Listen to "Canticle 1, A Song of Creation" (*The Hymnal 1982*, S177; *We Sing of God*, S3) on the *Children Sing!* tape. Play it a second time and sing along.

CONNECTING/SPEAKING OUT
(Time: 15–20 minutes)

Option 1. Group Discussion

At the top of a large piece of newsprint (or on a chalkboard), print Joshua's name. Divide the remaining space in half vertically. On the left side, print the word "Qualities." On the opposite side, print the word "Action." As a group, identify the qualities and characteristics of Joshua as a leader of God's people. (See *Deuteronomy 34:9 and Joshua 1:5-9.*) What did Joshua actually do? (See especially *Joshua 1:10; 3:1-6, 11.*)

Under "qualities," list the group's conclusions. Possible responses: Joshua had faith in God, wisdom, strength, courage, lack of fear, and the assurance that God was with him wherever he went.

Under "action," note that God enabled Joshua to lead the Hebrew people into the promised land, fulfilling the promise made to Moses.

Option 2. Current Events

The roles of Joshua and the judges who followed him represented an era of tribal life for God's people. Each chosen judge had to chart a course most likely to keep all the tribes together as worshippers of the one God who had brought them out of slavery and into their own land.

Ask the students to think about the schools they attend. What holds a school together? Who helps all the classes to know and understand the school rules and traditions?

What holds our nation together from generation to generation? In today's world, what happens when people in a nation no longer recognize their leaders' authority?

REFLECTING
(Time: 10 minutes)

Share the following possibilities for the students' personal reflection:

Throughout the period of the judges, the people were continually tempted to break the Covenant and follow false gods. We face the same temptations today.

Why do you think people find it hard to remain faithful to God's laws?

What helps us to return to a closer relationship with God?

Put your thoughts down in writing or in a drawing. At the end of your reflection, add a prayer.

Add the sheets from this session to the "Reflection Collection" envelopes. Envelopes can be started at any time during the Unit.

LEARNING SKILLS
(Time: 10–15 minutes)

Option 1. Class Memory Challenge

Review the list of Old Testament books that have been memorized in the three previous sessions. (See the chart in the student newspaper, *Covenant Times*, Unit I, Issue 4.) Ask a volunteer to go to a chalkboard or newsprint easel to write, from memory, the initial letters of the books, *Genesis* through *Esther*. Then ask the class members to call out the names in unison as you point to each initial letter in turn. You may want to divide into teams for this exercise.

Option 2. Learning Scripture

Add cards and symbols to the classroom Scripture Banner prepared for this Unit for any students who have memorized verses.

Remind the class members that any verse cited during this Unit may be memorized at any time. The complete list of passages for the Unit appears in the student newspaper, *Covenant Times*.

Unit I. Covenant—Session 4
Shell Year Intermediate—Copyright © 2000 Virginia Theological Seminary and Morehouse Publishing

Invite the students to choose either of the following to be learned before the next class session: *Deuteronomy 10:5* or *Joshua 24:15b, e*.

ONGOING PROJECT
(Time: 5–10 minutes)

Add to the class timeline the symbol of the Ark of the Covenant, the words Joshua/Judges, and the Scriptures cited for this session. Joshua's rule began around 1250 BCE, and the period of the judges was approximately 1230-1050 BCE.

SYMBOL CARD and TREASUREBOOK

Card 4 has an Ark of the Covenant on one side, with a Scripture verse, and an explanation on the back.

Suggest that the students read about the biblical books of *Joshua* and *Judges* in Part I, Section 5, or the *Shell Year Treasurebook*. Which of the judges was a woman? What did she do?

GOING FORTH

Gather the group. The teacher or a student will say:
I ask your prayers for all who seek God, or a deeper knowledge of him.
Pray that they may find and be found by him.
Silence

[Learners may add their petitions.]

Praise God for those in every generation in whom Christ has been honored especially those whom we remember today.
Pray that we may have grace to glorify Christ in our own day.

From The Prayers of the People
The Book of Common Prayer, p. 386

Teacher: Let us go forth in the name of Christ.
Students: Thanks be to God.

TEACHER'S ASSESSMENT

The students are likely to have a clear understanding of the stories of Abraham through Moses, and they may also know about Kings David and Solomon. Are they able to state what happened between Moses and King David? As you reflect on the students' work and their discussions, what are the indications that they can now place Joshua and the judges in biblical history?

LOOKING AHEAD

The next session focuses on the period of the kings and the building of a temple in Jerusalem. Consider the significance of permanent places of worship—places where people gather, generation after generation, to glorify God in prayer and song. Where are places of worship that have been important to you?

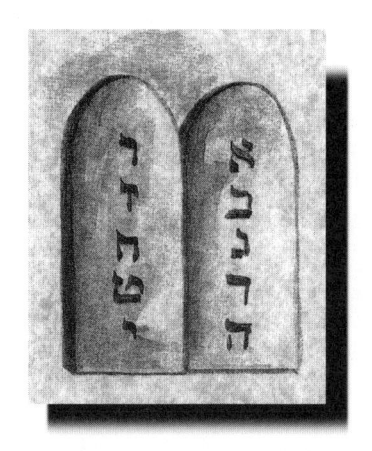

COVENANT
SESSION 5
A PLACE FOR THE ARK OF THE COVENANT

FOCUS

After the period of the judges, Israel moved to a new form of government. A series of kings ruled over the covenant people: Saul, David, and Solomon. Solomon built the temple that had been a dream of his father, David. It became the permanent home of the Ark of the Covenant. The students should be able to describe the shift in government, name the three kings, and explain in their own words the importance of the temple as a place for the Ark.

GETTING READY

In Israel's struggles with enemies and in an effort to stay together under the judges, the people lost a firm sense of the covenant Moses had made with God.

In this session, we move to the next great period in Israel's history. The Israelites shifted to a new form of governance. No longer would the people be a pure theocracy (ruled by God alone); they would become more like other nations—ruled by kings.

In *I Samuel*, chapters 8-10, we can sense the tension over this change. Some favored establishing the kingship while others opposed it. Samuel warned the people of the "ways of the king" (*I Samuel 8:9*). He knew that kings would be tempted to make Israel serve their own purposes, forgetting that they were bound by covenant to the Lord God of heaven and earth.

God reluctantly conceded to the people's wish. Samuel, in the role of God's prophet, took the initiative to find and anoint Saul as the first king of Israel.

The role of the king in early Israel was remote from that of her ancient neighbors. The kingship of Israel was instituted in response to internal and external threats from their enemies, the Philistines. By contrast, kingship in other nations was regarded as a divinely ordained political order that had existed from the beginning of time.

This session offers a survey of the reigns of the three great kings of Israel—Saul, David, and Solomon. It culminates with the construction and dedication of the temple under Solomon. At last the Ark of the Covenant (a constant reminder of the Commandments given to Moses) had a permanent resting place.

Intermediate-age students may be familiar with stories about these kings. This session challenges them to think about the thread of "covenant" through this period in the story of God's people.

Almighty and ever-living God, source of all wisdom and understanding, be present with those who take counsel for the renewal and mission of your Church. Teach us in all things to seek first your honor and glory. Guide us to perceive what is right, and grant us both the courage to pursue it and the grace to accomplish it; through Jesus Christ our Lord. *Amen.*

For a Church Convention or Meeting
The Book of Common Prayer, p. 818

TEACHING TIP

The six-pointed Star of David has always had special meaning for Jewish people. Many intermediate-age students have read stories or seen movies about the Holocaust during World War II in Europe. Jewish people were forced to wear a yellow star of David to set them apart from others. Explain that the symbol itself has no negative connotations. Jewish people throughout the world proudly display the Star of David as a symbol of their faith.

GATHERING

Display Poster No. 5 of the Star of David from the Teacher's Packet. As the students arrive, invite them to comment on the poster. What do they associate with it? Why? Where have they seen a Star of David?

When everyone is present, say:

Let us pray. (Use the prayer "For a Church Convention or Meeting," above, or a prayer of your own choosing.)

The chosen student lector reads from the class Bible:

A Reading from the Book of First Samuel, chapter 8, verses 1 through 9.

When Samuel became old, he made his sons judges over Israel. The name of his firstborn son was Joel, and the name of the second, Abijah; they were judges in Beer-sheba. Yet his sons did not follow in his ways, but turned aside after gain; they took bribes and perverted justice.

Then all the elders of Israel gathered together and came to Samuel at Ramah, and said to him, "You are old and your sons do not follow in your ways; appoint for us, then, a king to govern us, like other nations. But the thing displeased Samuel when they said, "Give us a king to govern us." Samuel prayed to the Lord, and the Lord said to Samuel, "Listen to the voice of the people in all that they say to you; for they have not rejected you, but they have rejected me from being king over them. Just as they have done to me, from the day I brought them up out of Egypt to this day, forsaking me and serving other gods, so also they are doing to you. Now then, listen to their voice; only—you shall solemnly warn them, and show them the ways of the king who shall reign over them."

Reader: The Word of the Lord.
Response: Thanks be to God.

INTRODUCING THE STORY
(Time: 10–20 minutes)

Begin by describing the shift from judges to kings as rulers of Israel. Until the time of the prophet Samuel, God alone was the ruler of Israel. But this did not work out, for the people were continually falling short and disobeying God.

The people grew tired of living under a succession of judges. They wanted a king like other nations. Samuel warned them of the dangers of a monarchy. He knew that having kings would tempt the people to forget that they were bound to God in a covenant.

But God instructed Samuel to do as the people asked, and to take the initiative in finding a king for Israel.

Tell the story of the anointing of Saul as the first king for Israel, the rise of David as the second king of Israel, and the events surrounding Solomon's succession to the throne:

• Saul, a renowned military leader from the mountain village of Gibeah, dedicated his reign to defeating the Philistines.

• David, from Bethlehem in Judah, was the second and most powerful king. He unified all of Israel and made it an independent state. He made Jerusalem the capital and first Holy City of Israel. He brought the Ark of the Covenant there and dreamed of a future temple for the worship of God.

• Solomon, the son of David and Bathsheba, was the third king of Israel. His wisdom surpassed the wisdom of his people: His massive building program included the magnificent temple in Jerusalem, which took seven years to complete. Emphasize the significance of the temple as a great symbol of the presence of God with the people and the home of the Ark of the Covenant. Read the student newspaper, ***Covenant Times*** (Unit I, Issue 5) for details about the temple construction, including a floorplan that shows where the Ark was kept.

The reign of Solomon was viewed as the "golden age" of Israel. Ask the students to turn in their Bibles to *I Kings 8:20-21* for a story about Solomon's speech at the dedication of the great temple. What does he say about the temple? about the ark of the covenant?

Next to Poster No. 5 used at the Gathering, display a sheet with these words: Kings of Israel, Saul, David, and Solomon. (Note that the Star of David symbolizes the period of kings in the history of the covenant people of God.)

EXPLORING
(Time: 15–20 minutes)

Option 1. Role Play

Role play the dedication of the temple (*I Kings 8*). Divide the class members into small groups or teams, each responsible for acting out one aspect of the story. Give each group an opportunity to look up the passage and decide how to present one of the following scenes (Note: If you made a replica of the Ark in the previous session, use it in the reenactment):

a. Solomon standing in front of the Temple, the elders and leaders of all the tribes before him, and the priests carrying the Ark of the Covenant (verses 1-4).

b. The people gathering to sacrifice oxen and sheep (verse 5).

c. The Ark placed in the inner sanctuary underneath the wings of the cherubim (verses 6-7).

After each group has presented its scene, talk about the event and what it meant to the people of Israel.

Option 2. Mural

Create a mural showing the scenes at the dedication of the temple (see listing under Option 1, above). This can be sketched directly onto a long sheet of paper, or drawn on separate pieces and attached to a background. When this is completed, ask a volunteer to stand next to the mural and read aloud *I Kings 8:14-21*.

Option 3. Word Puzzle

Ask the students to turn in the student newspaper, *Covenant Times*, Unit I, Issue 5, to "Temple Dedica-tion." This word puzzle can be completed by individuals, teams, or the whole group.

MUSIC
(Time: 10 minutes)

Sing or chant "Canticle 1, A Song of Creation" (*The Hymnal 1982*, S177; *We Sing of God*, S3) using the *Children Sing!* tape.

CONNECTING/SPEAKING OUT
(Time: 15–20 minutes)

Option 1. Group Discussion

Before the emergence of the kingship, early Israel was ruled by clan chieftains. Discuss with students the following: What led to the development of the kingship in Israel? How did the prophet Samuel feel about the idea? How would you describe the reign of King Saul? David's reign? Solomon's rule?

Was life better for Israel under kings than it had been under the judges? Why? Why not?

Option 2. Current Events

Stories from history (about kings and queens, priests, judges, and prophets) give students a chance to discover similarities and differences between past and present societies. The Israelite kings acknowledged their dependence on God. Solomon, the king, built a temple for God. Ask students to share some of the things they know about present-day countries and the role that religious faith plays in their national life. Bring in news clippings that might be shared on this topic.

REFLECTING
(Time: 10 minutes)

Share the following possibilities for the students' personal reflection:

Solomon offered a long prayer, re-dedicating himself and the people to a life of obedience to God's covenant. If you were to pray to God for help, what would you say? Name some thoughts and actions you would like to dedicate to God. You could begin your letter with: Dear God, please help me to . . . .

Add the sheets from this session to the "Reflection Collection" envelopes. Envelopes can be started at any time during the Unit.

LEARNING SKILLS
(Time: 10–15 minutes)

Option 1. Class Memory Challenge

Review briefly the books of the Old Testament that have been learned thus far. Then introduce the five books of poetry. Here is a way to remember them, in order: The first is Job. It is followed by two books that begin with P—*Psalms* and *Proverbs*. The last two are *Ecclesiastes* and *The Song of Solomon*. On a chalkboard or easel, write two P's followed by blanks. Put a blank above the P's, and two blanks below them. Point to the five blank areas repeatedly, calling on the group to fill them in.

When the five new books have been learned, go through the entire list from *Genesis* through *The Song of Solomon*. Refer to the chart in the student newspaper, *Covenant Times*, Unit I, Issue 5.

Option 2. Learning Scripture

If class members have memorized verses suggested in previous sessions, add cards and symbols to the Scripture Banner.

Invite the students to commit to memory one or both of the following: *II Chronicles 3:1* or *Psalm 51:15*. See "Learning Scripture" in the student newspaper, *Covenant Times*.

ONGOING PROJECT
(Time: 5–10 minutes)

Add to the class timeline the symbols of a Star of David and of Solomon's Temple, the names of the Kings Saul, David, and Solomon, and Scripture passages used in this session. The period of the three kings of united Israel was approximately 1050-925 BCE.

SYMBOL CARD and TREASUREBOOK

Card 5 has a symbol of a temple, a Scripture verse, and an explanation on the back.

Ask the students to look again at *Shell Year Treasurebook*, Part I, Ch. 3, to discover the "four large ideas" that led to the writing of the Old Testament. What are they?

GOING FORTH

Gather the group. The teacher or a student says:
I ask your prayers for all who seek God, or a deeper knowledge of him.
Pray that they may find and be found by him.
Silence

[Learners may add their petitions.]

Praise God for those in every generation in whom Christ has been honored especially those whom we remember today.
Pray that we may have grace to glorify Christ in our own day.
              From The Prayers of the People
              The Book of Common Prayer, p. 386

Teacher: Let us go forth in the name of Christ.
Students: Thanks be to God.

TEACHER'S ASSESSMENT

Consider the five symbols introduced so far in this Unit: rainbow (covenant with Noah); the field of stars (covenant with Abraham); tablets of the law (covenant with Moses); Ark of the Covenant (period of Joshua and the judges); Star of David and temple (period of the kingships of Saul, David, and Solomon). How well do the students connect the symbols and their respective periods in the Biblical narrative? the flow of the account from *Genesis* through *I Kings*? What actions or comments of the students suggest that they are making the associations?

LOOKING AHEAD

The next session introduces trouble and division in the kingdom of Israel. As you plan ahead for the discussion of the divided kingdoms of Israel and Judah, reflect on the suffering and turmoil that accompany major national divisions. Often these are paralleled in our own institutions, communities, families, and personal lives. Think about your own experiences with painful division.

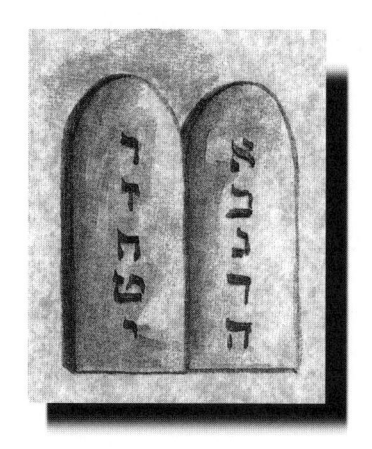

COVENANT
SESSION 6
COVENANT PEOPLE DIVIDED

FOCUS

In time, the kingdom of God's people was divided—Israel in the north and Judah in the south. The students should be able to describe the division, locate on a map the areas occupied by Israel and Judah and their neighboring nations, and explain in their own words the concept of "covenant faithfulness."

GETTING READY

Disobedience to the covenant brought tragic consequences for the people of Israel. In this session, we explore what happened after the death of Solomon:
  a. Rehoboam, son of Solomon, continued his father's harsh policies of heavy taxation and forced labor.
  b. Jeroboam led a revolt by ten northern tribes that resulted in a division into two kingdoms.
  c. The ten northern tribes formed the kingdom of Israel. The tribe of Judah became the kingdom of the south.
  d. For centuries, the two kingdoms continued—each one ruled by a succession of kings.

To get a better view of this whole period of covenant history, read *I Kings 11:41* to *II Kings 23:37*. The books of the Kings were probably one book originally, detailing the long struggle over what it meant to be God's chosen people.

Some of the kings dropped the concept of a covenant relationship with God; others tried to serve both God and their own desires. Some attempted valiantly to make Israel into the kind of kingdom they thought would be pleasing to God.

Throughout this era of about four centuries, in the ebb and flow of the kingdoms' histories, it was the prophets who took the lead in turning kings and people back to God. Sometimes the priests would side with the prophets, but usually they acceded to the kings' desires.

O God, the Father of all, whose Son commanded us to love our enemies: Lead them and us from prejudice to truth; deliver them and us from hatred, cruelty, and revenge; and in your good time enable us all to stand reconciled before you; through Jesus Christ our Lord. *Amen.*
  For our Enemies
  The Book of Common Prayer, p. 816

TEACHING TIP

While the stories of the Hebrew kings can be very exciting, young people may dismiss them unless you can relate them to their world. The events and personalities that resulted in the divided kingdom have parallels in recent history. Help students understand that their struggle to be true to God and fit in with their peers is not unlike the struggles of the Hebrew people.

GATHERING

As the students arrive, explain that new rules of conduct will apply for today's class time. (Some suggested rules might be: absolutely no talking without permission; no one will leave a seat without permission; all students will have homework to complete during the coming week; if today's activities are not completed during the allotted time period, there will be a punishment.)

After the new rules have been presented, urge class members to share the rules with others who may arrive later. Proceed with the class.

The Gathering activity will be the subject of the

discussion in Connecting/Speaking Out. Students will probably be more than ready to talk about the new rules, and should also see the connection with Rehoboam's arbitrary behavior introduced in the session.

When everyone is present, say:

Let us pray. (Use the prayer "For our Enemies," above, or a prayer of your own choosing.)

The chosen student lector reads from the class Bible:

A Reading from the Book of First Kings, chapter 12, verses 16 through 20.

When all Israel saw that the king would not listen to them, the people answered the king,
"What share do we have in David?
We have no inheritance in the son of Jesse.
To your tents, O Israel!
Look now to your own house, O David."
So Israel went away to their tents. But Rehoboam reigned over the Israelites who were living in the towns of Judah. When King Rehoboam sent Adoram, who was taskmaster over the forced labor, all Israel stoned him to death. King Rehoboam then hurriedly mounted his chariot to flee to Jerusalem. So Israel has been in rebellion against the house of David to this day.

When all Israel heard that Jeroboam had returned, they sent and called him to the assembly and made him king over all Israel. There was no one who followed the house of David, except the tribe of Judah alone.

Reader: The Word of the Lord.
Response: Thanks be to God.

INTRODUCING THE STORY
(Time: 10–20 minutes)

Using information from Getting Ready (above), *I Kings,* chapters 11 and 12, and the student newspaper, **Covenant Times** (Unit I, Issue 6) tell the story about the division of the kingdom.

In the last years of Solomon's reign, he was harsh and demanding. To accomplish his building projects, he established forced labor and severe rules.

During this period, a young man named Jeroboam came to Solomon's attention as a threat to his leadership. When Solomon wanted to kill him, Jeroboam fled to Egypt and remained there until Solomon died.

After Solomon's death, his son Rehoboam was all set to become king over Israel. But suddenly Jeroboam reappeared. Rehoboam became very angry and promised to punish the people even more gravely than his father had done. Jeroboam was unafraid, and he led the people in an uprising that resulted in a divided kingdom.

Ten tribes of Israel stayed together with Jeroboam as their king. Rehoboam was left with only the tribe of Judah. Direct the students' attention to the map of the kingdoms on Poster No. 6 in the Teacher's Packet, with Israel in the north and Judah in the south.

Ask the students to turn in their Bibles to *I Kings 12:12-16* to read about the initial meeting Rehoboam and Jeroboam. (The word scorpion, used by Rehoboam, refers to a stinging whip, much more cruel than an ordinary whip.) Ask: To whose advice did Rehoboam listen? Why? How did the people respond?

EXPLORING
(Time: 15–20 minutes)

Option 1. Oral History

The names and places of the characters in the story for this session can often be confusing. Help the students remember the people and places by composing a rap song about Rehoboam and Jeroboam. Work on the song as a group, or assign parts of the story to small groups. Use a tape recorder to capture the final product. Rhythm instruments will add to the performance.

The following could be included (see *I Kings 12* for more ideas):

• All Israel comes to Shechem to make Rehoboam king.

• The people promise to serve him if he lightens the heavy yoke (burden) that his father had put on them.

• The old men counsel Rehoboam to listen to the people, but the young men say scornfully, "Add more to their yoke."

• Rehoboam says, "My father disciplined you with whips, but I will discipline you with scorpions."

• Israel goes away to their tents.

• Rehoboam sends Adoram to be taskmaster, but the people stone him to death.

- Jeroboam, true to God, arises to lead the people of Israel.
- Rehoboam retreats to rule over Judah.

Option 2. Plaster Map

Provide each student with a sheet of corrugated paper stock on which to construct a relief map of the kingdoms of Israel and Judah. Use salt dough, flour dough, or plaster-of-paris mixed to a mayonnaise consistency. Vegetable coloring can be added to make the two kingdoms in different colors.

Draw outlines of the two kingdoms on the cardboard as a first step. Keep the dough or plaster within the sketched borders. Use the map on Poster No. 3 in the Teacher's Packet to help the students know where to put elevated areas.

Option 3. Jumbled Words

Invite the students to do the word jumble, "Keeping the Covenant," found in the student newspaper, *Covenant Times*, Unit I, Issue 6. Work as a group or in teams, or as individuals, to unscramble the ten Scripture words. Students may use their Bibles to check their answers.

MUSIC
(Time: 10 minutes)

Sing "God has spoken to his people" *(The Hymnal 1982*, 536; *We Sing of God*, 85) with the tape *Children Sing!*

Call attention to the name of the music ("Torah song"), noted in small print at the bottom of the page. Write the name on a board or newsprint. "Torah" means instruction, guidance, and law. (Torah Ora means "The law is our light.") "Hallelujah" is Hebrew for "Praise the Lord."

CONNECTING/SPEAKING OUT
(Time: 15–20 minutes)

Option 1. Group Discussion

Talk about the Gathering for this session and the sudden imposition of rules. Ask: How did it feel to have these rules suddenly introduced? What were your reactions?

Encourage the students to compare their experience in this session with what happened among the people under Rehoboam's harsh rule. How did they feel and react to their king?

Recall how Jeroboam and the people rebelled. If you had been there, how would you have reacted? Whose leadership would you have preferred? Why?

Option 2. Current Events

In every generation, groups of people rebel against established authority. These "revolutions" lead to the forming of new governments with different laws and customs. The twentieth century has been marked by many such revolutions, with the names of countries changing and rapid shifts in leadership.

If possible, bring in current maps to compare with maps of the former Soviet Union, the continent of Africa from the late 1950s, or Europe in the 1970s. Ask the student to find differences in the maps. Share the reasons for the changes you or the students may know. Are there leaders today who are like Rehoboam or Jeroboam?

REFLECTING
(Time: 10 minutes)

Share the following possibilities for the students' personal reflection:

Think about a time when people took sides in an argument at school, a scout meeting, or a sports event.

How did you feel? Did you want to bring both sides together? Did you take sides?

At the end of your reflection, write a prayer for forgiveness.

Add the sheets from this session to the "Reflection Collection" envelopes. Envelopes can be started at any time during the Unit.

LEARNING SKILLS
(Time: 10–15 minutes)

Option 1. Class Memory Challenge

Review the books of the Old Testament that have been learned thus far (*Genesis* through *The Song of Solomon*). Then introduce the list of books known as the major prophets: *Isaiah, Jeremiah, Lamentations, Ezekiel,* and *Daniel*. Refer to the chart in the student newspaper, *Covenant Times*, Unit I, Issue 6.

A convenient way to commit the major prophets to memory is to recall the sentence, "IJ led." The IJ stands for *Isaiah* and *Jeremiah*. The word "led" is formed from the initial letters of *Lamentations, Ezekiel,* and *Daniel*.

Option 2. Learning Scripture

Place cards and symbols on the Scripture Banner for students who have memorized verses suggested previously.

Invite the students to memorize before the next class session any or all of the following: *I Kings 12:16b; Psalm 122:1; Psalm 124:8.* (All these are verses used repeatedly in the worship of both Jewish and Christian congregations.) See "Learning Scripture" in the student newspaper, *Covenant Times.*

ONGOING PROJECT

(Time: 5–10 minutes)

Add to the class timeline the symbols of a twelve-pointed star and a lion's head. (The star represents the unified twelve tribes of Israel. The lion's head stands for the people of Judah, ancestors of David, who were left as a separate kingdom after the division under Rehoboam.) Alongside, write the words Israel and Judah, and the Scripture citation, *I Kings 12:1-20.* The approximate dates of the divided kingdom are 925-587/586 BCE.

SYMBOL CARD and TREASUREBOOK

Card 6 has a twelve-pointed star and a lion's head, a Scripture verse, and an explanation on the back.

Recommend that the students review the summaries of *I and II Kings* in the *Shell Year Treasurebook,* Part I, Section 5. Who followed Solomon as king? What happened?

GOING FORTH

Gather the group. The teacher or a student says:
I ask your prayers for all who seek God, or a deeper knowledge of him.
Pray that they may find and be found by him.
Silence

[Learners may add their petitions.]

Praise God for those in every generation in whom Christ has been honored especially those whom we remember today.
Pray that we may have grace to glorify Christ in our own day.

From The Prayers of the People
The Book of Common Prayer, p. 386

Teacher: Let us go forth in the name of Christ.
Students: Thanks be to God.

TEACHER'S ASSESSMENT

When a covenant is broken or an agreement is not working, a relationship is harmed and ruptured. What did the students say about the concepts of separation and division? As they thought about the dividing of God's people into separate kingdoms, did the students sense the pain and brokenness of the people?

LOOKING AHEAD

The next session focuses on the destruction of the kingdoms and the captivity in Babylon that followed. God's people were in a strange land, far from their temple site. Going into exile has been a recurring experience for various peoples of the earth. Have you ever felt that you were in exile?

COVENANT

SESSION 7
COVENANT PEOPLE IN EXILE

FOCUS

God's covenant people fell victim to the king of Babylon, and many were carried into exile. There they wept and longed to be back in their own land. The students should be able to summarize orally the story of the exile, explain the symbol of the harp in a willow tree, and describe the plight of exiled peoples in every period of history (including our own).

GETTING READY

The people of Israel and of Judah, so often rebellious and disobedient, fell upon hard days, and large groups of them were led into Babylon as captives.

This policy of deportation was practiced by many ancient powers:

Assyria deported part of the Northern Israel population in 722 BCE *(II Kings 17:6)*. Babylon deported King Jehoiachin and members of the royal family in 597 BCE *(II Kings 24:15-16)*.

The second deportation—led by the Babylonian King Nebuchadnezzar in 587-586 BCE—was devastating for Jerusalem. The temple, palace, and houses were burned. The city walls were broken down and large numbers of people were taken into exile *(II Kings 25:8-12)*.

Students do not need to memorize the precise dates and details of the Babylonian captivity. They do need to understand the sadness of the exile as a never-to-be-forgotten experience in the life of God's people. The imagery of being among strangers, away from the familiar surroundings of home and temple, is conveyed in *Psalm 137:1-4*, written just after the people's return from the exile. Read and think about this psalm as you prepare to teach.

O God our Father, whose Son forgave his enemies while he was suffering shame and death: Strengthen those who suffer for the sake of conscience; when they are accused, save them from speaking in hate; when they are rejected, save them from bitterness; when they are imprisoned, save them from despair; and to us your servants, give grace to respect their witness and to discern the truth, that our society may be cleansed and strengthened. This we ask for the sake of Jesus Christ, our merciful and righteous Judge. *Amen.*

For those who suffer for the sake of Conscience
The Book of Common Prayer, p. 823

TEACHING TIP

Students at the intermediate-age level are able to memorize impressive amounts of information. For instance, young people can recall details from their baseball card collections or all the lyrics of popular songs and commercials. This is a good time to offer the chance to memorize the books of the Bible, names of key figures, timelines, Scripture verses, and hymns if it is fun and meaningful.

GATHERING

Arrange a display of pictures showing people who had to leave their homelands. Consult a public library for books or find clippings from the media. Some examples would be Palestinians in camps in the Middle East, Cubans leaving their country in the 1960s and today, the Vietnamese boat people of the 1970s, Haitian boat people, or the Albanians of the 1990s.

As the students arrive, think aloud with them about what it might be like to lose possessions, homes, and jobs—and to be sent to a refugee camp.

If you know persons in your community or congregation who have had such an experience, you might want to share some details about their lives.

When everyone is present, say:

Let us pray. (Use the prayer "For those who suffer for the sake of Conscience," above, or a prayer of your own choosing.)

The chosen student lector reads from the class Bible:

A Reading from the Book of Second Kings, chapter 25, verses 8 through 12.

In the fifth month, on the seventh day of the month—which was the nineteenth year of King Nebuchadnezzar, king of Babylon—Nebuzaradan, the captain of the bodyguard, a servant of the king of Babylon, came to Jerusalem. He burned the house of the Lord, the king's house, and all the houses of Jerusalem; every great house he burned down. All the army of the Chaldeans who were with the captain of the guard broke down the walls around Jerusalem. Nebuzaradan the captain of the guard carried into exile the rest of the people who were left in the city and the deserters who had defected to the king of Babylon—all the rest of the population. But the captain of the guard left some of the poorest people of the land to be vinedressers and tillers of the soil.

Reader: The Word of the Lord.
Response: Thanks be to God.

INTRODUCING THE STORY
(Time: 10–20 minutes)

Begin by reading aloud *Psalm 137:1-4*. Explain that the psalm is probably a lament written during a tragic time in the history of God's covenant people.

Remind the students that the people of God were divided into two kingdoms—Israel in the north, and Judah in the south. For a period of nearly four centuries, each of the two kingdoms had a long succession of kings.

The kings and religious leaders were never able to keep the covenant with God as they should. They formed alliances with neighboring peoples and sometimes worshiped strange gods. They placed their reliance on power and wealth instead of obedience to God. They neglected the poor and failed to work for God's justice.

Prophets arose to warn that God would bring judgment upon the people for their lack of faithfulness. The prophets Amos, Micah, and Hosea wrote stern warnings to both Israel and Judah.

Around 586 BCE, the prophets' predictions came true. The king of Babylon destroyed the temple, burned the people's homes, and broke down the walls of Jerusalem. Ask students to turn in their Bibles to *II Kings 25* to locate the story of the destruction of Jerusalem. Large numbers of the people were taken into captivity in Babylon. They were settled in colonies around and about the city.

Describe, in your own words, how these exiles would feel—far from their own land and without all that they held dear. For ideas, refer to an imaginary report about the deportation of Judah's people in the student newspaper, **Community Times** (Unit I, Issue 7). The paper includes a description of how the exiles felt and notes on the present-day location of the Babylonian region.

The exile lasted fifty years or so before some of the people (or their descendants) were able to go back home. The final period of migration back to the Hebrew homeland came nearly a hundred years after that.

During the exile, the prophets Jeremiah and Ezekiel spoke words of comfort and assurance of hope. Share the picture of the prophet Jeremiah found on Poster No. 5 in the Teacher's Packet.

EXPLORING
(Time: 15–20 minutes)

Option 1. Illustration

Supply each student with a large sheet of white construction paper, and crayons or markers. Invite the class members to draw their own illustrations of the destruction of Jerusalem as described in *II Kings*, chapter 25. As they work, the students may share phrases and descriptions from the chapter. Suggest that the illustrations include the people being driven into captivity in Babylon.

Option 2. Contrasting Collages

Divide the class into two groups. Each group will make a large collage on a piece of poster board using pictures or words clipped from magazines or newspapers. Ask one group to concentrate on the theme of people in distress, such as those who are exiled to a strange land. Ask the other group to focus on comfortable surroundings of "home."

Remind both groups to consider all the emotions, living situations, and scenery that will convey their respective themes. Afterwards, talk about the collages and what the pictures and words represent. Display the finished products in the classroom.

Option 3. Acrostic

Turn, in the student newspaper, *Covenant Times*, Unit I, Issue 7, to the puzzle titled "Exile in Babylon." This acrostic can be done by individuals, teams, or the whole class.

MUSIC
(Time: 10 minutes)

Sing "God has spoken to his people" (*The Hymnal 1982*, 536; *We Sing of God*, 85) with the *Children Sing!* tape.

The rhythm of the music is particularly appealing. The students may clap their hands, use pencils to tap on the table, shake coins in their hands, or find things in the classroom to make different sounds.

CONNECTING/SPEAKING OUT
(Time: 15–20 minutes)

Option 1. Group Discussion

Imagine what it was like for individuals among God's people who spent so many years in the Babylonian exile. Ask for volunteers to talk about situations in which they felt homesick: being away at camp, on an extended vacation, or staying overnight at someone else's house. Ask: What feelings did you experience? What did you miss? Did you have a choice about when you could go home? Or was the period away from home pre-determined? How was life "different" when you were away? Did other people understand your feelings?

Refer to the pictures of refugees (exiles) displayed at the Gathering. How would you describe the feelings of the people?

Option 2. Current Events

Within our country, groups of people have endured the suffering of involuntary exile. For example: Native Americans were placed on reservations. Africans were forcibly taken from their country and made slaves. Japanese Americans were placed in internment camps during World War II. (Share other examples.)

Ask: Were you aware of these "exiles"? What would it feel like to be an exile in your own country? In another country? What would you want to take with you?

REFLECTING
(Time: 10 minutes)

Share the following possibilities for the students' personal reflection:

Suppose you are going to be away from home for several months. What do you think you would miss most? Would you miss worshipping at your church? What do you like about worship at your church?

How would you worship God while you were away from home?

You may wish to end your reflection with a short prayer.

Add the sheets from this session to the "Reflection Collection" envelopes. Envelopes can be started at any time during the Unit.

LEARNING SKILLS
(Time: 10–15 minutes)

Option 1. Class Memory Challenge

Review briefly the list of five major prophetic writings, learned in the previous session. Note that there is only one remaining task—to learn the books of the twelve minor prophets: *Hosea, Joel, Amos, Obadiah, Jonah, Micah, Nahum, Habukkuk, Zephaniah, Haggai, Zechariah,* and *Malachi*. See the chart in the student newspaper, *Covenant Times*, Unit I, Issue 7.

List the twelve on a chalkboard or on newsprint for all to see. Lead the group in a slow, deliberate chant of the names. Stress all the syllables of the names. Repeat at least three times. Divide the group into teams and challenge each one to be able to say the twelve names aloud together after a short period of study. Allow each team to do so.

Option 2. Learning Scripture

Allow time for students who have memorized verses from suggestions offered in previous sessions to add cards and symbols to the Scripture Banner.

Invite the students to choose one or both of the following verses to be committed to memory before the next class session: *Psalm 137:1-2*, or *4*. See "Learning Scripture" in the student newspaper, *Covenant Times*.

ONGOING PROJECT
(Time: 5–10 minutes)

Add to the class time-line the symbol of a harp in a willow tree, with the word "exile" and the Scripture cited for this session *(II Kings 25:8-12)*. You may want to add the dates 586-444 BCE, the approximate period from the beginning of the exile to the return of the last group quite some time after the reconstruction of the Jerusalem temple.

SYMBOL CARD and TREASUREBOOK

Card 7 has the symbol of a harp in a willow tree, a Scripture verse, and an explanation on the back.

Challenge the students to read *Shell Year Treasurebook* and prepare a true/false quiz based on facts from Part I, Section 5.

GOING FORTH

Gather the group. The teacher or a student says:
> I ask your prayers for all who seek God, or a deeper knowledge of him.
> Pray that they may find and be found by him.
>
> *Silence*
>
> [Learners may add their petitions.]
>
> Praise God for those in every generation in whom Christ has been honored especially those whom we remember today.
> Pray that we may have grace to glorify Christ in our own day.
>   From The Prayers of the People
>   *The Book of Common Prayer*, p. 386

Teacher: Let us go forth in the name of Christ.
Students: Thanks be to God.

TEACHER'S ASSESSMENT

How did students respond to the anguish of the Babylonian exile? Were they sympathetic to the plight of exiled peoples from the past? Did they seem able to generalize about exiles at any time in history?

LOOKING AHEAD

In the next session, the students will examine the edict of Cyrus that made it possible for the Hebrew people to return to their land. Think about homecoming events that you have experienced. What were the occasions? Who was there? What did you do? Why do you remember these times?

COVENANT
SESSION 8
COVENANT PEOPLE RETURN

FOCUS

Cyrus, king of Persia, permitted many of the people of God to return from their time of exile and begin rebuilding the temple in Jerusalem. The students should be able to tell the story of the people's return and describe the renewal of Hebrew faith and practice.

GETTING READY

This session concludes this Unit's exploration of the covenant concept in Hebrew history. First, we explored two great covenants in *Genesis* (Noah and Abraham) and the covenant in *Exodus* (Moses). Then, in rapid succession, we glimpsed key periods in the life of God's people since their entry into the promised land under Joshua's leadership: the time of the judges; the period of three kings—Saul, David, and Solomon; the divided kingdom; and the exile.

We turn now to the following events:

a. Cyrus, king of Persia, conquered Babylon.
b. He issued a decree that allowed the people of Judah to return to Jerusalem and begin reconstructing the destroyed temple.
c. Over a period of many decades, other groups of exiles (or their descendants) returned to their homeland.
d. The walls of Jerusalem were rebuilt.

Through this whole time, prophets of God delivered two kinds of messages to the covenant people: 1. stern warnings of coming doom; 2. words of hope for eventual freedom and restoration in their own land. Their deportation was not to be the final word. At no time did the prophets proclaim the end of God's covenant.

The prophet Isaiah said that God had inspired King Cyrus to issue his edict. He spoke of Cyrus as God's "anointed" through whom God's plan for the people would be realized.

For an account of the return from exile and the reconstruction that followed, we turn to the books of *Ezra* and *Nehemiah*. These books have always been considered by Jews to be one book covering the period from the first year of Cyrus' reign (539 BCE) through the thirty-second year of the reign of Artaxerxes, King of Persia (432 BCE).

The books of *Ezra* and *Nehemiah* share how much had to be done to repair all the ruin of the years in captivity: Traditions had to be re-established, the city and the sanctuary had to be rebuilt, and life under the Law had to be renewed. The writer tells of each successive stage in accomplishing the tasks of building the altar, the new temple, and the walls of the city. A new sense of a holy community was encouraged—with true worship and obedience to the God who called them to covenant faithfulness so long ago.

> Look with pity, O heavenly Father, upon the people in this land who live with injustice, terror, disease, and death as their constant companions. Have mercy upon us. Help us to eliminate our cruelty to these our neighbors. Strengthen those who spend their lives establishing equal protection of the law and equal opportunities for all. And grant that every one of us may enjoy a fair portion of the riches of this land; through Jesus Christ our Lord. *Amen.*
>
> For the Oppressed
> *The Book of Common Prayer*, p. 826

TEACHING TIP

Students at the intermediate level enjoy learning in creative ways (through skits, murals, and games). They like to cooperate in teams and can handle the job of dividing tasks and coordinating efforts. Organize class activities to capitalize on the students' interest in group work.

GATHERING

Put up a simple banner that says, "Welcome home!" On a nearby table, set out some items that might be appropriate for a homecoming party, such as hats, horns, balloons, and confetti. As students arrive, talk with them about any homecoming celebrations they know about or have participated in.

When everyone is present, say:

Let us pray. (Use the Collect "For the Oppressed," above, or a prayer of your own choosing.)

The chosen student lector reads from the class Bible:

A Reading from the Book of Ezra, chapter 1, verses 2 through 4.

"Thus says King Cyrus of Persia: The Lord, the God of heaven, has given me all the kingdoms of the earth, and he has charged me to build him a house at Jerusalem in Judah. Any of those among you who are of his people—may their God be with them!—are now permitted to go up to Jerusalem in Judah, and rebuild the house of the Lord, the God of Israel—he is the God who is in Jerusalem; and let all survivors, in whatever place they reside, be assisted by the people of their place with silver and gold, with goods and with animals, besides freewill offerings for the house of God in Jerusalem."

Reader: The Word of the Lord.
Response: Thanks be to God.

INTRODUCING THE STORY
(Time: 10–20 minutes)

Begin by recalling the situation of the people of God who had been in exile in Babylon for many years.

In your own words, tell the story of the return of the people of God. For background, read about Ezra's reading of the law in the student newspaper, ***Covenant Times*** (Unit I, Issue 8). It includes an interview with Nehemiah describing his leadership in restoring safety to the city of Jerusalem and in renewing the people's obedience to the covenant. Key figures in the history of Israel and Judah are also highlighted in background sketches. In your story include the following:

• Explain the "Edict of Cyrus" (see *Ezra 1:2-4*). This Persian king was the one who allowed the people of God to return to Jerusalem and start the rebuilding of the temple. In fact, the prophet Isaiah called Cyrus the "Lord's anointed" *(Isaiah 45:1-3)*. This was like saying, "Cyrus is God's agent because he is allowing us to return."

• It took nearly twenty years to rebuild the temple; there were many interruptions. Harvests were poor. People grew discouraged and would not work. Neighboring peoples were hostile.

• People trickled back from exile in Babylon but did not want to live in Jerusalem because its walls were in ruins. Obedience to the covenant and faithful worship had all but disappeared.

• Nehemiah was a servant of the Persian king (not Cyrus, but one of his successors). He was appointed governor over Judah. He oversaw the rebuilding of the walls of Jerusalem. Once the city was more secure, he turned to the task of calling the people back to faithful observance of the covenant law.

• Ezra, a priest and scribe of the temple, had returned from Babylon after Nehemiah did. He brought with him a copy of the law of Moses. He was shocked by the way the people in Judah were living.

• Ezra read aloud the entire law as the people listened. Nehemiah was there. It was the beginning of a new period of faithfulness among God's people. To this day, Jewish people honor Ezra as the one who helped them to become "people of the book."

EXPLORING
(Time: 15–20 minutes)

Option 1. Expressions of Joy

This session's theme lends itself to artistic expression, either realistic or abstract. Provide paper, crayons, markers, colored pencils, chalk, or paint. Invite the students to portray the joy of the Hebrew people upon hearing Cyrus' proclamation.

Option 2. Homecoming

Plan a party to celebrate the return of the exiles from Babylon. Divide into three groups to prepare for the celebration. The first group will decorate the room using items from the Gathering display. They can make signs, hang balloons, or create construction paper chains to represent the exile and freedom.

The second group will be in charge of games. Let them know if the games are to be indoors or outside. Encourage them to plan two or three games that will include everyone in the group.

The third group will prepare the tables, set up the snack, and make name tags for everyone in the group. Save about twenty minutes for the party at the end of the class session.

Option 3. Making New Words

Ask the students to complete "Words from Ezra," found in the student newspaper, *Covenant Times*, Unit I, Issue 8. Students may work as individuals, in teams, or as a total group.

Examples of words that can be formed: Persia, Israel, Lord, spirit, gold, build, rebuild. Suggest that the group keep a list of other key words that *cannot* be formed from the letters in the sentence, including: Cyrus, Judah, Jerusalem, offerings, house.

MUSIC
(Time: 10 minutes)

Sing again "God has spoken to his people" (*The Hymnal 1982*, 536; *We Sing of God*, 85) with the *Children Sing!* tape.

If possible, ask someone to play this song on the guitar for the class. Invite the students to pretend they are returning from Babylon and singing along the way. Which words and phrases would have special meaning?

CONNECTING/SPEAKING OUT
(Time: 15–20 minutes)

Option 1. Group Discussion

Discuss the following with students: How would you explain why the people of God became captives in Babylon? How faithful had they been to the covenant with God?

Have you ever stopped talking or seeing a friend because you were angry? Did you give that person a second chance? Why do you think God gave the people of Israel another chance?

Have you ever been asked to take a "time out" by a parent or a teacher? What was that like? How did you feel when you were allowed to be a part of the family or group again?

Option 2. Current Events

To live in freedom is to enjoy greater opportunity, but it also entails taking on personal responsibility for yourself and the welfare of others. All of us often take our freedom for granted. In recent times, many people in the world have suffered the fate of being deprived of their freedom. Some have been detained against their will as hostages and prisoners. (If possible, display articles and books related to people who have been political captives.)

Ask the students to share their opinions about the use of force to overcome or change peoples and nations. What causes leaders of groups to deprive others of their freedom? What are some of the freedoms that are lost by the victims? Why does this keep happening? Why do we care?

REFLECTING
(Time: 10 minutes)

Share the following possibilities for the students' personal reflection:

Think about a time when you were away from your home and familiar surroundings (such as going to camp or having a long visit with relatives elsewhere). Recall how it felt to come back and resume your regular activities. What was it like? What were you grateful for? Invite students to record their ideas in writing.

You may wish to add a prayer at the end of your reflection.

Add the sheets from this session to the "Reflection Collection" envelopes.

LEARNING SKILLS
(Time: 10–15 minutes)

Option 1. Class Memory Challenge

Review all the books of the Old Testament. Place on a board or newsprint the names of the sections: Torah (Pentateuch), Historical Books, Poetry, Major Prophets, Minor Prophets. The students can call out the names of the books in unison for each heading. Which section do they find easiest to recall? Why? (Refer to the chart in the student newspaper, *Covenant Times*, Unit I, Issue 8.)

Option 2. Learning Scripture

Provide opportunity for students to add cards and symbols to the classroom Scripture Banner for the verses they have memorized.

Challenge the students to memorize *Isaiah 40:3, 4,* or *5* before the next class session. See "Learning Scripture" in the student newspaper, *Covenant Times.*

ONGOING PROJECT
(Time: 5–10 minutes)

Add to the class timeline the symbol of the hand of God, the words "Israel returns" and "Temple rebuilt," and a Scripture verse chosen from the first chapter of the *Book of Ezra.* Write the dates 539-520 BCE on the card. These are the approximate years of Judah's return to their homeland. Other exiles did not return until the following century.

SYMBOL CARD and TREASUREBOOK

Card 8 has the symbol of a scroll, a Scripture verse, and an explanation on the back.

Invite the students to read *Shell Year Treasurebook,* Part I, Section 6. Which books in the Old Testament repeat the same stories found in other books?

GOING FORTH

Gather the group. The teacher or a student says:
> I ask your prayers for all who seek God, or a deeper knowledge of him.
> Pray that they may find and be found by him.
> *Silence*

[Learners may add their petitions.]

> Praise God for those in every generation in whom Christ has been honored especially those whom we remember today.
> Pray that we may have grace to glorify Christ in our own day.
>> From The Prayers of the People
>> *The Book of Common Prayer,* p. 386

Teacher: Let us go forth in the name of Christ.
Students: Thanks be to God.

TEACHER'S ASSESSMENT

Think back over this Unit. The students have reexamined covenants God made with Noah, Abraham, and Moses. In a rapid survey, they have been introduced to these periods in biblical history: Joshua and the judges; the rise and rule of Kings Saul, David, and Solomon; the division of the kingdoms after Solomon; the Babylonian captivity; and the people's return to their own land. How well do you think the students have grasped the flow of the story, which covers hundreds of years? Are they able to identify key figures? Can they put the main events into correct sequence?

LOOKING AHEAD

The session that follows is designed for use on the Sunday nearest All Saints' Day (November 1).

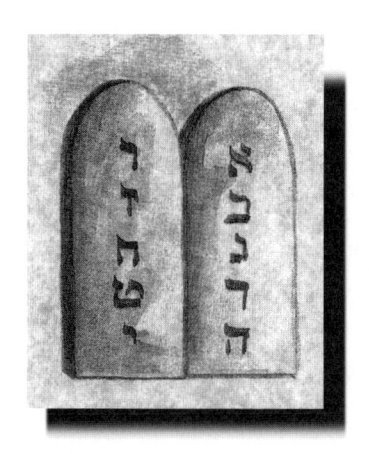

COVENANT
SESSION 9
ALL SAINTS

FOCUS

At the Feast of All Saints, we remember all our forebears who have believed and followed God—from Abraham until now. God is faithful and merciful to every generation, and we celebrate and praise God for this kindly providence. The students should be able to link the biblical theme of God's covenant faithfulness with All Saints' Day.

GETTING READY

The celebration of All Saints' Day is related to the covenant history of God's people. On this major Feast Day of the Church, we include the remembrance of the Hebrew leaders, prophets, and followers who were called out to be a chosen people in the world. They are among those whom we honor as saints of God.

The session is designed to be used at the appropriate time in the Church Year and can stand alone.

God's covenant faithfulness is unique in that God stands at the center. Divine initiative and faithfulness allow the people to respond with fidelity. The long line of saints in the Christian and Hebrew traditions are those who accept God's word and promise as trustworthy.

The covenant faithfulness between God and his people results in an exclusive demand of obedience (*Genesis,* chapter 6; *Exodus 20:3*). Since the faith of the saints is always reflective of God's fidelity and loving kindness, it must be expressed in both obedience and praise. This we recall each time we renew our own covenant relationship begun at baptism.

We give thanks to you, O Lord our God, for all your servants and witnesses of time past: for Abraham, the father of believers, and Sarah his wife; for Moses, the lawgiver, and Aaron, the priest; for Miriam and Joshua, Deborah and Gideon, and Samuel with Hannah his mother; for Isaiah and all the prophets; for Mary, the mother of our Lord; for Peter and Paul and all the apostles; for Mary and Martha, and Mary Magdalene; for Stephen, the first martyr, and all the martyrs and saints in every age and in every land. In your mercy, O Lord our God, give us, as you gave to them, the hope of salvation and the promise of eternal life; through Jesus Christ our Lord, the first-born of many from the dead. *Amen.*

For the Saints and Faithful Departed
The Book of Common Prayer, p. 838

TEACHING TIP

Most students at this age enjoy expressing ideas by drawing pictures. Some will produce realistic scenes, with almost photographic detail. Others will draw abstract images whose shape or color will convey varying moods. While you can offer a few suggestions when introducing an art project, it is best to avoid too many instructions. Students often enjoy brainstorming together, to stimulate their creativity and generate new ideas.

GATHERING

Ahead of time, cut out the names and individual letters found on the All Saints' Poster No. 7 in the Teacher's Packet. If you wish, these can be mounted on heavier paper stock. The names are Abraham, Sarah, Moses, Aaron, Miriam, Joshua, Deborah, Gideon, Samuel, Hannah, Isaiah, Mary (mother of Jesus), Peter, Paul, Martha, Mary Magdalene, Stephen. The six letters are S, A, I, N, T, S.

As the students arrive, invite them to create a

display on a board or table top. The letters are to be arranged to form a title word for the display. The names may be placed in any positions that appeal to the class members. As they work, encourage them to talk about the individuals who are named.

When everyone is present, say:

Let us pray. (Use the thanksgiving "For the Saints and Faithful Departed.") Distribute Prayer Books to the group. The chosen student lector leads in a responsive reading of *Psalm 145:8-21* (BCP, p. 802). The lector reads verse 8, the group reads verse 9, and the reading continues in this pattern to the end. (If Prayer Books are not available, make photocopies of the passage.)

The chosen student lector reads from *The Book of Common Prayer*.

Let us read responsively by whole verse, Psalm 145, verses 8 to 21.

The Lord is gracious and full of compassion,
   slow to anger and of great kindness.
The Lord is loving to everyone
   and his compassion is over all his works.
All your works praise you, O Lord,
   and your faithful servants bless you.
They make known the glory of your kingdom
   and speak of your power;
That the peoples may know of your power
   and the glorious splendor of your kingdom.
Your kingdom is an everlasting kingdom;
   your dominion endures throughout all ages.
The Lord is faithful in all his words
   and merciful in all his deeds.
The Lord upholds all those who fall;
   he lifts up those who are bowed down.
The eyes of all wait upon you, O Lord,
   and you give them their food in due season.
You open wide your hand
   and satisfy the needs of every living creature.

The Lord is righteous in all his ways
   and loving in all his works.
The Lord is near to those who call upon him,
   to all who call upon him faithfully.
He fulfills the desire of those who fear him;
   he hears their cry and helps them.
The Lord preserves all those who love him,
   but he destroys all the wicked.

INTRODUCING THE STORY
(Time: 10 minutes)

Ask the students to turn to the thanksgiving "For the Saints and Faithful Departed," found in *Covenant Times,* Unit I, Issue 9. Suggest that they match the names on their display prepared at the Gathering (above) with the phrases of the Collect. With the students' help, describe briefly each of the saints named in the prayer.

Review the meaning of God's covenant faithfulness the the people of God. From the call of Abraham through the whole history of the people of Israel (with all their triumphs and trials), and from the coming of Jesus Christ to the present-day Church, God's faithfulness and mercy extend to every generation.

Ask the students what they think about when they hear the word "saint." Write their ideas on a piece of newsprint. Then describe the two-fold definition of the word "saints":

• God has dedicated and "set apart" individuals (saints) in every generation who are remembered and honored as persons with extraordinary faith in God. Through these "holy ones," God's covenant is sustained and renewed. (These are represented by the names in the Collect, above.)

• In the Christian church, all baptized persons belong to the "communion of saints." Each of us is joined with all the followers of Christ in all previous generations.

Compare these definitions with the words or phrases written on the newsprint. Add new words, including the names of each person in the class. Then invite the students to add names to the display prepared earlier—either biblical figures not mentioned in the Collect or contemporary Christians whom they would regard as saints.

Ask the students to turn, in *The Book of Common Prayer,* to An Outline of the Faith (The Catechism), page 862. Locate the Question, "What is the communion of saints?" Ask: Did you realize that a person whom you have hurt is a saint? Would knowing that make you treat this person differently?

EXPLORING
(Time: 15–20 minutes)

Option 1. All Saints' Alphabet

Using the alphabet, list at least one biblical character, a Saint on the Church's calendar, or a saintly quality alongside each letter. You may need to supply suitable words for the letters q, x, and z (such as Quiet, "eX-traordinary," and Zealous). Possibilities might include:

A   Abraham
B   Baptist, Benjamin
C   Christians . . . . etc.

You may want to point out that God in Christ is "the Alpha and the Omega, the beginning and the end" (as represented by the first and last letters of the Greek alphabet). See *Revelation 21:6*.

Option 2. Psalm Illustration

Provide the students with construction paper, crayons, and markers. Ask them to work individually or in pairs to produce their own illustrations of selected verses from *Psalm 145:8-21*. (For reference, use Prayer Books or copies made for the Gathering, above.)

Some of the students may choose to do literal pictures, such as an open hand to illustrate verse 7. Others may simply create pictures that suggest the mood of the passage, such as rays of color extended downward over the page. Still others may elect to draw scenes of biblical events that seem to them to portray particular verses, such as Moses praying to God, to illustrate verse 19.

Option 3. Shields

Ask the students to work individually on the "Saints' Shields," found in the student newspaper, *Covenant Times*, Unit I, Issue 9. When the task is completed, the students may wish to share how they filled in the shields.

MUSIC
(Time: 10 minutes)

Practice singing "For all the saints who from their labors rest" (*The Hymnal 1982*, 287; *We Sing of God*, 46) with the *Children Sing!* tape.

The students might enjoy looking over each stanza and choosing the words that bring pictures to mind, such as Stanza 2, with images of a rock, a fortress, a captain, darkness, and light.

CONNECTING/SPEAKING OUT
(Time: 15–20 minutes)

Option 1. Group Discussion

Begin a group discussion by noting that we sometimes speak of saints with a capital *S* (the great figures of the past whom we honor in the Church), and saints with a small *s* (all the baptized people of God, both living and dead). Ask: How does it make you feel to be considered a saint? When we think of ourselves as saints, how does it affect the way we live?

In *Hebrews 12:1-2*, the saints of the past are called a "cloud of witnesses." The writer asks us to take up the Christian way of life, looking to Jesus as an example. Jesus is called a "pioneer." Ask: How would you explain the words "cloud of witnesses" and "pioneer"? Who are some of the saints you would include in the "cloud"? How is Jesus a pioneer?

Option 2. Current Events

Using current newspapers and magazines, ask students to find articles about individuals or groups whose deeds suggest saint-like behavior and faith in God.

Afterwards, share the stories and explain the reasons for their selection. Talk about the people in the stories. Ask: Why did you select this person or story? Is this person different from people you know? What makes a person "saintly"?

REFLECTING
(Time: 10 minutes)

Share the following possibilities for the students' personal reflection time:

Who are the people who have inspired you the most? What do you admire about them? What have they done or said? Would you want to be like one of these people? Why?

Write down your thoughts and conclude your reflection with a prayer.

Add the sheets from this session to the "Reflection Collection" envelopes. Envelopes can be started at any time during the Unit.

LEARNING SKILLS
(Time: 10–15 minutes)

Option 1. Class Memory Challenge

If the students wish to do so, review the names, in order, of all the Old Testament books learned thus far in this Unit. See the charts in the student newspaper, *Covenant Times*, Unit I, Issue 1-8.

Option 2. Learning Scripture

Allow time for students who have memorized verses since the last class meeting to add cards and symbols to the classroom Scripture Banner.

Invite the students to look at *Psalm 145:10 or 13* and choose a verse to be committed to memory before the next class session. See "Learning Scripture" in the student newspaper, *Covenant Times*.

ONGOING PROJECT

(Time: 5–10 minutes)

Look over the timeline produced thus far in the Unit. Which people named on the timeline would you include in the great "cloud of witnesses"?

SYMBOL CARD and TREASUREBOOK

Card 9 shows a silhouette of a head, with a nimbus or halo to symbolize sainthood, a Scripture verse, and an explanation on the back.

Encourage the students to read the *Shell Year Treasurebook*.

GOING FORTH

Gather the group. The teacher or a student says:
I ask your prayers for all who seek God, or a deeper knowledge of him.
Pray that they may find and be found by him.
Silence

[Learners may add their petitions.]

Praise God for those in every generation in whom Christ has been honored especially those whom we remember today.
Pray that we may have grace to glorify Christ in our own day.

From The Prayers of the People
The Book of Common Prayer, p. 386

Teacher: Let us go forth in the name of Christ.
Students: Thanks be to God.

TEACHER'S ASSESSMENT

From the students' comments and general participation in this session, what evidence do you find that they have a personal definition of "saints"? Do they appear to sense the significance of the feast of All Saints' Day?

Note: The following letter is for teachers and parents of children in the Intermediate level of church school. These two pages can be reproduced or used as a model for a personalized letter.

Episcopal Children's Curriculum
Unit II: Miracles

Dear Parents and Guardians,

In the next unit your child will be looking at New Testament passages and themes. Each time we say together the Church's creeds, we confess anew our faith in Jesus Christ. We know Jesus was sent from God as our Messiah and Savior. In him, God made a New Covenant with humankind.

The sessions of Unit II for this year fall into two groups: five sessions of the prophets' visions fulfilled related to Advent, Christmas, and Epiphany, and four sessions on the miracles, Jesus' deeds of power.

We encourage you to spend time talking with your child about what he or she is learning in church school. You can do this by reading the Scripture passages listed below, discussing the **Symbol Cards** and *Covenant Times* sent home each week, and by exploring the New Testament section of the ***Shell Year Treasurebook***, a reference book for students.

Prophets' Vision Fulfilled

Here is a brief summary of the first five sessions in the Miracles Unit that are to be used in the weeks surrounding the nativity, the fulfillment of the prophetic vision of the coming of the Messiah. Jesus would establish a New Covenant written on the hearts of God's people.

Session 1: "Prophets Vision: A New Covenant" highlights the twofold character of the season of Advent. We prepare for the celebration of the Nativity, and we declare our belief in the return of the Lord. Your child will be introduced to a common theme from about 500 years of prophetic ministry: God would establish a new covenant. Christians believe that this has indeed come to pass in Jesus of Nazareth. He is the embodiment of the vision found in the prophecies of Jeremiah, Micah, and Ezekiel. (*Jeremiah 31:31-34*)

Session 2: "Isaiah's Vision: Salvation" concentrates on the vision of salvation found in the *Book of Isaiah*. Each year in Advent, the most-quoted prophet is Isaiah. The Church sees the life and work of Jesus Christ to be the beginning of the new reign of God. The students may listen to selected passages from Handel's *Messiah* that include lines from *Isaiah*. The students will be challenged to think about what it would be like to be a prophet. (*Isaiah 35:1-6*)

Session 3: "Gabriel Speaks of Visions Fulfilled" looks at Gabriel's announcement to Mary that she would bear a child. Students will have an opportunity to enter into the roles of the archangel, Mary, Joseph, and Elizabeth. They will be asked how each character might narrate the story of the annunciation. Gabriel's words makes clear the early Church's understanding of God's purpose in sending Jesus to be born of a woman. Through this act, God entered into our human situation as Savior and Redeemer. (*Luke 1:26-38*)

Session 4: "Mary's Song for Christmas," designed for use near Christmas Day, focuses on Mary's Song, the *Magnificat* found in *Luke 1:46-55*. Mary praises God for having chosen her to bring the Messiah to the world. She also sings of God's care for the lowly, the powerless, and the poor. Mary celebrates God's fulfillment of promises made since the time of Abraham and proclaims the mercy of God for all people throughout history. (*Luke 1:39-55*)

Session 5: "Magi Seek the Christ Child," scheduled for Epiphany, helps students learn more about the origin of this festival. Teachers will help them explore the meaning of the word "epiphany" and how the church celebrates this season. The Magi, who appear only in the *Gospel of Matthew*, were the first persons in the Gentile world to offer homage to Jesus Christ. (*Matthew 2:1-12*)

Jesus' Deeds of Power

The remaining portion of the Miracles Unit is devoted to great deeds of power accomplished by Jesus in his earthly ministry.

Session 6: "Blind Bartimaeus" links the cry of the blind beggar, with the "Kyrie eleison" (Lord, have mercy) of Christian worship. Bartimaeus was healed by Jesus and became one of his followers. Jesus places the emphasis on the man's faith rather than on the cure itself. (*Mark 10:46-52*)

Session 7: "Healing the Paralytic" is about the story of Jesus healing a man who is paralyzed. Teachers will emphasize the faith and persistence of the man's friends, the connection between divine forgiveness and healing, and the beginning of strong opposition to Jesus' ministry. While Bartimaeus pleaded his own case with Jesus, the paralyzed man needed the assistance of his friends. This session encourages students to think about how the man's friends were showing love for their neighbor while respecting his dignity. (*Mark 2:1-12*)

Session 8: "Cleansing of the Ten Lepers" is about the healing of ten lepers. Once again, their cry to Jesus is a reminder of the Kyrie eleison (Lord, have mercy). The story links healing with obedience, faith, and gratitude. Only one member of the group returned to give thanks to Jesus for the miracle of health. He was a Samaritan—a person that Jewish people during that time would least expect to do the right thing. Teachers will help children explore the Church's contemporary ministries of healing and service to the sick. (*Luke 17:11-19*)

Session 9: "Raising of Lazarus" looks at the most dramatic of Jesus' miracles—the raising of his friend Lazarus from the dead. In the *Gospel of John*, this miracle is the climax of a series of signs showing that Jesus is the expected Messiah. The raising of Lazarus also intensified the opposition of religious leaders to Jesus. Jesus loved Lazarus and his sisters, Martha and Mary, and wept openly at the grave of his dear friend. (*John 11:1-44*)

Yours in Christ,

Church School Teachers

MIRACLES
SESSION 1
PROPHET'S VISION: A NEW COVENANT

FOCUS

In the season of Advent, we look in two directions: backward to the story of God's covenant people, and forward to the celebration of the Nativity. We recall the Hebrew prophets' vision of a Messiah who would come to establish a new covenant. The students should be able to describe the prophets' vision that God did not desert his creation, but stays with the original purpose, sending Christ and the Spirit in a new way.

GETTING READY

This session introduces the Hebrew prophets' vision of a Messiah. We reflect on their message of a coming day when God would establish a new covenant. Over a period of at least 500 years, prophets spoke of a descendant of King David who would establish the reign of God.

Examples of this vision may be found in the prophets' books listed below.

Micah 5:1-5 (about 725). This passage about a just ruler who would come out of Bethlehem is quoted in the *Gospel of Matthew* (chapter 2), in the story of the wise men who came when Christ was born.

Jeremiah 31:31-34; 33:14-16 (about 626). After the fall of Jerusalem, the more influential members of the population were deported to Babylon. Jeremiah remained behind, identifying with the poor people who were his neighbors. But Jeremiah still offered hope. God would establish a new covenant and restore the people.

Ezekiel 37:24-28 (about 593). This prophet went into exile with his people who were deported to Babylon. He sought to comfort the homesick and lift them from their despair. He, too, kept alive a strong hope for the people's return and a renewed covenant with God.

The *Book of Isaiah* contains the most tender messages about the coming of the Messiah, and in Session 2 we will focus on these words alone.

Almighty God, give us grace to cast away the works of darkness, and put on the armor of light, now in the time of this mortal life in which your Son Jesus Christ came to visit us in great humility; that in the last day, when he shall come again in his glorious majesty to judge both the living and the dead, we may rise to the life immortal; through him who lives and reigns with you and the Holy Spirit, one God, now and for ever. *Amen.*
First Sunday of Advent
The Book of Common Prayer, p. 211

TEACHING TIP

By this time, students have discarded the myth of Santa Claus. While they are still focused on the excitement of receiving and giving presents at Christmas, they can think about the true meaning of the season. During the weeks of Advent, discuss what it means to await the coming of Jesus Christ as Savior.

GATHERING

During the season of Advent, make a classroom Advent wreath. If you have a regular circular form to hold the four candles, ask students to surround it with greens. Or they can make a wreath from a styrofoam ring or molding clay. Invite the students to replenish the greens each week and to tend the candles.

When everyone is present, gather around the wreath as the first candle is lighted. Invite the students to read together "Hark! a thrilling voice is sounding," found on Poster No. 7 in the Teacher's Packet. (The poster includes stanzas 1 and 5 of this hymn from *The Hymnal 1982,* 59.)

The teacher then says:

Let us pray. (Use the Collect "First Sunday of Advent," above, or a prayer of your choice.

The chosen student lector reads from the class Bible:

A Reading from the Book of Jeremiah, chapter 31, verses 31 through 34.

The days are surely coming, says the Lord, when I will make a new covenant with the house of Israel and the house of Judah. It will not be like the covenant that I made with their ancestors when I took them by the hand to bring them out of the land of Egypt—a covenant that they broke, though I was their husband, says the Lord. But this is the covenant that I will make with the house of Israel after those days, says the Lord: I will put my law within them, and I will write it on their hearts; and I will be their God, and they shall be my people. No longer shall they teach one another, or say to each other, "Know the Lord," for they shall all know me, from the least of them to the greatest, says the Lord; for I will forgive their iniquity, and remember their sin no more.

Reader: The Word of the Lord.
Response: Thanks be to God.

Since the candles of the Advent wreath will be lit during the Gathering for each week in Advent, extinguish them after the reading above. They can be re-lit just before the Going Forth.

INTRODUCING THE STORY
(Time: 10–20 minutes)

Talk with the students about the season of Advent, which begins a new church year. Advent means "coming," and the season has a double purpose (see the student newspaper):

1. We spend the four weeks before the celebration of Jesus' birth recalling what it was like for the people of God to wait for the expected Messiah.

2. We declare our belief in our Lord's promise to return.

Tell the story of how God's people waited for the coming of a Messiah. Refer to the story in the student newspaper, *Covenant Times* (Unit II, Issue 1) about the prophet Jeremiah who told the people about a new covenant between God and Israel.

Jeremiah was often in trouble because he foretold the destruction of Jerusalem. But the king and the other nobles would not listen to him. When the city lay in ruins, Jeremiah offered new hope for a covenant that would be written on the hearts of the people.

A succession of Hebrew prophets spoke out following the division of the kingdom of Israel—and both during and after the Babylonian captivity. As God's messengers, they called on the people to be obedient and faithful. They also foretold a day when a new covenant would be established.

Ask students to work individually or in teams to look up *Micah 5:1-5* and *Ezekiel 37:24-28*. Ask: What is the "vision" of each of these prophets? Was their message similar to Jeremiah's? (The student newspaper, *Covenant Times*, includes stories about their prophecies.)

During Advent, we give thanks for the message of prophets who kept alive the vision of God's reign. They pointed to the time when God entered our lives in the person of Jesus Christ.

The word Christ is Greek for "the anointed one" (the Messiah). The child who was born to Mary at Bethlehem was destined to be the Christ for whom God's people had waited so long.

EXPLORING
(Time: 15–20 minutes)

Option 1. Statues

Play a game of "Statues" to help students think about waiting during Advent. Move chairs and tables to the sides of the room. Play music (such as the music selection on the *Children Sing!* tape). Encourage students to move freely in the center of the room, acting out parts of the story or words from the hymn.

At some point, stop the action by saying, "Freeze" and turning off the music. Students must stop moving immediately and become like statues. If someone moves, he or she comes to the side of the room while the rest of the group starts moving around again.

Continue playing until no one is left in the center. Discuss the concept of waiting.

Option 2. Prophet Stand-ups

List these three prophets on newsprint or chalkboard: Jeremiah, Micah, and Ezekiel. Give each student a piece of sturdy posterboard (about 9 x 12 inches) and three strips of construction paper in different colors (about 1.5 x 6 inches).

Invite the students to devise creative ways to print the names of the three prophets on their paper strips. Borders can be added with colorful markers or with bits of decorative material such as foil and tissue. When the name strips are completed, arrange them on the posterboard pieces in a variety of patterns and angles. They can experiment with folding and shaping the strips in various ways. Supply loops of masking tape to attach the names to the posterboard pieces to make the names stand out from the background.

Option 3. Word Puzzle

Turn in the student newspaper, *Covenant Times,* Unit II, Issue 1, to the word puzzle titled "Names for the Messiah."

Students may work individually, in pairs, or as a total group.

MUSIC
(Time: 10 minutes)

Introduce the Advent hymn, "Come, thou long expected Jesus" *(The Hymnal 1982,* 66). Listen to it on the *Children Sing!* tape and then read the words of the first two stanzas. Ask: How do these stanzas remind us of the Hebrew prophets?

CONNECTING/SPEAKING OUT
(Time: 15–20 minutes)

Option 1. Group Discussion

God called Jeremiah to be a prophet when he was still a teenager. He questioned God because he did not believe someone like him could be a prophet. However, God touched his mouth to let Jeremiah know that God would give him the words to speak.

Ask the students if they have ever been asked to do something for which they were not prepared. For example, completing an assignment from a teacher at school or taking on a new position on a sports team. What was that experience like? Were you successful? Why?

Talk about new challenges students face at school, at home, on teams, and at church. Ask: Where can you go for help? Are challenges good? How can you tell if a challenge might be harmful?

Option 2. Current Events

Talk with the students about what they see and hear in stores, malls, and in the media during the weeks of Advent. How would they describe the spirit of this season in the commercial world?

In contrast, how does your congregation observe these weeks of Advent? What do the students see and hear in the services of worship? What is emphasized? Why? What does Advent mean for you?

REFLECTING
(Time: 10 minutes)

For this Unit, set up a "Reflection Center" to encourage students to make personal responses to the session themes. Supply a box of materials to invite artistic expression (colorful drawings, collages, and bright paper). Students who prefer to write can compose journal entries, poems, or essays. Plan to add new materials and replenish the supplies as needed for each session's work. (This activity may be done at each session or occasionally during the Unit.)

Use the envelopes from Unit I or provide new envelopes approximately 9 x 12 inches in size for each student. The class members may add their names and decorate the envelopes, which will be used to store items produced during the sessions. Assure the students that the contents are private and may be taken home at the end of the Unit.

Offer direction for student responses like the following:

Imagine that you were one of ten finalists to take part in the first space trip to Mars. You have read everything you can find. As a finalist, you get to talk to astronauts to learn about space travel.

Now all you can do is wait. First there are problems with funding, then there's a glitch in the computer that guides the craft. You continue to prepare physically and mentally, knowing you may not even go. What would it be like to wait? How would you keep your hopes up? The people of Israel waited over 500 years for a Messiah. How do you think they felt?

When you have completed either your drawing or your writing, you may compose a brief prayer.

LEARNING SKILLS
(Time: 10–15 minutes)

Option 1. Class Memory Challenge

For this Unit, the memory challenge is related to the life of Jesus in the four Gospels. Begin by naming the four Gospels in order and introducing the Church's traditional symbols for them: Matthew (winged man); Mark (winged lion); Luke (winged ox); John (rising eagle). A way of remembering this information is to learn a long word, "manlionoxeagle." When the word is separated into its four parts, they are in the right order to go with *Matthew, Mark, Luke,* and *John.* See the student newspaper, *Covenant Times,* Unit II, Issue 1, for an explanation of the symbols.

Option 2. Learning Scripture

Offer the students the opportunity to learn one of the following Scripture verses before the next class session: *Isaiah 9:6* or *Jeremiah 31:33b* (in any version or translation). All the verses for the Unit are listed under "Learning Scripture" in the student newspaper, *Covenant Times.*

For this Unit, prepare a scroll made from sturdy paper, approximately 11 inches wide and 70 inches long. Mark off the scroll's length into five-inch blocks so that the two verses for each of the next seven sessions can be printed in a separate block. (Leave plenty of blank space within the block under each verse.) The scroll may be attached to dowels or sticks so that it can be rolled and unrolled easily.

Indicate on the scroll (under each verse) the number of students who memorized each verse by drawing a small candle for each student.

ONGOING PROJECT
(Time: 5–10 minutes)

During the seasons of Advent/Christmas/Epiphany (Sessions 1–5), consider developing a series of five billboards to announce a Scriptural theme. When completed, each board will be like an eye-catching public announcement. For example, the billboard for this session might have the headline, "Prophets Share A Vision."

Use a large background such as posterboard or other sturdy material. The students may work as a group to design and complete each billboard. Select Scripture or create slogans to highlight each session's theme. Display the billboards.

SYMBOL CARD and TREASUREBOOK

Card 10 contains the Greek letters Alpha and Omega, a Scripture verse, and an explanation.

Suggest that the students review *Shell Year Treasurebook*, Part II, Sections 2-3 about the New Testament. Why do we use these Greek letters as a Christian symbol?

GOING FORTH

Re-light the two candles on the Advent wreath. The teacher or a student will say the following, pausing for the students' response of "Lord, have mercy":

With all our heart and with all our mind, let us pray to the Lord, saying, "Lord, have mercy."

For the peace from above, for the loving-kindness of God, and for the salvation of our souls, let us pray to the Lord.
Lord, have mercy.

For the peace of the world, for the welfare of the holy Church of God, and for the unity of all people,
let us pray to the Lord.
Lord, have mercy.

For ____[learners may add their own petitions], let us pray to the Lord.
Lord, have mercy.
    From The Prayers of the People
    The Book of Common Prayer, pp. 383-384

Teacher: Let us go forth in the name of Christ.
Students: Thanks be to God.

TEACHER'S ASSESSMENT

Do the students understand the role of the Hebrew prophets? Is Jesus Christ seen as the fulfillment of the prophets' Messianic vision? Have the students discussed about the reason for Advent in the Church?

LOOKING AHEAD

The next session focuses on the *Book of Isaiah,* which includes tender words about the coming of a Messiah. Spend some time reading and reflecting on one of the following: chapters 11, 35, and 40.

MIRACLES
SESSION 2
ISAIAH'S VISION: SALVATION

FOCUS

The prophet Isaiah painted a word picture of a day when God would save the faithful, and all of creation would sing God's praise. In Advent, we are reassured by this vision of God's salvation. The students should be able to recite one or more lines from Isaiah's vision and explain its relationship to our time of waiting in the season of Advent.

GETTING READY

Each year in Advent the Lectionary readings for Holy Eucharist include passages from *Isaiah*. They comprise some of the most beautiful poetry in all the Hebrew Scriptures, and they offer visions of the coming of the Messiah.

Consider, for example:

Isaiah 11:1-3: "There shall come forth a shoot from the stump of Jesse, and a branch shall grow out of his roots. And the spirit of the Lord shall rest upon him, . . ."

Isaiah 9:6: "For to us a child is born, to us a son is given; and the government will be upon his shoulder, and his name will be called `Wonderful Counselor, Mighty God, Everlasting Father, Prince of Peace.'"

Isaiah 40:3: "A voice cries: 'In the wilderness prepare the way of the Lord, make straight in the desert a highway for our God.'"

Scholars generally believe there were at least two Isaiahs. The first wrote chapters 1-39 during the eighth century BCE. The second prophet—perhaps a follower of the first—wrote chapters 40-55 following the destruction of Jerusalem in 587. The final part of the book is a collection of writings that were produced after the exile.

The vision of First Isaiah in chapter 35 is a great burst of joyful confidence that God's people will be saved. This passage, read in Advent in Lectionary Year A, offers great comfort and hope. A helpless people will be strengthened, and all creation will break out into new life and beauty in the presence of God's creative power.

The people's refusal to honor the covenant with God resulted in the exile. Over and over again, they turned away from God. The coming of Christ was God's attempt to bring the people back through a new and final covenant.

The Church has long interpreted these *Isaiah* passages as descriptions of the life and mission of Jesus Christ. In him, the vision of salvation is still unfolding.

Intermediate-age students, who are beginning to use analogies and metaphors with greater ease, can be challenged to think of the coming celebration of Christ's birth as a time to be grateful for the visions in the *Book of Isaiah*.

Merciful God, who sent your messengers the prophets to preach repentance and prepare the way for our salvation: Give us grace to heed their warnings and forsake our sins, that we may greet with joy the coming of Jesus Christ our Redeemer; who lives and reigns with you and the Holy Spirit, one God, now and for ever. *Amen.*

Second Sunday of Advent
The Book of Common Prayer, p. 211

TEACHING TIP

Intermediate-age learners are increasingly able to analyze and discuss issues. But they also need non-verbal experiences, such as art projects and games. In your teaching, strive for a balance of activities. Along with reading, writing, and discussion, include opportunities for creative projects, musical expression, and games.

GATHERING

As the students arrive, ask them to prepare the Advent wreath with fresh greens. On a piece of paper next to the wreath, ask each person to write down one way to prepare for Christmas that has nothing to do with gift-giving or parties.

When everyone is present, gather around the wreath. Light two candles, and invite the students to read together "Hark! a thrilling voice is sounding" from Poster No. 7 in the Teacher's Packet. (The poster includes stanzas 1 and 5 of this Advent hymn from *The Hymnal 1982*, 59.)

The teacher then says:

Let us pray. (Use the Collect "Second Sunday of Advent," above, or a prayer of your choice.)

The chosen student lector reads from the class Bible:

A Reading from the Book of Isaiah, chapter 35, selected verses ending at verse 6:

The wilderness and the dry land shall be glad,
    the desert shall rejoice and blossom;
like the crocus it shall blossom abundantly,
    and rejoice with joy and singing. . . .
Strengthen the weak hands,
    and make firm the feeble knees.
Say to those who are of a fearful heart,
    "Be strong, do not fear!
Here is your God. . . .
    He will come and save you."

Then the eyes of the blind shall be opened,
    and the ears of the deaf unstopped;
then the lame shall leap like a deer,
    and the tongue of the speechless sing for joy.
For waters shall break forth in the wilderness,
    and streams in the desert; . . .

Reader: The Word of the Lord.
Response: Thanks be to God.

Extinguish the candles after the reading (above). They can be re-lit just before the Going Forth.

INTRODUCING THE STORY
(Time: 10 minutes)

Begin by looking at the ideas the students wrote during the Gathering. Ask: How do these ideas help us prepare for Christmas? How did people prepare for the Messiah long ago?

In your own words, describe the prophecies of Isaiah about the birth of a child whose name would be Immanuel, which means God with us. Use the story in the student newspaper, *Covenant Times* (Unit II, Issue 2) as a guide for your discussion.

Isaiah's prophecy came during an encounter with King Ahaz of Judea. The king was being pressured to join with the northern kingdoms of Israel and Syria in an alliance against Assyria. Isaiah was opposed to this alliance. When the king refused to ask God for a sign, Isaiah announced that God would send a sign—the child who was to be called Immanuel.

Identify Isaiah as one of several Hebrew prophets. Prophets were unique persons who felt called to speak out, or announce, what God desired or would do. Not only did they warn people of coming judgments but they also shared visions of a day when God would rule over all.

Ask students to look at the Lectionary listings for the four Sundays of Advent, in *The Book of Common Prayer*, pp. 889, 900, and 911. Note especially the readings from the Old Testament (Hebrew Scriptures).

In Year A, all four readings are from *Isaiah*. Three of the four readings in Year B are from *Isaiah*. Passages from the prophetic books of *Zechariah*, *Zephaniah*, and *Micah* are used in Year C. Isaiah is the most-quoted prophet during Advent.

As an example, read aloud *Isaiah 9:6*. Invite the students to indicate if they have heard this line before. When? (Consider playing portions of a recording of the *Messiah* by Handel that contain words from *Isaiah*.)

Ask students to turn in their Bibles to *Isaiah 40:3-5*. Read the passage aloud in unison. Ask: What is this poem about? If you were going to draw a picture to go with it, what would you include? Point out that John the Baptist was considered to be the voice "crying out in the wilderness" when he was preaching and baptizing before Jesus began his ministry. (See *Matthew 3:1-3*.) John fulfilled Isaiah's vision of God's people being called back to faithful worship and obedient living.

Explain that the Christian Church has always declared the life and work of Jesus Christ to be the beginning of the new reign of God that Isaiah was describing.

EXPLORING
(Time: 15–20 minutes)

Option 1. Prophets' Relay

Play a Prophet Relay Game. Bring in old shoes, robes, and towels to use as head coverings. Prepare ahead of time cards with the words of Scripture verses from the Learning Scripture section of the *Covenant Times*. Divide into two or more teams. Make sure each team has enough cards for each person and one set of shoes, a robe, and a towel. Put the cards and clothing at the end of the room. Indicate a starting point with masking tape on the opposite side of the room. Ask the teams to line up behind the tape.

The goal of the game to is give each person a chance to be a prophet. At your signal, the first person from each team walks quickly to a pile of clothing and puts everything on. He or she then selects one card and reads it as dramatically as possible. He or she removes the clothes and walks back to tag the next person in line. The game is over when everyone has had a turn.

Option 2. Crayon Resist

Give each class member a piece of sturdy paper, and make available a good supply of wax crayons.

Ask the students to turn to *Isaiah 40:3-5* and draw their interpretations of these words. The drawings should then be colored with crayons, leaving narrow spaces between colors and sections of their work. (Use bright colors and press firmly.)

When the students' colored illustrations are finished, brush them with a light coat of diluted black tempera paint. This will create a stained-glass window effect as the black paint seeps into the paper and fills the blank spaces.

Option 3. Crossword Puzzle

Turn in the student newspaper, *Covenant Times*, Unit II, Issue 2, to the crossword puzzle, "Prophets' Visions." Students may work individually, in pairs, or as a total group.

MUSIC
(Time: 10 minutes)

Listen again to "Come, thou long expected Jesus" (*The Hymnal 1982*, 66) on the *Children Sing!* tape.

Ask: How is Jesus described in this hymn? (See stanzas 1 and 2). What do stanzas 3 and 4 say Jesus will do? How does this Advent hymn remind us of the prophet Isaiah?

CONNECTING/SPEAKING OUT
(Time: 15-20 minutes)

Option 1. Group Discussion

Hebrew prophets filled a special role. They had an ability to see and talk about what God was doing, and would do, in the life of God's people. Ask: How do you think it would feel to be a prophet? What risks would you be taking? What would you do or say if people grew angry at your words?

When the visions in the *Book of Isaiah* were written, God's people were waiting for the day when God would rule in a new way. Ask: How do you think these words of the prophet helped them to wait?

Why do you think we read and sing the prophecies from *Isaiah* during the season of Advent? How do these words help us to wait during these days?

Option 2. Current Events

Who are the people who act like prophets today? Ask students to look through several recent newspapers and news magazines. Scan headlines and articles. Who is speaking out about events and conditions in the world? in the nation? in the community? What are they saying? How are people reacting?

If Hebrew prophets like Jeremiah and Isaiah were to read these news reports, what do you think they would say? Where would they find signs of hope? What would Isaiah say today?

REFLECTING
(Time: 10 minutes)

Distribute the students' reflection envelopes and set up the Reflection Center, as described in Session 1.

Offer direction for the students' responses like the following:

Imagine you are a prophet today. What will you say? Who will your message be for? Where and how will you speak out?

When you have completed either drawing or writing your reflections, write a brief prayer.

LEARNING SKILLS
(Time: 10–15 minutes)

Option 1. Class Memory Challenge

Encourage the students to begin memorizing an outline of events in Jesus' life, along with citations from the Gospels. For this session, concentrate on the following:

Jesus' birth and infancy in Bethlehem—*Luke*, chapter 2
The visit of the Magi—*Matthew*, chapter 2
Jesus in the temple at age 12—*Luke*, chapter 2

Point out that these stories appear only in these chapters; they are not in the other Gospels. Suggest that the students work in pairs and quiz one another on the three headings in the list. Refer to the chart in the student newspaper, *Covenant Times*, Unit II, Issue 2.

Option 2. Learning Scripture

Ask whether class members have learned verses given in the previous session. If so, add symbols under the verses on the scroll, as described in Session 1.

Encourage the students to memorize *Isaiah 11:1-2* or *40:1* before the next class session.

See "Learning Scripture" in the student newspaper, *Covenant Times*.

ONGOING PROJECT
(Time: 5–10 minutes)

Work with the students to develop a billboard related to the session theme about the prophecy of the coming of a Messiah. See Session 1 for a description of this project. A possible headline for this session might be "The Messiah Is Coming." As they plan, encourage the students to think about the work of the prophet Isaiah, and to consult his words in the Old Testament.

SYMBOL CARD and TREASUREBOOK

Card 11 illustrates a scroll, and includes a verse of Scripture, with an explanation of the symbol on the back.

Ask the students to discover, in *Shell Year Treasurebook* (Part II, Sections 1-3), about the coming of a Messiah. Where did Isaiah make his prophecy?

GOING FORTH

Re-light the two candles on the Advent wreath. The teacher or a student will say the following, pausing for the students' response of "Lord, have mercy":

> With all our heart and with all our mind, let us pray to the Lord, saying, "Lord, have mercy."
>
> For the peace from above, for the loving-kindness of God, and for the salvation of our souls, let us pray to the Lord.
> *Lord, have mercy.*
>
> For the peace of the world, for the welfare of the holy Church of God, and for the unity of all people, let us pray to the Lord.
> *Lord, have mercy.*
>
> For _____ [learners may add their own petitions], let us pray to the Lord.
> *Lord, have mercy.*
>
> From The Prayers of the People
> *The Book of Common Prayer,* pp. 383-384

Teacher: Let us go forth in the name of Christ.
Students: Thanks be to God.

TEACHER'S ASSESSMENT

Do the students sense the significance of prophecies from the *Book of Isaiah* for the season of Advent? Which images from these writings emerged as important to the class members? Are the students able to define Advent as a time of waiting?

LOOKING AHEAD

The next session is on the angel Gabriel's announcement to Mary that she is to be the mother of Jesus. Think of times when you have received unexpected good news that may have changed your life. What were your feelings?

MIRACLES
SESSION 3
GABRIEL SPEAKS OF VISIONS FULFILLED

FOCUS

When the angel Gabriel appeared to the Virgin Mary, he announced that she would bear a son who would fulfill the prophets' vision of a Messiah for the people of God; in him the new covenant and salvation would be made known. The students should be able to tell the story of the Annunciation and explain why Christians link it with God's promises declared by the prophets.

GETTING READY

In the first two sessions of this Unit, we looked briefly at the Hebrew prophets' messages concerning the Messiah, through whom God would establish a new covenant with us. These prophetic writings comforted and inspired many generations of Jewish believers as they waited for signs of the reign of God.

Now we turn to the story of the angel Gabriel's visit to the Virgin Mary to give her the news that she will bear a son, whom she is to name Jesus *(Luke 1:26-38)*. This child is to be the descendant of David who is destined to be called "Son of the Most High." This meant that Jesus would be the long-awaited Messiah. The prophets' vision was coming true!

Gabriel is an "archangel" (an angel high in rank) in Jewish and early Christian thought. He appears as both a messenger from God and an interpreter for the people to whom he is sent. The focus of Gabriel's announcement to Mary is the radical newness of God's saving action.

Mary was mystified by Gabriel's greeting. She was the highly favored one, not because of something she had done but because of her having been chosen for a unique role in the salvation of God's people. She accepted the incredible news that she would conceive as a virgin, and she submitted with grace to the will of God.

Intermediate-age students have heard this story before, but now they are able to place it on a timeline and grasp its relationship to the history of God's covenant people.

Pour your grace into our hearts, O Lord, that we who have known the incarnation of your Son Jesus Christ, announced by an angel to the Virgin Mary, may by his cross and passion be brought to the glory of his resurrection; who lives and reigns with you, in the unity of the Holy Spirit, one God, now and for ever. *Amen.*
The Annunciation
The Book of Common Prayer, p. 240

TEACHING TIP

Many students are involved in Advent and Christmas liturgies in their churches as acolytes, members of choirs, or in Nativity pageants. Try to relate each of the session activities to what is happening in your congregation at this time of year. Talk with the learners about worship and the choices of hymns and prayers.

GATHERING

Hang Poster No. 8 from the Teacher's Packet of the Annunciation near the Advent wreath. As the students arrive, ask them to place fresh greens around the Advent wreath. While they work, encourage them to talk about the poster. Who are the two people in the poster? What is happening?

When everyone is present, light three candles and invite the students to join in a choral reading, using the poster, "Hark! a thrilling voice is sounding," found in the Teacher's Packet. (The poster includes stanzas 1 and 5 of this Advent hymn from *The Hymnal 1982,* 59.)

Unit II. Miracles—Session 3
Shell Year Intermediate—Copyright © 2000 Virginia Theological Seminary and Morehouse Publishing

The teacher then says:

Let us pray. (Use the Collect "The Annunciation," above, or a prayer of your own choosing.)

The chosen student lector reads from the class Bible:

A Reading from the Gospel of Luke, chapter 1, verses 26 through 38.

In the sixth month the angel Gabriel was sent by God to a town in Galilee called Nazareth, to a virgin engaged to a man whose name was Joseph, of the house of David. The virgin's name was Mary. And he came to her and said, "Greetings, favored one! The Lord is with you." But she was much perplexed by his words and pondered what sort of greeting this might be. The angel said to her, "Do not be afraid, Mary, for you have found favor with God. And now, you will conceive in your womb and bear a son, and you will name him Jesus. He will be great, and will be called the Son of the Most High, and the Lord God will give to him the throne of his ancestor David. He will reign over the house of Jacob forever, and of his kingdom there will be no end." Mary said to the angel, "How can this be, since I am a virgin?" The angel said to her, "The Holy Spirit will come upon you, and the power of the Most High will overshadow you; therefore the child to be born will be holy; he will be called Son of God. And now, your relative Elizabeth in her old age has also conceived a son; and this is the sixth month for her who was barren. For nothing will be impossible with God." Then Mary said, "Here am I, the servant of the Lord; let it be with me according to your word." Then the angel departed from her.

Reader: The Word of the Lord.
Response: Thanks be to God.

Extinguish the candles after the reading. Re-light them just before the Going Forth.

INTRODUCING THE STORY
(Time: 10 minutes)

Review the Advent theme explored in the previous sessions—the Hebrew prophets' message from God that a Messiah would come to establish a new covenant. As we shift to the New Testament, we discover that the vision of Isaiah came true with the birth of Jesus.

Write on a chalkboard or easel the following: 1. The angel Gabriel; 2. Mary; 3. Elizabeth; 4. Joseph.

Divide the class members into four teams, and assign one of these roles to each team. Ask them to meet and prepare to tell briefly the story found in *Luke 1:24-38,* from the viewpoints of their characters. Encourage them to read the story about the Annunciation in the student newspaper, ***Covenant Times*** (Unit II, Issue 3). To assist the groups in developing their stories, copy and distribute question sheets (or cards), as follows:

Group 1 (Gabriel): What has God asked you to tell Mary? How will you greet her? How will you feel when you give her the news? How will you answer her questions?

Group 2 (Mary): Where are you living? How will it feel to be visited by an angel? How will he look? What will you say when he greets you? What does the angel's message mean for you? How will other people feel about what Gabriel has told you?

Group 3 (Joseph): You are mentioned in Luke's story. When Mary tells you about Gabriel's visit, what will you say? How do you feel about the news from the angel? What will you do?

Group 4 (Elizabeth): What unusual thing has happened to you? Why does the angel Gabriel tell Mary you are going to have a baby? What will you to say to Mary?

Move among the teams to answer questions and help them decide on what to share. Ask each group to make their presentations, in order.

EXPLORING
(Time: 15–20 minutes)

Option 1. Constructing Gabriel

Make a life-size illustration of Gabriel to display in the classroom. Ask a volunteer to lie down on a large piece of butcher paper or several pieces of newsprint taped together. Ask the person to spread his or her arms out like wings. Trace the outline of the volunteer except for the lower part of the arms, which will be made into wings.

Put the image on a table so several people can work on the drawing at once. The students can draw features such as those on Poster No. 8, or use bits of foil and colored paper for an abstract illustration.

Make more than one Gabriel if the class is large. Display the angels.

Option 2. Lift-up Picture

Supply sheets of sturdy white construction paper, pencils, rulers, and scissors. Invite each student to make a straight base-line horizontally, about a third of the way up from the bottom of a sheet. The next task is to draw outlines of the angel Gabriel and Mary, facing each other on the line (closer to the center of the paper than to the outside borders). The figures should be solid, with simple lines and no sharp details.

When the drawings are completed, show the students how to insert the points of their scissors at the outside lines of the two figures. They are to cut around both Mary and the angel, then lift them up and fold sharply at the base—taking care not to cut in any direction except around the drawings.

The result will be a lift-up picture; the left-over portion of the sheet rests on a table or other surface to support the scene.

Option 3. Acrostic

Turn in the student newspaper, *Covenant Times*, Unit II, Issue 3, to the acrostic titled "Gabriel Speaks." Students may work individually, in pairs, or as a total group.

MUSIC
(Time: 10 minutes)

Introduce the carol, "Lo, how a Rose e'er blooming" *(The Hymnal 1982,* 81) found on the *Children Sing!* tape. Ask the students to identify Biblical persons who are mentioned. Who are they?

Jesse is the father of King David and ancestor of Jesus; the "seers" are the prophets. Isaiah is a key prophetic name in the Bible. Mary is the mother of Jesus.

CONNECTING/SPEAKING OUT
(Time: 15–20 minutes)

Option 1. Group Discussion

Encourage the class members to look at the Annunciation scene on Poster No. 8 from the Teacher's Packet. Ask: What do you think of the artist's way of picturing the angel Gabriel? If you were to paint Gabriel, how would he look? What do angels do? Where do they come from?

Talk about angels as God's messengers in both the Old and New Testaments. They have a human-like form, but they do not necessarily have wings. They are inhabitants of God's spiritual world.

Invite the students to do research on the presence of angels in the Gospel accounts of the Nativity. Write these references on a board or easel: *Luke 1:26-38; Matthew 1:20; Luke 2:8-16.* Suggest that the class members work individually or in teams to answer these questions: In each passage, who sees and hears the angels? What do the angels have to say? When do they disappear?

Option 2. Current Events

In the Advent season, many congregations are involved in service and giving to other people. Consider, with the students, any ways they could take part in outreach projects, such as programs for assisting mothers and children or food collections.

Talk with the class members about community needs. What are some of the helpful tasks the class members can undertake?

REFLECTING
(Time: 10 minutes)

Hand out the students' reflection envelopes, and set up the Reflection Center, as described in Session 1.

Offer directions for the students' responses such as the following:

When Mary asked Gabriel how the news he brought could possibly be true, he replied that nothing is impossible for God.

What are some personal situations or relationships that seem very hard to handle just now? Does anything seem just impossible? Where can you turn for help?

Write or draw your thoughts or feelings about one or more events or relationships in your life. When you have finished, add a written prayer.

LEARNING SKILLS
(Time: 10–15 minutes)

Option 1. Class Memory Challenge

Review the memory tasks of the preceding sessions, and move on to introduce three more headings in the story of Jesus' life:

John baptizes Jesus—*Matthew*, chapter 3; *Mark*, chapter 1; *Luke*, chapter 3

Unit II. Miracles—Session 3
Shell Year Intermediate—Copyright © 2000 Virginia Theological Seminary and Morehouse Publishing

Jesus' temptations—*Matthew,* chapter 4; *Mark,* chapter 1; *Luke,* chapter 4

Jesus chooses disciples—*Matthew,* chapter 10; *Mark,* chapter 3; *Luke,* chapter 6

Note that we now begin to work with stories that appear in more than one Gospel. The Gospels are listed as they appear in the Bible—*Matthew, Mark, Luke,* and *John.* (See the chart in the student newspaper, *Covenant Times,* Unit II, Issue 3.)

One possibility for committing the chapter numbers to memory is to associate number patterns with key words, such as Baptism 3-1-3; Temptations 4-1-4; Disciples 10-3-6. Here is an example of how to translate the code: The first of the three numbers is linked with *Matthew,* the second number with *Mark,* and the third with *Luke.* So 3-1-3 (for Jesus' Baptism) becomes: *Matthew,* chapter 3; *Mark,* chapter 1; *Luke,* chapter 3.

An extra memory task could be to learn the names of the disciples.

Option 2. Learning Scripture

Ask whether class members have learned verses given in the previous sessions. If so, add symbols to the scroll described in Session 1.

Encourage the students to memorize *Psalm 40:8* or *Luke 1:30* before the next class session. (The line from Psalm 40 is included in the liturgy for the Annunciation, the feast celebrating Gabriel's visit to Mary.)

See "Learning Scripture" in the student newspaper, *Covenant Times.*

ONGOING PROJECT

(Time: 5–10 minutes)

See Session 1 for a description of this project. A possible headline for this session's billboard might be "Gabriel Surprises Mary." As they plan, encourage the students to review the story of the Annunciation in *Luke 1:26-38.*

SYMBOL CARD and TREASUREBOOK

Card 12 contains a picture of an angel with a lily, a Scripture verse, and an explanation on the back.

Ask the students to discover in the *Shell Year Treasurebook,* Part II, Section 4, where to find the story of Jesus' birth in the Gospels.

GOING FORTH

Re-light the two candles on the Advent wreath. The teacher or a student will say the following, pausing for the students' response of "Lord, have mercy":

With all our heart and with all our mind, let us pray to the Lord, saying, "Lord, have mercy."

For the peace from above, for the lovingkindness of God, and for the salvation of our souls, let us pray to the Lord.
Lord, have mercy.
For the peace of the world, for the welfare of the holy Church of God, and for the unity of all people, let us pray to the Lord.
Lord, have mercy.

For _____ [learners may add their own petitions], let us pray to the Lord.
Lord, have mercy.
　　From The Prayers of the People
　　The Book of Common Prayer, pp. 383-384

Teacher: Let us go forth in the name of Christ.
Students: Thanks be to God.

TEACHER'S ASSESSMENT

In this Advent season, are the students gaining greater insight into the relationship between the Old Testament prophets' visions and the events surrounding Jesus' birth? In your opinion, are the class members able to retell the Annunciation story with some sense of the drama and feelings of the participants?

LOOKING AHEAD

The next session focuses on the meeting of Mary and her cousin Elizabeth. Read and think about the versions of the Magnificat in *Luke 1:46-55,* in *The Book of Common Prayer,* p. 91, and in *The Hymnal 1982,* 437.

MIRACLES
SESSION 4
MARY'S SONG FOR CHRISTMAS

FOCUS

As Mary and her cousin Elizabeth exchanged greetings before the births of their children, Mary said a song we call the Magnificat. She praised God for the coming birth of Jesus. The students should be able to say in their own words how Mary's vision speaks to us at Christmas. They should also be able to recite the first two lines of the Magnificat.

GETTING READY

This session, designed to be used near Christmas Day, focuses on the Song of Mary *(Luke 1:46-55)*. The words are especially appropriate as Advent ends; the song is the Gospel lesson for the Fourth Sunday in Lectionary Year C.

These lines of praise are appropriate for study during our celebrations of the Nativity because they describe God's powerful intervention in human history. The Nativity culminates a longstanding, divine process of overthrowing proud human expectations and exalting the lowly. Mary praises God for selecting her to be a participant in this mighty act; for God's care for the lowly, the powerless, and the poor; and especially for God's bringing to fulfillment the promise made to Abraham and his descendants. Mary's word for God's goodness is "mercy."

In the Latin translation of this song, the first word is "Magnificat," hence its name in our Christian liturgies. (This Latin word is reflected in our English version of the first line, "My soul *magnifies* the Lord, . . .")

Intermediate-age students are able to memorize and sing canticles and hymns with ease. The Song of Mary is appealing because of its association with the mother of Jesus.

O God, you have taken to yourself the blessed Virgin Mary, mother of your incarnate Son: Grant that we, who have been redeemed by his blood, may share with her the glory of your eternal kingdom; through Jesus Christ our Lord, who lives and reigns with you, in the unity of the Holy Spirit, one God, now and for ever. *Amen.*

Saint Mary the Virgin
The Book of Common Prayer, p. 243

TEACHING TIP

Intermediate-age students may be experiencing an emotional "overload" during the days surrounding Christmas Day. Like younger learners, they are distracted by all the preparations for the holiday, including the activities that happen at church, such as pageants and special services. Find ways to reduce the tensions the students may be feeling at this time of year. Plan quiet times for them to reflect on the true meaning of the season.

GATHERING

As the students arrive, ask them to replenish the greens on the Advent wreath. As they work, ask them to think about one gift of time they could give to a family member or friend.

When everyone is present, light four candles. Invite the students to read together, "Hark! a thrilling voice is sounding," found on Poster No. 7 in the Teacher's Packet. (The poster includes stanzas 1 and 5 of this Advent hymn from *The Hymnal 1982*, 59.)

The teacher then says:

Let us pray. (Use the Collect "Saint Mary the Virgin," above, or a prayer of your own choosing.)

The chosen student lector reads from the class Bible:

A Reading from the Gospel of Luke, chapter 1, verses 39 through 47.

In those days Mary set out and went with haste to a Judean town in the hill country, where she entered the house of Zechariah and greeted Elizabeth. When Elizabeth heard Mary's greeting, the child leaped in her womb. And Elizabeth was filled with the Holy Spirit and exclaimed with a loud cry, "Blessed are you among women, and blessed is the fruit of your womb. And why has this happened to me, that the mother of my Lord comes to me? For as soon as I heard the sound of your greeting, the child in my womb leaped for joy. And blessed is she who believed that there would be a fulfillment of what was spoken to her by the Lord."

And Mary said, "My soul magnifies the Lord, and my spirit rejoices in God my Savior, for he has looked with favor on the lowliness of his servant. Surely, from now on all generations will call me blessed; . . ."

Reader: The Word of the Lord.
Response: Thanks be to God.

Extinguish the candles on the wreath, and plan to re-light them at the Going Forth. If your wreath has a fifth, white Christ Candle, talk about how it is to be lit on Christmas Day and through the twelve days of the season.

INTRODUCING THE STORY
(Time: 10 minutes)

Set the stage for Mary's words of praise that we call the Magnificat. Begin by recalling that Mary learned two important things from the angel Gabriel: that she would bear God's Son, and that her cousin Elizabeth would bear a son as well. Mary hurried to visit her cousin Elizabeth who greeted her with joy.

Mary responded with a song of praise, or the Magnificat. It gets its name from the word "magnifies" in the first line, "My soul magnifies the Lord, . . ."

Ask the students to find *Luke 1:39-56* in their Bibles. Suggest that they work in pairs to compile a list of all that Mary says God has done. How does she describe what God has done for her?

We can imagine that Mary would have this song in her heart all through the time she waited for her son to be born. She might have said the words to herself again and again at Bethlehem when Jesus' birth occurred. She could have sung it all through the time Jesus was growing up. (Call attention to Poster No. 9 of the nativity, from the Teacher's Packet.)

The Song of Mary is a canticle in *The Book of Common Prayer,* and it appears also in *The Hymnal 1982.* For many centuries Christians have used it in their worship. The main subject in this poem is God. Mary sings about what God has done in sending Jesus Christ. God has kept promises made to the people of God.

EXPLORING
(Time: 15–20 minutes)

Option 1. Nativity Scene

Suggest that the students create three-dimensional Nativity scenes using popsicle sticks and liquid glue. Encourage the class members to share creative ideas for this project:

How can the figures of Mary, Joseph, and the child Jesus be assembled? Will shepherds be included? What is the best way to position the figures? Will any animals be included?

How can a simple creche be formed from the sticks? Wood shavings or grasses may be used to simulate straw. How could tiny bits of fabric be used to add clothing for the figures? Glue the finished scenes to cardboard bases.

The group may want to work out an assembly-line approach, assigning tasks to individuals or teams. Cover work tables with newspapers to protect them from spilled glue.

Option 2. Shape Cards

Make Christmas greeting cards in selected shapes.

Give each student a rectangle of sturdy paper approximately 6 x 10 inches. Supply pens, markers, and scissors.

Fold the paper over to form a double thickness of 5 x 6 inches.

Design a half-pattern of a seasonal "shape" (such as half of a bell, half of a manger, half of a star, or half of a rose). Place the pattern against the fold in the paper. Trace and cut so that the unfolded sheet will form the complete shape. Decorate the cards with markers or cover the designs in foil wrap. Write Christmas messages on the inside.

Suggest that students take the cards home and send them to a grandparent, other relative, or friend.

Option 3. Fill-in-the-Blank Puzzle

Turn in the student newspaper, *Covenant Times*, Unit II, Issue 4, to the fill-in-the-blank puzzle titled "The Nativity." Students may work individually, in pairs, or as a total group.

MUSIC
(Time: 10 minutes)

Listen on the *Children Sing!* tape to "Tell out, my soul, the greatness of the Lord!" (*The Hymnal 1982*, 437 or 438). Encourage the students to compare the hymn's words with the Magnificat.

Also, sing or listen again to the carol, "Lo, how a Rose e'er blooming" (*The Hymnal 1982*, 81).

CONNECTING/SPEAKING OUT
(Time: 15–20 minutes)

Option 1. Group Discussion

Use Poster No. 9 of the Nativity from the Teacher's Packet to introduce a discussion of the events surrounding Jesus' birth. What do the Gospels of *Matthew* and *Luke* share about what happened *before* the scene in the poster? What will happen *after* this scene?

Note aloud that many of the Christmas creches we see in this season include the wise men bearing their gifts. Their visit, however, took place quite some time after Jesus was born, perhaps even as much as two years later. (It is appropriate to save the figures of the wise men through the twelve days of Christmas and place them in the creche on Epiphany, January 6.)

Ask: What gift could you bring to the Christ child? What will you do after Christmas?

Option 2. Current Events

Encourage the class members to share what they have read or heard about the celebration of Christmas in other parts of the world and to bring in books about Christmas traditions in other countries. What are some of the special customs or events in other cultures? If current newspapers have included articles about celebrations of the holiday, clip and display these.

/REFLECTING
(Time: 10 minutes)

Give out the reflection envelopes, and arrange the Reflection Center as described in Session 1.

Offer direction for the students' responses, using the following:

At the time of Jesus' birth, Mary gave thanks for the great things God had done for her. Think about your own life this Christmas season. What good things has God done for you?

When you have completed either drawing or writing your reflections, write a brief prayer. You may want to begin with Mary's words, "My soul magnifies the Lord . . . ," adding your own thoughts.

LEARNING SKILLS
(Time: 10–15 minutes)

Option 1. Class Memory Challenge

At this session, which is designed for use near Christmas Day, suggest that the students recall the Gospel account of Jesus' birth and also their favorite carols. Arrange for a few minutes of quiet time in which each class member chooses a line or stanza to be shared. (Bibles and hymnals may be used.) At a designated time, the students may share aloud what they selected.

Option 2. Learning Scripture

For each student who has learned a verse, add a symbol to the scroll described in Session 1. Encourage the students to memorize *Luke 1:47* or *2:11* before the next class session.

See "Learning Scripture" in the student newspaper, *Covenant Times*.

ONGOING PROJECTS
(Time: 5–10 minutes)

See Session 1 for a description of this project. The headline related to this session could be something like "Mary Rejoices." As they plan, encourage the students to review the Magnificat and the nativity story (*Luke 1:39-48* and chapter 2).

SYMBOL CARD and TREASUREBOOK

Card 13 contains a rose, a Scripture verse, and an explanation on the back.

Ask the students to read again about three passages from Luke set to music for Christian

Unit II. Miracles—Session 4
Shell Year Intermediate—Copyright © 2000 Virginia Theological Seminary and Morehouse Publishing

worship in the *Shell Year Treasurebook,* Part II, Section 7. Which one do you like best?

GOING FORTH

Re-light the two candles on the Advent wreath. The teacher or a student will say the following, pausing for the students' response of "Lord, have mercy":

With all our heart and with all our mind, let us pray to the Lord, saying, "Lord, have mercy."

For the peace from above, for the loving-kindness of God, and for the salvation of our souls, let us pray to the Lord.
Lord, have mercy.

For the peace of the world, for the welfare of the holy Church of God, and for the unity of all people, let us pray to the Lord.
Lord, have mercy.

For _____ [learners may add their own petitions], let us pray to the Lord.
Lord, have mercy.
From The Prayers of the People
The Book of Common Prayer, pp. 383-384

Teacher: Let us go forth in the name of Christ.
Students: Thanks be to God.

TEACHER'S ASSESSMENT

How did the students respond to the story of Mary's song (the Magnificat)? Are they able to say the opening lines? What kinds of questions do the students have about the season of Christmas?

LOOKING AHEAD

The next session will be the last in a series of five sessions related to Advent, Christmas, and Epiphany. This part of the Unit has been designed to help the students get a more cohesive picture of how the Messianic visions of the Hebrew prophets, the story of Jesus' birth, and the Epiphany season all fit together. What do these seasons mean in your own life?

MIRACLES
SESSION 5
MAGI SEEK THE CHRIST CHILD

FOCUS

The wise men, arriving in Jerusalem, sought out Hebrew priests to learn where the child Jesus might be. They were told that his birth would be in Bethlehem, to fulfill the words of a Hebrew prophet. The students should be able to retell the story of the Magi and explain how Epiphany is celebrated today.

GETTING READY

This session on the theme of Epiphany is based on *Matthew 2:1-12*—the familiar story of the wise men (Magi) who came from afar to worship the Christ Child. The Magi are portrayed as astrologers "from the East" who had observed the appearance of an unusual star. They followed it to Jerusalem where they asked Herod how they might find the child.

At Epiphany, we celebrate the "manifestation" or "showing forth" of Jesus to the Gentiles (the non-Jewish world). The wise men, believed to be from Persia, are considered to be the first Gentiles to pay homage to Christ. They were unaware of the spiritual prophecy that the Hebrews' Messiah would come from Bethlehem. Herod, the governor, referred the Magi to "priests and scribes of the people" for the information they needed. The priests pointed to *Micah 5:2,* with its mention of Bethlehem.

The tradition that there were three Magi is based on the list of three gifts (gold, frankincense, and myrrh) that were presented. Only Matthew's Gospel includes the story of their journey.

A Christian calendar of the Church of Rome in 354 CE mentioned December 25 as the feast day honoring the birth of Christ. No mention was made of Epiphany, which had been the traditional time for celebrating the Nativity in the Eastern Orthodox Churches. Later in the fourth century, the Church in Rome introduced the Epiphany on January 6.

Intermediate-age students, with their developing capacity to imagine and dramatize scenes, enjoy the Feast of Epiphany.

Almighty God, whose Son our Savior Jesus Christ is the light of the world: Grant that your people, illumined by your Word and Sacraments, may shine with the radiance of Christ's glory, that he may be known, worshiped, and obeyed to the ends of the earth; through Jesus Christ our Lord, who with you and the Holy Spirit lives and reigns, one God, now and for ever. *Amen.*
Second Sunday after the Epiphany
The Book of Common Prayer, p. 215

TEACHING TIP

Epiphany comes as a kind of "mini-beginning" for intermediate-age students, both at church and at school. The busy-ness of the Christmas season is ending, and routines are getting back to normal. Talk with class members about this time of new beginnings as an opportunity for learning and growth.

GATHERING

As the students arrive, invite them to reflect on the Advent wreath. Its candles may be burned low by now. The seasons of Advent and Christmas have been observed. Ask students to share their best memory of this season.

When everyone is present, gather around a Christ Candle and light it. (This may be the fifth candle of the wreath, or you may need to provide a large white candle for this session.)

Invite the class members to say or sing together the words of the first stanza of "We three kings of

Orient are" (*The Hymnal 1982*, 128; *We Sing of God*, 27).

The teacher then says:

Let us pray. (Use the Collect "Second Sunday after the Epiphany," above, or a prayer of your own choosing.)

The chosen student lector reads from the class Bible:

A Reading from the Gospel of Matthew, chapter 2, verses 1 through 12.

In the time of King Herod, after Jesus was born in Bethlehem of Judea, wise men from the East came to Jerusalem, asking, "Where is the child who has been born king of the Jews? For we observed his star at its rising, and have come to pay him homage." When King Herod heard this, he was frightened, and all Jerusalem with him; and calling together all the chief priests and scribes of the people, he inquired of them where the Messiah was to be born. They told him, "In Bethlehem of Judea; for so it has been written by the prophet: 'And you, Bethlehem, in the land of Judah, are by no means least among the rulers of Judah; for from you shall come a ruler who is to shepherd my people Israel.'"

Then Herod secretly called for the wise men and learned from them the exact time when the star had appeared. Then he sent them to Bethlehem, saying, "Go and search diligently for the child; and when you have found him, bring me word so that I may also go and pay him homage." When they had heard the king, they set out; and there, ahead of them, went the star that they had seen at its rising, until it stopped over the place where the child was. When they saw that the star had stopped, they were overwhelmed with joy. On entering the house, they saw the child with Mary his mother; and they knelt down and paid him homage. Then, opening their treasure chests, they offered him gifts of gold, frankincense, and myrrh. And having been warned in a dream not to return to Herod, they left for their own country by another road.

Reader: The Word of the Lord.
Response: Thanks be to God.

Extinguish the Christ Candle, and plan to re-light it for the Going Forth.

INTRODUCING THE STORY
(Time: 10 minutes)

Display Poster No. 10 of the wise men from the Teacher's Packet. Tell the story of the Magi in your own words, similar to the fictional story in the student newspaper, **Covenant Times** (Unit II, Issue 5). The story is written in the form of an interview with Caspar, the youngest of the three astrologers. He describes how they saw a star in the western sky and heard that a king was to be born in Judea.

They brought gifts befitting a king: gold, the symbol of wealth; frankincense, the perfume of the divine; and myrrh, the ointment of death.

Ask the students to find *Matthew 2:6* in their Bibles. The priests whom Herod called to speak with the wise men used these lines from the Messianic vision in the prophet Micah. Suggest that the students find *Micah 5:2* and compare the two texts.

Show the students a current calendar with Christmas Day and the twelve days of the Christmas season. Explain that January 6 is the Feast of Epiphany, when we remember the journey of the Magi to present gifts to the Christ Child—a story shared only in Matthew's Gospel.

Explain that the word "epiphany" means "making known" or "showing forth." The Church uses candles to symbolize this meaning.

The story of the Magi is important because it makes clear that the Messiah's birth was for all people. Epiphany is one of the oldest Christian festivals. Not only do Christians around the world celebrate the visit of the Magi but also they remember the baptism of Jesus and his first miracle—the changing of water to wine at a wedding in Cana.

EXPLORING
(Time: 15–20 minutes)

Option 1. Gift Charades

On a piece of newsprint, write the three gifts the Magi brought Jesus: gold, frankincense, and myrrh. Ask the group to brainstorm different items that represent each category. (For more information about the gifts, see the Discussion activity.) For example, gold might be a bracelet, a ring, or money; frankincense could be anything that smells good; myrrh could be a cream or ointment for healing, such as aloe salve used for burns.

Quickly write each idea on a slip of paper. Divide into two groups for a game of charades. Give one person on each team a card. See how fast the group can guess the gift.

Option 2. Folding Stars

Supply colored paper, straws, or pipe cleaners. Encourage the students to experiment with folding Epiphany stars (with five or ten points).

Thread or yarn may be attached for hanging the finished stars from a coat hanger or paper towel tube.

Option 3. Word Scramble

Turn in the student newspaper, *Covenant Times,* Unit II, Issue 5, to the word scramble titled "Words from Matthew." Students may work individually, in pairs, or as a total group.

MUSIC
(Time: 10 minutes)

Sing "Brightest and best of the stars of the morning" *(The Hymnal 1982,* 117 or 118) with the *Children Sing!* tape.

Ask: In what section of the hymnal is this hymn found? How many other hymns are included in this section?

Note that stanza 3 lists the gifts of the Magi. (The "odors of Edom" are from frankincense.) The word "oblation" means gifts.

CONNECTING/SPEAKING OUT
(Time: 15–20 minutes)

Option 1. Group Discussion

Explain that the gifts the Magi gave to Jesus were also symbols. As a group, discover the meaning of these symbols in the following way:

On each of three sheets of construction paper (one grey, one yellow or gold, and one green), draw an outline in the shape of a treasure chest. Write on these chests: *gold* (yellow), *frankincense* (grey), and *myrrh* (green).

Discuss the uses and symbolism of the three gifts, using the following outline:

Gold was associated with kings and rulers. It was used for crowns and for making coins. To have gold was to be wealthy.

Frankincense was used by priests at times of prayer and public worship.

Myrrh was a spice used for healing and for anointing a body at the time of burial. It was used as a perfume.

Ask the students to speculate about the connection between these gifts and the events of Jesus' life.

Option 2. Current Events: Epiphany Party

Make plans for an Epiphany party to be celebrated on or near January 6. Some possible activities for such a gathering might be:

• Arrange for a burning of the greens. Be sure to check local fire and environmental regulations.

• Prepare a simple dinner to be shared after an Epiphany service.

• Make an Epiphany cake. (Three beans are added to the batter and baked in the cake. The three people who find them wear crowns during a closing celebration.)

• Reenact *Matthew 2:1-12.* Include the singing of "We three kings of Orient are" *(The Hymnal 1982,* 128).

Distribute slips of paper for each person to finish this sentence: "One gift I would like to offer Jesus this year is . . . ." Collect the slips and present them as an offering at the Going Forth.

REFLECTING
(Time: 10 minutes)

Distribute the reflection envelopes, and set up the Reflection Center as described in Session 1.

Direct the students to think about the following:

What are some of the gifts you would like to offer to Jesus this year? What are some qualities you would like to develop? What behaviors would you like to change? Could you make a contribution to the church? Could you devote time to a worthwhile community project? How?

When you have finished writing or drawing your reflections, write a brief prayer.

LEARNING SKILLS
(Time: 10–15 minutes)

Option 1. Class Memory Challenge

Resume the memory project by reviewing the chart that appears in the student newspaper, *Covenant Times,* Unit II, Issue 5. The task for this session is to learn the locations for the following examples of Jesus' teaching:

Sermon on the Mount—*Matthew,* chapters 5, 6, 7
The Lord's Prayer—*Matthew,* chapter 6 (in the Sermon on the Mount) and *Luke,* chapter 11
Parable of the Good Samaritan—*Luke,* chapter 10
Parables of the lost sheep, lost coin, and lost son—*Luke,* chapter 15

Note that these are all very familiar passages, and

it is helpful to be able to find them easily. Write the headings on a chalkboard or easel, under the caption, "Examples of Jesus' Teaching." Provide cards with the citations printed on them. Allow teams of students to take turns placing the cards with the correct headings, using removable tape.

Explain that, while the Gospels contain about thirty parables, only *Luke* shares the four parables in this list.

Option 2. Learning Scripture

Determine whether class members have learned verses given in the previous sessions. If so, add symbols to the scroll described in Session 1.

Encourage the students to memorize *Isaiah 60:1* or *Matthew 2:11c* before the next class session.

See "Learning Scripture" in the student newspaper, *Covenant Times*.

ONGOING PROJECT
(Time: 5–10 minutes)

See Session 1 for a description of this project. The headline for this session's billboard could be "Magi Find the King." Encourage the students to review *Matthew 2:1-12* as they prepare.

This is the fifth and last of the billboard series. Decide what to do with the billboards that have been on display. Can they be saved for a future use?

Another ongoing project will replace this one in the remaining sessions of the Unit.

SYMBOL CARD and TREASUREBOOK

Card 14 shows the three gifts of the Magi, and includes a Scripture verse with an explanation on the back.

Suggest that the students read in the *Shell Year Treasurebook*, Part II, Section 1, about the Graeco-Roman world at the time of Jesus' birth. How did the Magi fit into this world?

GOING FORTH

Re-light the two candles on the Advent wreath. The teacher or a student will say the following, pausing for the students' response of "Lord, have mercy":

With all our heart and with all our mind, let us pray to the Lord, saying, "Lord, have mercy."

For the peace from above, for the loving-kindness of God, and for the salvation of our souls, let us pray to the Lord.
Lord, have mercy.

For the peace of the world, for the welfare of the holy Church of God, and for the unity of all people, let us pray to the Lord.
Lord, have mercy.

For _____ [learners may add their own petitions], let us pray to the Lord.
Lord, have mercy.

From The Prayers of the People
The Book of Common Prayer, pp. 383-384

Teacher: Let us go forth in the name of Christ.
Students: Thanks be to God.

TEACHER'S ASSESSMENT

In what ways did this session contribute to the students' understanding of Epiphany? What were some of the gifts shared within the session (such as laughter, joy, spontaneity, energy, or helpfulness)? Which of these do you cherish most?

LOOKING AHEAD

The next session is the first of a series on healing miracles performed by Jesus. The story is on blind Bartimaeus. Spend time thinking about the words of the hymn, "Amazing grace! how sweet the sound" (*The Hymnal 1982*, 671).

MIRACLES
SESSION 6
BLIND BARTIMAEUS

FOCUS

Jesus restored the sight of a blind beggar, Bartimaeus. He did so in response to the beggar's plea for mercy. Bartimaeus called Jesus "son of David" and "teacher." When he received his vision again, he followed Jesus. The students should be able to retell the story of this miracle and explain the similarity of Bartimaeus' plea to the "Kyrie eleison" (Lord, have mercy).

GETTING READY

This session begins a series of studies on healing miracles of Jesus. These deeds of power show that Jesus was the Messiah whose birth was heralded at Christmas and Epiphany. God in Christ is Lord of God's creation. When he renews the covenant, God acts to make creation whole by healing. These are symbolic of God's ultimate restorative purposes for the creation. God takes responsibility for creation in the new covenant and redemption.

This session, like the three that follow, is designed to offer class members a close look at one of the miracles performed by Jesus. It is in these acts that Jesus manifested the role of Messiah—the One who fulfilled the visions of the Hebrew prophets. He healed the sick, and he caused the lame to walk, the deaf to hear, and the blind to see.

In the *Gospel of Mark*, the disciples of Jesus are slow to grasp who he was. In *Mark 8:18*, Jesus asked the Twelve why they, "having eyes," did not see and understand what he was doing in their presence. He had fed 5,000 people miraculously, yet they did not comprehend the fact he was God's Son in their midst. In a way, they were blind to his true mission.

Jesus then performed a miraculous healing of a blind man at Bethsaida (chapter 8:22-26).

What follows in this Gospel is a series of Jesus' teachings as he moved about with his disciples. The instruction ended in Jericho as Jesus was approached by a blind man named Bartimaeus, who pleaded for attention from Jesus. In chapter 10:46-52, we can read Mark's story of how Bartimaeus' sight was restored.

Thus, Jesus' teaching begins and ends with two stories of blind men being healed. This can be seen as a kind of object lesson for the disciples: Open your own eyes, and end your blindness to the work of God.

The cure of Bartimaeus is unique. He cried out, "Son of David, have mercy on me." Up to this time, only demons have called Jesus by a title for the Messiah. (See *Mark 3:7-12*.)

Jesus asks the man the same question he had posed earlier to his disciples, James and John: "What do you want?" The disciples had asked for seats of honor in the kingdom of God, but Bartimaeus asked only to have his sight.

Jesus healed him instantly, saying that it was his faith that made him well. Jesus chose to underscore Bartimaeus' faith rather than the cure itself.

Luke and Matthew included this story in their Gospels, but they did not mention Bartimaeus by name. (See *Luke 18:35-43* and *Matthew 20:29-34*.)

O God, the source of all health: So fill my heart with faith in your love, that with calm expectancy I may make room for your power to possess me, and gracefully accept your healing; through Jesus Christ our Lord. Amen.
For Trust in God
The Book of Common Prayer, p. 461

TEACHING TIP

Younger children are often frightened by the physical appearance of people with severe handicaps. In contrast, more mature students have empathy for these people. They want to know what is wrong and why and look for appropriate ways of offering assistance. Be direct and truthful when discussing causes and effects of physical handicaps. Stress the importance of respecting individuals and seeing them for who they are, not just for what they can or cannot do.

GATHERING

From the Teacher's Packet, display the Poster No. 11 showing Jesus healing a blind man. As the students arrive, invite them to examine the details in this painting. Ask: What seems to be happening? What do you think the people in the scene are feeling?

When everyone is present, the teacher says:

Let us pray. (Use the prayer "For Trust in God," above, or a prayer of your own choosing.)

The chosen student lector reads from the class Bible:

A Reading from the Gospel of Mark, chapter 10, verses 46 through 52.

They came to Jericho. As he and his disciples and a large crowd were leaving Jericho, Bartimaeus son of Timaeus, a blind beggar, was sitting by the roadside. When he heard that it was Jesus of Nazareth, he began to shout out and say, "Jesus, Son of David, have mercy on me!" Many sternly ordered him to be quiet, but he cried out even more loudly, "Son of David, have mercy on me!" Jesus stood still and said, "Call him here." And they called the blind man, saying to him, "Take heart; get up, he is calling you." So throwing off his cloak, he sprang up and came to Jesus. Then Jesus said to him, "What do you want me to do for you?" The blind man said to him, "My teacher, let me see again." Jesus said to him, "Go; your faith has made you well." Immediately he regained his sight and followed him on the way.

Reader: The Word of the Lord.
Response: Thanks be to God.

INTRODUCING THE STORY
(Time: 10 minutes)

Begin with a preview of Sessions 6-9 of this Unit. The next four sessions are about deeds of power performed by Jesus.

Present in your own words the story of Bartimaeus. For storytelling ideas, read the article about the healing of Bartimaeus on page 1 of the student newspaper, **Covenant Times** (Unit II, Issue 6).

Bartimaeus was a blind beggar who encountered Jesus on a road outside the city of Jericho. Instead of asking for money when Jesus came near, he asked that Jesus have mercy on him. Jesus healed him, and Bartimaeus became a follower.

Note that Bartimaeus' cry, "Son of David," is significant. It is a title for the long-expected Messiah. This is the first time in Mark's Gospel that Jesus has been greeted openly by such a title. Previously, only the demons (unclean spirits) had called him "Son of God."

Bartimaeus also uses the words, "have mercy on me." Remind the students of the Greek phrase "Kyrie eleison" used sometimes at the Eucharist. It means "Lord, have mercy on us."

An important part of this story is Bartimaeus' humility. He does not ask for anything but his sight. Jesus, in response, focuses on the blind man's faith rather than the cure itself.

Invite the students to locate the story of Bartimaeus in *Mark 10:46-52* in their Bibles and compare the story with *Luke 18:35-43* and *Matthew 20:29-34*.

EXPLORING
(Time: 15–20 minutes)

Option 1. Illuminated Kyrie

From Poster No. 7 the Teacher's Packet, make photocopies of the open-lettered "Lord, have mercy on us." Provide one of these for each student, along with fine-point felt-tip pens in a variety of colors. Invite the students to make their own illuminations by adding color and detail to each letter. If possible, supply a few pens with which to add gold effects.

The finished sheets may be glued to black construction paper to simulate frames. Display the sheets in the classroom for the remainder of this Unit.

Option 2. Role Play

Suggest that the students act out the scene of the blind man's healing. Decide where the roadside will be and the time period in which to set your drama. For example, if you decide to set it in the present, where would Jesus most likely encounter a beggar in your community or city?

Assign the parts of Jesus and Bartimaeus, disciples, and members of the crowd. Ask the actors: How would Bartimaeus know Jesus was near? How did the crowd treat Bartimaeus at first? How do you think Bartimaeus reacted when the crowd told him to go to Jesus? What did Bartimaeus do after receiving his sight? When everyone is prepared, start the action. End with Bartimaeus joining those following Jesus.

Option 3. Crossword Puzzle

Turn in the student newspaper, *Covenant Times*, Unit II, Issue 6, to the crossword puzzle titled "A Blind Man Sees." Students may work individually, in pairs, or as a total group.

MUSIC
(Time: 10 minutes)

Listen to the *Children Sing!* tape: "What wondrous love is this" (*The Hymnal 1982*, 439; *We Sing of God*, 73). Point out that this American folk hymn is in the hymnal's section titled "Jesus Christ our Lord."

You may want to call attention to words in the stanzas that may be less familiar to the students: "Bliss" is spiritual joy (the happiness of being with God); "I AM" is the title for God in the story of Moses and the burning bush; "eternity" is forever—beyond all time.

CONNECTING/SPEAKING OUT
(Time: 15–20 minutes)

Option 1. Group Discussion

As a group, do some brainstorming about Bartimaeus' life before and after he met Jesus. Ask: What was his life like? How was he treated by others? What was his lifestyle? Write down the students' thoughts on a chalkboard or newsprint easel.

Some possible responses:

Before—dependent on others, poor, sad, unable to travel, lonely.

After—able to appreciate beautiful things, follower of Jesus, helper of others, sympathetic.

Discuss: What do we expect when we say "Lord, have mercy on us" as Bartimaeus did? What else did Bartimaeus receive from Jesus in addition to his sight?

Option 2. Current Events

Talk with the students about "blindness" as a word to describe human indifference, lack of awareness, or insensitivity. An example of a person's blindness is recounted in a story in the student newspaper about John Newton, who wrote the words to the hymn "Amazing Grace." Once a slave trader, he encountered God during a storm at sea. Gradually his life changed, and he became a priest in the Church of England.

Encourage the group to list current events or conditions in our society to which people may be "blind," such as drug abuse, racial slurs, violence, poverty, and homelessness. Ask: What causes people to see what they had been ignoring or neglecting? How are our eyes "opened" to conditions around us?

When do people follow orders or rules without really thinking? How is this like being blind? Conclude by reading the first stanza of "Amazing grace! how sweet the sound" (*The Hymnal 1982*, 671), emphasizing the final words, "was blind but now I see."

REFLECTING
(Time: 10 minutes)

Distribute the students' reflection envelopes, and arrange the Reflection Center as described in Session 1.

For this session, offer the following directions:

Jesus asked Bartimaeus, "What do you want me to do for you?" Imagine that Jesus asked you the same question. What would you ask for? Why?

Write or draw your thoughts or feelings. When you have finished, compose a short prayer.

LEARNING SKILLS
(Time: 10–15 minutes)

Option 1. Class Memory Challenge

Continue to memorize headings for the outline of Jesus' life and ministry. For this session, prepare a chalkboard or easel with the words "Examples of Jesus' Healing." The following have been selected:

Blind Bartimaeus—*Matthew*, chapter 20; *Mark*, chapter 10; *Luke*, chapter 18

The Paralytic—*Matthew*, chapter 9; *Mark*, chapter 2; *Luke*, chapter 5

Ten Lepers—*Luke*, chapter 17

Peter's Mother-in-Law—*Matthew*, chapter 8

Divide the class members into pairs. Supply paper and pencils, and dictate the headings and citations so that each pair has the full list to study. Note that two of these four miracles appear in three Gospels, one is in *Luke* only, and one is in *Matthew* only.

Print one of the chapter citations on each of four cards. Write the headings on the board. After the teams have had a chance to memorize their lists, ask them to put away their papers and take turns placing each card with the correct heading.

Explain that many more healing stories appear in the Gospels; these four have been chosen as good illustrations of Jesus' ministry.

Look for the past and new memory challenges in the student newspaper, *Covenant Times*, Unit II, Issue 6.

Option 2. Learning Scripture

Find out whether class members have learned verses given in the previous sessions. If so, add symbols to the scroll described in Session 1.

Encourage the students to memorize *Isaiah 35:5-6* or *Mark 10:52a* before the next class session.

See "Learning Scripture" in the student newspaper, *Covenant Times*.

ONGOING PROJECT
(Time: 5–10 minutes)

As an ongoing project for Sessions 6-9, the class members may want to develop a series of pictures and captions that tell stories of Jesus' deeds of power.

Make all the scenes on the same size paper, and tape them together (in sequence) in one long roll. The roll can then be attached to a cardboard shipping tube, which would allow the pictures to be unrolled as if they were appearing on a television screen. The completed project can be shared with learners in other classes.

Supply paper and crayons or markers. For this session, ask the students to draw and color a series of pictures showing the healing of Bartimaeus, and add appropriate lines chosen from *Mark 10:46-52*. Suggested divisions for as many as eleven scenes and captions: verse 46, verse 47, verse 48a, verse 48b, verse 49a, verse 49b, verse 50, verse 51a, verse 51b, verse 52a, verse 52b.

SYMBOL CARD and TREASUREBOOK

Card 15 contains a picture of a sun, with a Scripture verse and explanation on the back.

Ask the students to read in the *Shell Year Treasurebook*, Part II, Sections 4-5, a description of the differences and similarities among the four Gospels. Which three are most closely related?

GOING FORTH

Gather the group for the dismissal. The teacher or a student will say the following, pausing for the students' response of "Lord, have mercy":

With all our heart and with all our mind, let us pray to the Lord, saying, "Lord, have mercy."

For the peace from above, for the loving-kindness of God, and for the salvation of our souls, let us pray to the Lord.
Lord, have mercy.

For the peace of the world, for the welfare of the holy Church of God, and for the unity of all people, let us pray to the Lord.
Lord, have mercy.

For _____ [learners may add their own petitions], let us pray to the Lord.
Lord, have mercy.

From The Prayers of the People
The Book of Common Prayer, pp. 383-384

Teacher: Let us go forth in the name of Christ.
Students: Thanks be to God.

TEACHER'S ASSESSMENT

What aspects of the story of Bartimaeus had the greatest appeal for the students? What were their questions? To what degree were they able to relate to the concept of "blindness" as a common human condition (indifference, lack of knowing, or insensitivity)?

LOOKING AHEAD

The next session will explore the healing of the paralytic. In preparation, be alert to your own community's provision for the physically handicapped. Could more be done?

MIRACLES
SESSION 7
HEALING THE PARALYTIC

FOCUS

Jesus was asked to heal a paralytic by the man's faith-filled friends. With his act of healing, Jesus linked forgiveness and God's ultimate restorative purposes for the creation. The students should be able to tell the story in their own words.

GETTING READY

The story of Jesus' healing of the paralytic man *(Mark 2:1-12)* has three very important dimensions:
a. The faith and persistence of the man's four friends is an example of human caring.
b. Jesus grants forgiveness to the paralytic, and the healing is linked to divine forgiveness.
c. This healing, very near the beginning of Jesus' ministry, marks the first evidence of strong opposition to Jesus on the part of religious leaders.

It is easy to visualize the scene. Jesus returned to his own region, and the news spread that he was back home. People gathered in great numbers to hear him preaching God's word. On this occasion they were jammed into a private home.

The friends of the paralytic, seeing that they had no hope of carrying him through the press of the crowd, decided to lower him through the roof. We can appreciate their devotion to a friend and the closeness they would feel to one another while carrying out their plan.

Palestinian houses had flat roofs and outside stairways for climbing to them. According to Luke's version of the story *(Luke 5:17-26)*, the roof was made of tiles.

The key emphasis in this episode is on Jesus' demonstrated power to forgive sins. The religious scribes who witnessed what Jesus said to the paralytic were shocked. Only God can forgive sin. Did Jesus claim to be God? Jesus did not retreat from their charge. He said to the paralytic, "I say to you, rise, take up your pallet and go home." *(Mark 2:11)*.

For intermediate-age students, the story focuses on the issue of faith in Jesus Christ and the forgiveness he extends to us.

> Most merciful God,
> we confess that we have sinned against you
> in thought, word, and deed,
> by what we have done,
> and by what we have left undone.
> We have not loved you with our whole heart;
> we have not loved our neighbors as ourselves.
> We are truly sorry and we humbly repent.
> For the sake of your Son Jesus Christ,
> have mercy on us and forgive us;
> that we may delight in your will,
> and walk in your ways,
> to the glory of your Name. Amen.
> Confession of Sin
> *The Book of Common Prayer*, p. 79

TEACHING TIP

Intermediate-age students are beginning to be skeptical about whether miracles in the Bible actually happened. Class members may raise questions about the healing of the paralytic, such as: Can anyone get well that quickly? Did his sins make him paralyzed? Encourage the students to talk about the issues. Be careful, however, that students do not over-generalize and equate all sickness with a need to be forgiven.

GATHERING

Display Poster No. 12 in the Teacher's Packet showing the healing of the paralytic man. As the students arrive, direct their attention to the picture of the man's four friends letting him down through the roof. Ask questions like: Where is this scene? Why are the men on the roof? What will happen next?

When everyone is present, the teacher says:
Let us pray. (Use the "Confession of Sin," above, or a prayer of your own choosing.)

The chosen student lector reads from the class Bible:

A Reading from the Gospel of Mark, chapter 2, verses 1 through 12.

When he returned to Capernaum after some days, it was reported that he was at home. So many gathered around that there was no longer room for them, not even in front of the door; and he was speaking the word to them. Then some people came, bringing to him a paralyzed man, carried by four of them. And when they could not bring him to Jesus because of the crowd, they removed the roof above him; and after having dug through it, they let down the mat on which the paralytic lay. When Jesus saw their faith, he said to the paralytic, "Son, your sins are forgiven." Now some of the scribes were sitting there, questioning in their hearts, "Why does this fellow speak this way? It is blasphemy! Who can forgive sins but God alone?" At once Jesus perceived in his spirit that they were discussing these questions among themselves; and he said to them, "Why do you raise such questions in your hearts? Which is easier, to say to the paralytic, 'Your sins are forgiven,' or to say, 'Stand up and take your mat and walk'? But so that you may know that the Son of Man has authority on earth to forgive sins"—he said to the paralytic—"I say to you, stand up, take your mat and go to your home." And he stood up, and immediately took the mat and went out before all of them; so that they were all amazed and glorified God, saying, "We have never seen anything like this!"

Reader: The Word of the Lord.
Response: Thanks be to God.

INTRODUCING THE STORY
(Time: 10 minutes)

Begin by noting that this is the second in a series of sessions on Jesus' deeds of power in his ministry. In the previous session, blind Bartimaeus cried out to Jesus on his own. We turn now to the story of another man who needed Jesus' help, but who also needed assistance from his friends in order to be with Jesus.

In your own words, retell the story from *Mark 2:1-12* about Jesus healing the paralytic. Underscore the three dimensions of Mark's account from Getting Ready (above). Read the fictional eyewitness account of the story in the student newspaper, **Covenant Times** (Unit II, Issue 7) for ideas.

The story describes the man as being paralyzed for a long time. He could not get around on his own, and was dependent on the kindness of others. His friends cared about him enough to bring him to Jesus, even if it meant cutting through the roof of a house.

Conclude by reminding the students of the final two questions in The Baptismal Covenant (BCP, p. 305): Will you seek and serve Christ in all persons, loving your neighbor as yourself? Will you strive for justice and peace among all people, and respect the dignity of every human being?

Ask the students to consider how the paralytic's friends were showing love for a neighbor and respecting his dignity.

Ask students to work individually or in teams to look up *Matthew 9:2-8* and *Luke 5:17-26* and read the other versions of the story of the paralytic's healing. How do these accounts differ from *Mark*?

EXPLORING
(Time: 15–20 minutes)

Option 1. Radio Interview

Prepare a radio interview program to be broadcast from the scene just after the healing of the paralytic.

Decide who will play each of the parts: Interviewer, the paralytic, the four friends, the scribes (opposing religious leaders), Jesus, the owner of the house, and witnesses from the crowd. Name a production staff to be responsible for sound effects and a tape recording of the program.

Suggested questions for the interviewer:

(to people in the crowd/witnesses) What happened here?

(to the paralytic) How do you feel now? How will your life change? Where are you going now?

(to scribes) Why are you upset with Jesus? What do you oppose?

(to paralytic's friends) Why did you carry your friend here? Why did you tear up the roof?

(to Jesus) What really happened here? Where are you going from here? What is important about today?

(to the home owner) How do you feel about what happened to your house?

Option 2. Barrier Survey

Read the article about assisting the handicapped in *Covenant Times*. As a group, take a survey of the accessibility of different areas in your church. Borrow a baby stroller and put a ten-pound bag of flour in it to help you determine if areas are wheelchair accessible. Blindfold one person to help you identify barriers that might exist for the blind, and ask another in the group to put cotton in his or her ears to find out about difficulties faced by a person with a hearing problem. Assign at least one or two "friends" to assist each person with a "disability." Don't forget to check bathrooms, drinking fountains, dining rooms, and parking lots.

After completing your survey, share it with the buildings and grounds committee or other appropriate groups. Could changes be made easily?

Option 3. Word Search

Turn in the student newspaper, *Covenant Times*, Unit II, Issue 7, to the word search titled "A Lame Man Walks." Students may work individually, in pairs, or as a total group.

MUSIC
(Time: 10 minutes)

Listen to "What wondrous love is this" (*The Hymnal 1982*, 439; *We Sing of God*, 73) on the *Children Sing!* tape.

Note that this folk hymn was probably sung originally without instrumental accompaniment. Phrases are repeated intentionally to make the hymn easier to learn for people who cannot read.

CONNECTING/SPEAKING OUT
(Time: 15–20 minutes)

Option 1. Group Discussion

Discuss Jesus' act of forgiving the paralytic man. The man's friends had brought him to Jesus in the hope that he would be made well. Ask: How did the paralyzed person feel when he heard Jesus forgiving him?

Note that therapists (people in the healing profession) have recognized a relationship between health and forgiveness. Ask: How does it make us feel to know we need to be forgiven? What can we do about it?

Our Christian faith assures us that we are forgiven by God when we confess our sins. It is through Jesus Christ that we are forgiven of our sins. Ask: How does it feel to hear that we are forgiven?

Option 2. Current Events

Talk with the students about our concern for the physically disabled. The paralytic's friends had to carry him on a pallet. In what ways do we assist handicapped persons today? Who are some of the persons and groups who minister to the handicapped? (Note that physical disabilities need not bar people from productive lives. All people have abilities and gifts. We sometimes speak of everyone as "differently abled.")

If you surveyed your church looking for barriers, identify one or more changes with which this group could assist. For example, contact an agency that works with the blind to learn how to make signs in Braille for meeting rooms and bathrooms. Seating at the front of the church or near speakers could be reserved for those with hearing problems. What other ways could you be like the friends of the paralyzed man?

REFLECTING
(Time: 10 minutes)

Hand out the students' reflection envelopes, and prepare the Reflection Center, as described in Session 1.

Share directions for the students, such as the following:

The paralytic had four friends who carried him to Jesus. Why were they eager to do this?

In what ways could you help people who need physical assistance? Are you willing to offer such help on a regular basis? What does Jesus have to do with your service to others?

Write or draw your thoughts or feelings about helping your friends and neighbors.

LEARNING SKILLS
(Time: 10–15 minutes)

Option 1. Class Memory Challenge

Look in the student newspaper, *Covenant Times*, Unit II, Issue 7. Encourage the students to learn a list titled "Other Miracles of Jesus":

Water Changed to Wine—*John,* chapter 2
Calming the Sea—*Matthew,* chapter 8; *Mark,* chapter 4; *Luke,* chapter 8
Feeding the 5000—*Matthew,* chapter 14; *Mark,* chapter 6; *Luke,* chapter 9; *John,* chapter 6

Notice that only John tells the story of Jesus' first miracle, at a wedding in Cana of Galilee. The feeding of the 5000 is the only miracle of Jesus that appears in all four Gospels.

Calming the sea lends itself to the number pattern 8-4-8 (*Matthew, Mark, Luke*). Students may choose which of the four citations to learn for the feeding of the 5000.

Explain that Jesus' many miracles are sometimes described in three categories: healings, exorcisms (casting out spirits or demons), and nature miracles. The three examples above are all nature miracles.

Option 2. Learning Scripture

Ask whether class members have learned verses given in the previous sessions. If so, add symbols to the scroll described in Session 1.

Encourage the students to memorize *Jeremiah 17:14* or *Mark 2:12b* before the next class session.

See "Learning Scripture" in the student newspaper, *Covenant Times.*

ONGOING PROJECT
(Time: 5–10 minutes)

If the class members have begun making the enlarged paper filmstrip on Jesus' miracles (as described in Session 6), encourage them to illustrate *Mark 2:1-12* and attach their drawings to the roll.

Pictures could be drawn and colored for each of these segments of the story: verses. 1-2, verse 3, verse 4, verse 5, verses 6-7, verses 8-11, verse 12a, verse 12b. Write the appropriate captions.

SYMBOL CARD and TREASUREBOOK

Card 16 has a picture of an oil stock and a Scripture verse and an explanation on the back.

Ask the students to read about Jesus' conflict with religious authorities in the *Shell Year Treasurebook,* Part II, Section 6. Which groups were most critical of Jesus?

GOING FORTH

Gather the group for the dismissal. The teacher or a student will say the following, pausing for the students' response of "Lord, have mercy":

With all our heart and with all our mind, let us pray to the Lord, saying, "Lord, have mercy."

For the peace from above, for the loving-kindness of God, and for the salvation of our souls, let us pray to the Lord.
Lord, have mercy.

For the peace of the world, for the welfare of the holy Church of God, and for the unity of all people, let us pray to the Lord.
Lord, have mercy.

For _____ [learners may add their own petitions], let us pray to the Lord.
Lord, have mercy.

From The Prayers of the People
The Book of Common Prayer, pp. 383-384

Teacher: Let us go forth in the name of Christ.
Students: Thanks be to God.

TEACHER'S ASSESSMENT

Which dimension of this session's story was of greatest interest to the students? What was said about the religious leaders' opposition to Jesus? about healing and forgiveness? about friends' sensitivity to the physical handicaps of others? In which of these areas do the class members appear to need more time for exploration?

LOOKING AHEAD

The next session focuses on Jesus' cleansing of ten lepers. Consider the plight of lepers as social outcasts in Jesus' day. Who are the isolated and lonely people in our own time? In what ways can healing occur for all such persons?

MIRACLES
SESSION 8
CLEANSING OF THE TEN LEPERS

FOCUS

Jesus showed pity on ten lepers (outcasts of society) by healing them of their disease. He did so in response to their plea for mercy. Only one of the ten returned to give thanks to Jesus. The students should be able to tell the story of this healing, and restate the importance of gratitude for healing and for all who minister to the sick.

GETTING READY

Only the *Gospel of Luke* describes Jesus' healing of the ten lepers (*Luke 17:11-19*).

Leprosy in biblical times was not clearly defined; the term could refer to any kind of serious skin disease (including swelling, boils, and rashes). Because they were thought to be contagious, lepers were required to live outside of the camp, in isolation from the community. Elaborate means of purification were prescribed, requiring the service of a priest and including rituals of washing and changing clothes.

The lepers in Luke's story are both Jews and Samaritans. The desperation of their plight brought them together, for these groups were generally at odds with one another. When they approached Jesus, the lepers cried out, "Jesus, Master, have mercy on us." As in the story of Bartimaeus (Session 6), this plea reminds us of the "Kyrie Eleison" (Lord, have mercy).

The story links healing with obedience, faith, and gratitude. Jesus simply told the ten people to show themselves to priests, an act of religious obedience. They were cleansed at once, even before they could carry out this action. But only one member of the group—a Samaritan—came back to express his thanks. Jesus responded by saying that the man's faith had made him well.

Intermediate-age students, with their increasing capacity for empathy, may be able to appreciate the suffering of the lepers. They are also able to see the story's emphasis on the gratitude of one leper in contrast to the ingratitude of the other nine.

Almighty God and heavenly Father, we give you humble thanks because you have been graciously pleased to deliver from sickness your servant, in whose behalf we bless and praise your Name. Grant, O gracious Father, that your servant through your help, may live in this world according to your will, and also be a partaker of everlasting glory in the life to come; through Jesus Christ our Lord. *Amen.*

For the Restoration of Health
The Book of Common Prayer, p. 841

TEACHING TIP

Intermediate-age students can identify a variety of instances in which people feel isolated or excluded, like the lepers in the Bible. They may be experiencing such feelings themselves, or even excluding other people in their peer groups. Look for times that class members exhibit feelings of empathy or prejudice. Offer opportunities for them to describe their own experience of being harshly judged or left out. Encourage acts of compassion.

GATHERING

As the students arrive, call their attention to Poster No. 11 from the Teacher's Packet showing Jesus' healing of the lepers. Ask the class members to study the faces and postures of the people in the scene. What are their feelings?

When everyone is present, the teacher says:

Let us pray. (Use the thanksgiving "For the Restoration of Health," above, or a prayer of your own choosing.)

The chosen student lector reads from the class Bible:

A Reading from the Gospel of Luke, chapter 17, verses 11 through 19.

On the way to Jerusalem Jesus was going through the region between Samaria and Galilee. As he entered a village, ten lepers approached him. Keeping their distance, they called out, saying, "Jesus, Master, have mercy on us!" When he saw them, he said to them, "Go and show yourselves to the priests." And as they went, they were made clean. Then one of them, when he saw that he was healed, turned back, praising God with a loud voice. He prostrated himself at Jesus' feet and thanked him. And he was a Samaritan. Then Jesus asked, "Were not ten made clean? But the other nine, where are they? Was none of them found to return and give praise to God except this foreigner?" Then he said to him, "Get up and go on your way; your faith has made you well."

Reader: The Word of the Lord.
Response: Thanks be to God.

INTRODUCING THE STORY
(Time: 10 minutes)

Show a map of New Testament times that shows Samaria. (See the map in **Covenant Times** for this Unit, Issue 4, p. 3.) Briefly describe the long-standing enmity between Samaritans and Jewish people.

Relate the status of lepers in Jesus' time. Note that various skin diseases might be called "leprosy." People with these conditions were social outcasts because others feared the diseases to be contagious. They could not return to a normal life until a priest had declared them healed.

In your own words, retell the story of Jesus' healing of the ten lepers. For ideas, read the story in the student newspaper, **Covenant Times** (Unit II, Issue 8), of a fictional interview with one of the nine lepers who did not return to thank Jesus.

Focus principally on the ingratitude of the nine in contrast to the Samaritan who came back to thank Jesus. As in the case of the parable of the Good Samaritan, the hero of the story is someone who Jesus' hearers would least expect to do what is right.

Ask the students to work in pairs to find *Luke 17:11-19* and *Luke 5:12-16*. What is similar about the two stories? How do they differ?

EXPLORING
(Time: 15–20 minutes)

Option 1. "Kyrie Eleison" Mobile

Provide the students with pieces of lightweight cardboard (possibly in varied shapes), markers, glue and art supplies, paper punches, string, and coat hangers. Give directions for making a "Kyrie Eleison" mobile.

Each class member will need three pieces of cardboard on which to write these lines, respectively (both front and back):

Lord, have mercy.
Christ, have mercy.
Lord, have mercy.

If they want to write the words in Greek, see page 356 of *The Book of Common Prayer*. The three pieces can be decorated in any way the students wish, with markers or glued-on bits of paper, foil, or fabric.

Punch a hole in each piece, insert a string, and attach it to the hanger. Decide where to display the completed mobiles.

Option 2. Costumed Tableau

Invite the students to use brown paper bags and shreds of newspaper to make costumes of clothing that a leper might wear. Pieces may be taped together to cover students' bodies.

Ask each person to think of a reason that someone might be considered a leper today and write a descriptive word or phrase on his or her costume. For example, someone might write "AIDS" or "homeless" or "refugee." Stand in a circle and say a one-sentence prayer for each condition written on the costumes.

Option 3. Word Puzzle

Turn in the student newspaper, *Covenant Times*, Unit II, Issue 8, to the word puzzle titled "The Healing of the Lepers." Students may work individually, in pairs, or as a total group.

MUSIC
(Time: 10 minutes)

Listen again to "What wondrous love is this" (*The Hymnal 1982*, 439; *We Sing of God*, 73) on the *Children Sing!* tape. Imagine the tenth leper singing this hymn. Which words would he emphasize? Why?

CONNECTING/SPEAKING OUT
(Time: 15–20 minutes)

Option 1. Group Discussion

Briefly describe the disease of leprosy from information in the student newspaper, *Covenant Times*. True leprosy, or Hansen's disease, is a chronic, infectious disease that affects the skin and nerve endings and is caused by a bacillus. If not treated, it can result in severe disfigurement.

Engage the students in conversation about the lepers' attitudes toward Jesus. Ask: Would they have been surprised that he came to see them? What did they say to Jesus when he arrived in the village? After he healed them, what did they do?

Discuss the lepers' reactions to the healing they experienced. How do you think Jesus felt about the nine who were silent? Why do people fail to express gratitude when they have been helped? What would cause others to be like the Samaritan in the story? When have you felt that your own kindness was taken for granted by someone?

Option 2. Current Events

Look in newspapers and magazines for stories about compassionate caring—in hospices, AIDS ministries, rescue missions, church outreach programs, and as a response to natural disasters (such as a hurricane or a large forest fire).

What kinds of risks are involved in these acts of kindness? How do people generally respond when help is offered to them in times of need?

Ask the class members to think about forms of Christian ministry they could undertake to help people who experience suffering of any kind. For ideas, read the story about Christian ministry in the student newspaper. How can each of us reach out to people who feel isolated or excluded?

REFLECTING
(Time: 10 minutes)

Set up the Reflection Center, as described in Session 1. Distribute the reflection envelopes, and offer these directions:

Think about a time when you or someone in your family was helped by others during a time of sickness or other period of need.

Did you say thank you? How do you express your feelings of gratitude? When have you sometimes forgotten to do so?

Write or draw your responses. A brief prayer may be added.

LEARNING SKILLS
(Time: 10–15 minutes)

Option 1. Class Memory Challenge

The memory task for this session focuses on Holy Week. Invite the students to learn the following headings and citations in order:

Palm Sunday—*Matthew*, chapter 21; *Mark*, chapter 11; *Luke*, chapter 19; *John*, chapter 12

The Last Supper—*Matthew*, chapter 26; *Mark*, chapter 14; *Luke*, chapter 22; *John*, chapter 13

Good Friday—*Matthew*, chapter 27; *Mark*, chapter 15; *Luke*, chapter 23; *John*, chapter 19

Easter—*Matthew*, chapter 28; *Mark*, chapter 16; *Luke*, chapter 24; *John*, chapter 20

Suggest that the students may want to work in pairs, with each pair concentrating on a different Gospel. The Holy Week events, Palm Sunday through Easter, appear in the last few chapters of each Gospel. They are found in *Matthew*, chapters 21-28; *Mark*, chapters 11-16; *Luke*, chapters 19-24; and *John*, chapters 12-20.

Remind the class members that these are the most important events in the story of Jesus, and it is good to know where to read them in the New Testament. See the student newspaper, *Covenant Times*, Unit II, Issue 8.

Option 2. Learning Scripture

Ask class members who have learned verses given in the previous sessions to share these from memory. Add symbols to the scroll described in Session 1.

Encourage the students to memorize *Luke 17:19* or *John 11:25-26a* before the next class session.

See "Learning Scripture" in the student newspaper, *Covenant Times*.

ONGOING PROJECT
(Time: 5–10 minutes)

If the students are making the enlarged paper filmstrip on Jesus' miracles (as described in Session 6), ask them to illustrate *Luke 17:11-19* and attach their drawings to the roll.

Pictures may be drawn and colored for each of these segments in the story: verses 11-13, verse 14a, verse 14b, verses 15-16, and verses 17-19. Include an appropriate caption for each drawing.

You may want to discuss arrangements for visiting another classroom during the next session to share this project with other children or an adult group.

SYMBOL CARD and TREASUREBOOK

Card 17 has an illustration of the shield of St. Catherine of Siena, a Scripture verse, and an explanation on the back.

Ask the students to look through *Shell Year Treasurebook,* Part II, Sections 4-6, for references to Jesus' healing ministry. How would you describe his life's work?

GOING FORTH

Gather the group for the dismissal. The teacher or a student will say the following, pausing for the students' response of "Lord, have mercy":

> With all our heart and with all our mind, let us pray to the Lord, saying, "Lord, have mercy."

For the peace from above, for the loving-kindness of God, and for the salvation of our souls, let us pray to the Lord.
Lord, have mercy.

For the peace of the world, for the welfare of the holy Church of God, and for the unity of all people, let us pray to the Lord.
Lord, have mercy.

For _____[learners may add their own petitions], let us pray to the Lord.
Lord, have mercy.
> From The Prayers of the People
> *The Book of Common Prayer,* pp. 383-384

Teacher: Let us go forth in the name of Christ.
Students: Thanks be to God.

TEACHER'S ASSESSMENT

From your observation, were the students able to appreciate Jesus' healing of the ten lepers as an act of grace and mercy? How did they respond to the ingratitude of the "nine"? In what ways do the class members express empathy for people in need? Are they able to name ways they could serve others?

LOOKING AHEAD

The final session in this Unit is devoted to Jesus' raising of Lazarus. Read the story, in *John 11*. What does this account mean for you? In what ways can you see life overcoming death?

MIRACLES
SESSION 9
RAISING OF LAZARUS

FOCUS

As evidence of his role as the Messiah, Jesus raised his friend Lazarus from the dead. This deed foreshadowed his own coming resurrection. The students should be able to tell this story in their own words and explain that Jesus' miracles were a demonstration of God's great power and love for "all sorts and conditions" of people.

GETTING READY

The story of Lazarus, in *John 11:1-44,* is the climax in a series of miracles. Jesus, the good shepherd, is now revealed to be "the resurrection and the life."

At the command of Jesus, Lazarus was raised from the dead, and this deed of power anticipated Jesus' own death and resurrection. Jesus' miracle evidenced God's glory and presence. It was an epiphany of God's healing love, revealed through the work of God's Son.

In the Jewish community at the time of Jesus, burial followed death almost immediately. The days of mourning were usually a week long. Professional "mourners" might be hired to weep. The body was wrapped with long cloths, and spices were added. Hints of these customs are found in the account of Lazarus' restoration to life.

Ironically, it was this great miracle on Jesus' part that intensified opposition to his ministry and brought about his condemnation and death *(John 11:45-57).* To love his friend Lazarus and give him life, Jesus had to be willing to risk and lose his own.

Intermediate-age students can put themselves into the roles of the key figures of the story. They can also begin to articulate the central theme of the Christian gospel: God in Christ won a permanent victory over death. The ultimate power of God is on the side of life.

For none of us has life in himself,
and none becomes his own master when he dies.
For if we have life, we are alive in the Lord,
and if we die, we die in the Lord.
So, then, whether we live or die,
we are the Lord's possession.
   The Burial of the Dead: Rite II
   The Book of Common Prayer, p. 491

TEACHING TIP

By this time, most students have experienced the deaths of people in their families or in the community in addition to beloved pets. They know both the pain and finality of death. This session, with its emphasis on Jesus Christ's power over death, offers comfort and hope to Christians. Be alert to what students say about death and dying. Take their feelings seriously; listening may be the most appropriate way to do so. Avoid attempts to gloss over the reality of death. At the same time, do not hesitate to affirm your own hope in the risen Christ.

GATHERING

As the students arrive, direct their attention to Poster No. 12 in the Teacher's Packet that shows an artist's interpretation of the raising of Lazarus. Ask: What appears to be happening in the scene? What do the people seem to be feeling?

When everyone is present, the teacher says:

Let us pray. (Use the anthem "From The Burial of the Dead: Rite II," above, or a prayer of your own choosing.)

Note: The entire story of Lazarus' illness, death, and the events that followed *(John 11:1-44)* is a long reading. Read selected verses, as suggested below. The words in parentheses have been added for clarity.

The chosen student lector reads from the class Bible:

A Reading from the Gospel of John, chapter 11, selected verses.

Jesus said to (Martha), "Your brother (Lazarus, who is dead) will rise again." Martha said to him, "I know that he will rise again in the resurrection on the last day." Jesus said to her, "I am the resurrection and the life. Those who believe in me, even though they die, will live, and everyone who lives and believes in me will never die. Do you believe this?" She said to him, "Yes, Lord, I believe that you are the Messiah, the Son of God, the one coming into the world." . . .

When Mary came where Jesus was and saw him, she knelt at his feet and said to him, "Lord, if you had been here, my brother would not have died." When Jesus saw her weeping, and the Jews who came with her also weeping, he was greatly disturbed in spirit and deeply moved. He said, "Where have you laid him?" They said to him, "Lord, come and see." Jesus began to weep. So the Jews said, "See how he loved him!" But some of them said, "Could not he who opened the eyes of the blind man have kept this man from dying?"

Then Jesus, again greatly disturbed, came to the tomb. It was a cave, and a stone was lying against it. Jesus said, "Take away the stone." . . . So they took away the stone. . . . (Jesus) cried with a loud voice, "Lazarus, come out!" The dead man came out, his hands and feet bound with strips of cloth, and his face wrapped in a cloth. Jesus said to them, "Unbind him, and let him go."

Reader: The Word of the Lord.
Response: Thanks be to God.

INTRODUCING THE STORY
(Time: 10 minutes)

If the shortened reading (above) was used, retell in your own words the story of Jesus' raising of Lazarus, including some of the omitted details. Use the story in the student newspaper, *Covenant Times* (Unit II, Issue 9), for ideas.

Introduce the following dimensions of the story:

• Jesus had been a close friend of Lazarus and his sisters, Martha and Mary. He had spent time in their home. (See the student newspaper, *Covenant Times*, for a story about an earlier visit to their home.) Jesus wept with sorrow when he knew that Lazarus had died.

• Jesus' disciples were worried about his decision to go to Bethany. It was only about two miles from Jerusalem, where the religious leaders were opposed to Jesus' ministry. The apostle Thomas foresaw what was coming when he said, "Let us also go, that we may die with him." *(John 11:16b.)*

• Until now in the *Gospel of John*, Jesus' deeds of power were healings of the sick or nature miracles (like the changing of water to wine, or the feeding of the multitudes). In the raising of Lazarus, it is now clear that Jesus Christ holds final power over death itself. The raising of Lazarus points to Jesus' own death and resurrection.

Ask the students to turn in their Bibles to *John 11*. Suggest they work individually or in teams to answer these questions: What did Lazarus' two sisters say and do? What reason did Jesus give for raising Lazarus from the dead?

EXPLORING
(Time: 15–20 minutes)

Option 1. Graffiti: Life and Death

Prepare a surface to serve as a graffiti board—a large strip of butcher paper, two oversize pieces of newsprint, or possibly a sheet of white cloth. Near the top, write "Death" on the left and "Life" on the right. Supply markers, large crayons, or fabric paint.

Ask the students to think about the two words and add their own imaginative graffiti under the headings. They may write other words and phrases or draw pictures. Ask: What do you think about when you hear each of the words? The graffiti may be as elaborate as the students wish to make it.

Talk about the words and drawings. How many are hopeful? How does Jesus change the way we look at life and death?

Option 2. Peacock Sponge Paintings

Give each student a sheet of white paper, 12 x 18 inches. Supply pencils and markers, small bits of sponge, and thinned tempera paint of varying colors poured into shallow dishes. Encourage the students to make sponge paintings of a peacock, which is an ancient symbol of resurrection (new life). Its tail is constantly renewed, and each growth of feathers is more beautiful.

To make a painting, draw the narrow body of the bird in the lower center of the sheet. (For a drawing of a peacock, see Symbol Card No. 18.) Dip sponge bits into paint to create the fanned-out tail feathers in a variety of colors.

Option 3. Word Puzzle

Turn in the student newspaper, *Covenant Times*, Unit II, Issue 9, to the word puzzle titled "The Raising of Lazarus." Students may work individually, in pairs, or as a total group.

MUSIC
(Time: 10 minutes)

Listen once again to the hymn "What wondrous love is this" *(The Hymnal 1982,* 439; *We Sing of God,* 73)* on the *Children Sing!* tape. Read in unison the final stanza. Ask: Why might this be called "The Song of Lazarus?"

CONNECTING/SPEAKING OUT
(Time: 15–20 minutes)

Option 1. Group Discussion

Use the following questions and references as you lead the class members in discussing the story of Lazarus *(John 11)*:

• Why do you think Jesus stayed two days longer in the place where he was? (See verse 5.)
• What did Martha and Mary do that showed how they felt about Jesus? (See verses 2, 3, 20-27, 28, 32-34, 39b.)
• Why did Jesus weep?
• How do you suppose the crowd reacted when Lazarus came out of the tomb?
• What do you think Jesus meant when he said, "I am the resurrection and the life"? (See verse 25a)
• How do you think Lazarus' life was changed by what happened?

Option 2. Current Events

More people were attracted to Jesus after his miraculous raising of Lazarus. They wanted to tell others about him. Talk with the students about Christians' eagerness to tell and retell stories about Jesus Christ. The Church has always understood that it exists to share news about the risen Lord with the whole world. It is our mission (task). Ask: How do we carry out this mission?

If students focus on clergy persons as the ones who tell about Jesus, talk about the mission of lay persons as well. Share any articles or current events that demonstrate ways in which the lay people are active in sharing the gospel (good news) of Christ. Cite people in your congregation who help others through volunteer organizations or church programs. Note that we share through both the spoken word and concrete acts of service in Christ's name.

REFLECTING
(Time: 10 minutes)

Distribute the reflection envelopes, and prepare the Reflection Center as described in Session 1.

Offer these directions for the students' response:

Choose one or more people in the story of Jesus' raising of Lazarus: Mary, Martha, one of Jesus' disciples, a member of the crowd, or Lazarus himself. Imagine you are the person you chose. How would you react to seeing Lazarus walk out of the tomb? How would you feel about Jesus after Lazarus was raised? What would you want to say to Jesus?

When you have completed writing or drawing your reflections, write a brief prayer.

LEARNING SKILLS
(Time: 10–25 minutes)

Option 1. Class Memory Challenge

Survey all the headings in the chart of Jesus' life and ministry. (See the student newspaper, *Covenant Times*, Unit II, Issue 9.) Ask the students to work in groups and reconstruct the outline from memory. How well can they recall the list?

Introduce the final two headings:

Jesus' "Great Commission" to his disciples—*Matthew 28* (last paragraph of this Gospel)

Jesus' ascension into heaven—*Luke 24* (last paragraph of this Gospel)

Note that only *Matthew* contains the Great Commission, and only *Luke* describes the ascension. A way of keeping this in mind is to remember that the Gospels and the events are in the same order (*Matthew* with the Great Commission and *Luke* with the ascension).

Be sure to commend the students who have taken on this Unit's memory challenge. It has required effort and persistence. Remind the class members that they will be able to use the outline throughout their lives.

Option 2. Learning Scripture

Add symbols to the scroll described in Session 1 for scripture verses class members have learned from the previous sessions.

See "Learning Scripture" in the student newspaper, *Covenant Times*.

For this final session of the Unit, unroll the entire scroll and review all the Scripture verses that have been learned. In Unit III, another group of verses will be introduced with a way to record what has been memorized.

ONGOING PROJECT

(Time: 5–10 minutes)

If the students have worked on this paper film-strip roll, encourage them to make final scenes related to the story of Lazarus, from *John 11:1-44*. Pictures could reflect these verses in particular: 1 and 18a; 11; 20-22; 23-27; 33-35; 38-39a; 41-42; 43-44.

If the group has decided to share the completed project with other groups in the congregation, work out the final arrangements.

SYMBOL CARD and TREASUREBOOK

Card 18 has an illustration of a peacock, and a Scripture verse and explanation on the back.

Encourage the students to review *Shell Year Treasurebook,* Part II. Which parts were most interesting or helpful?

GOING FORTH

Gather the group for the dismissal. The teacher or a student will say the following, pausing for the students' response of "Lord, have mercy":

With all our heart and with all our mind, let us pray to the Lord, saying, "Lord, have mercy."

For the peace from above, for the loving-kindness of God, and for the salvation of our souls, let us pray to the Lord.
Lord, have mercy.

For the peace of the world, for the welfare of the holy Church of God, and for the unity of all people, let us pray to the Lord.
Lord, have mercy.

For _____[learners may add their own petitions], let us pray to the Lord.
Lord, have mercy.
From The Prayers of the People
The Book of Common Prayer, pp. 383-384

Teacher: Let us go forth in the name of Christ.
Students: Thanks be to God.

TEACHER'S ASSESSMENT

How did the students respond to the story of Lazarus? Were they able to relate the account to Jesus' mission and his own coming death and resurrection? As you look back over your experience in teaching this Unit, what were some of the memorable moments? Why?

Note: The following letter is for teachers and parents of children in the Intermediate level of church school. These two pages can be reproduced or used as a model for a personalized letter.

Episcopal Children's Curriculum
Unit III: Baptism—New Life

Dear Parents and Guardians,

An aim of Christian education in Episcopal churches is to assist every member, young and old, to live out the covenant made in Holy Baptism (*The Book of Common Prayer*, p. 304). In pursuit of that aim, the curriculum materials for each year focus on Scripture, sacraments, and the life of the Church. Through their exploration of these topics, children can begin to take their place as witnesses for Christ, faithful to the Baptismal Covenant in every dimension of their lives.

In the Shell year, children at each age level study a unit on the sacrament of Holy Baptism. Intermediate-age students are ready for a more detailed exploration of baptism. We will use many different teaching methods to help them understand more about the first of the two great sacraments given by Christ to his Church. (See the "Catechism" in *The Book of Common Prayer*, p. 858.)

We encourage you to continue to be involved in your student's study of the Bible and the Church. We suggest that you use the Scripture references provided in this letter, the *Shell Year Treasurebook*, and the student newspaper *Covenant Times* in your family discussions. You may want to create a display for the Take-Home Symbol Cards for this Unit. Encourage everyone in your family to learn about baptism symbols and look for them in your church. Each part of the curriculum provides a wealth of information about this sacrament.

From John the Baptist Until Now

The first five sessions of this unit are devoted to the origin of baptism, the Baptismal Covenant, and the service itself as the Church's rite of initiation.

Session 1: "The Baptism of Jesus" will help us to understand the sacrament as its beginning. In various forms, washing with water is an ancient practice found in almost all religious bodies. For Christians, the cleansing rite of baptism happens only once, often in infancy. Holy Baptism was instituted by Jesus who asked John the Baptist to baptize him in the Jordan River. The Holy Spirit descended upon Jesus, and his ministry as Messiah began at that time. (*Matthew 3:11-17*)

Session 2: "Baptism and Our Beliefs" focuses on the three "faith" questions of the Baptismal Covenant. In response to the three questions, the people of the congregation reaffirm their commitment to God, the undivided Trinity—in the words of the Apostles' Creed. This Creed dates back to the early Church and was probably composed for use by believers who came for baptism. (*Matthew 28:16-20*)

Session 3: "Baptism and Our Living" is devoted to the five "action" questions of the Covenant. These five questions describe what is needed to "keep God's holy will and commandments." The people's response to each question is, "I will, with God's help." We will help students realize that it is through prayerful reliance on God that we are able to live out these promises. Your student should be able to name all five questions or promises. (*John 15:1-5, 9-11*)

Session 4: "Baptized by Water and the Spirit" is centered on the prayer of thanksgiving over the water (BCP, p. 306). This prayer includes the rich imagery of God's Spirit moving over the waters of Creation, delivering Israel out of bondage from Egypt, and the saving water of baptism. The prayer is from the writings of the apostle Paul who spoke of baptism as burial with Christ in his death and being raised from the water as sharing in Christ's resurrection. (*Acts 2:38-41*)

Session 5: "Receiving the Newly Baptized" is devoted to the words of welcome at the end of the service. The people confess Christ, proclaim his resurrection, and share in his priestly ministry. After the welcome, the congregation joins in the ancient Christian tradition of passing the peace. (*Romans 15:5-7*)

Baptism, Holy Week, and Easter
The final four sessions of the unit are intended for use in the latter part of Lent and into the first weeks of the Easter season. They are devoted to the events of Maundy Thursday, Good Friday, and Easter.

Session 6: "Jesus Is Servant" is based on the account of the Last Supper in the *Gospel of John*. Jesus took the role of a servant and washed the disciples' feet. Jesus then gave them a new commandment that they should "love one another" (*John 13:34*). The word "Maundy" is from the Old English word for "commandment." (*John 13:1-9*)

Session 7: "Jesus Was Crucified" describes the event of Jesus' betrayal, trial, and crucifixion. Intermediate-age children can handle the Good Friday narrative. The focus, however, will be on the actual events of Holy Thursday and Good Friday and not on the painful physical details of Christ's suffering on the cross. (*John 18:1b-8*)

Session 8: "Jesus Was Raised From the Dead" shares the resurrection account according to the *Gospel of John*. The surprise of the empty tomb is viewed through the eyes of Mary Magdalene, Peter, Thomas, and the other apostles. We will look at the rich imagery of this season—such as the Easter Vigil, a traditional time for baptisms. (*John 20:1-10*)

Session 9: "Jesus Offers New Life" is devoted to the expression "newness of life" that the apostle Paul used to describe the journey of baptized people. We end the unit with a focus on the future. The learners are called to take their place in the baptized community, the Body of Christ. (*Romans 6:3-4*)

Yours in Christ,

Church School Teachers

BAPTISM: NEW LIFE
SESSION 1
THE BAPTISM OF JESUS

FOCUS

Jesus was baptized by John the Baptist in the Jordan River. The Holy Spirit came upon Jesus (like a dove), and John saw the power of Jesus. The students should be able to describe Jesus' baptism, explain the symbol of the dove, and affirm in their own words the significance of the sacrament of Holy Baptism.

GETTING READY

This is the first of five sessions on the sacrament of Holy Baptism. We begin with Jesus' own baptism by his cousin, John the Baptist *(Matthew 3:11-17)*. This event, which appears in the three Gospels of *Matthew, Mark,* and *Luke,* was the beginning of Jesus' formal ministry.

John's preaching was a strong indictment against the people of God, especially their leaders. They had sinned, John said. He called for them to repent (turn back to God from their lives of sin and selfishness). Why? Because the promised reign of God was coming soon, and the people must prepare themselves for it.

All the Gospel accounts stress John's climactic message that a "mightier One" would come to bring salvation. The Holy Spirit would be given to the obedient, and fierce judgment would come upon the wicked.

Jesus had no need to repent. He was without sin. It is understandable that John would protest when Jesus asked to be baptized. But Jesus insisted; he was fulfilling God's will.

For Christians, Holy Baptism is one of the two great sacraments (Baptism and Eucharist) that came directly from Jesus himself. We participate in Eucharist over and over. Baptism, however, happens only once for each of us. It is our formal rite of initiation into the Body of Christ.

Intermediate-age students are ready to learn more about the sacrament's meaning and the promises made for many of them by parents and sponsors at their own baptisms.

Father in heaven, who at the baptism of Jesus in the River Jordan proclaimed him your beloved Son and anointed him with the Holy Spirit: Grant that all who are baptized into his Name may keep the covenant they have made, and boldly confess him as Lord and Savior; who with you and the Holy Spirit lives and reigns, one God, in glory everlasting. *Amen.*

First Sunday after the Epiphany
The Book of Common Prayer, p. 214

TEACHING TIP

Students come from a variety of home settings. Some may be part of nuclear families with parents and siblings, some may live in single-parent households, and others may be living with step-parents or other relatives. The students themselves are aware of these differences. In discussions about baptism as initiation into the family of God's people, it will be important to be sensitive to the various types of family groups that are represented. Avoid making assumptions that the class members share common backgrounds, and listen for comments the students may make about their family situations.

GATHERING

Display the outline map of Palestine in Jesus' day from Poster No. 5 in the Teacher's Packet. As the students arrive, call their attention to the unlabeled blue areas. Challenge the class members to add labels to the map, including the names of all bodies of water (Dead Sea at the top, Sea of Galilee at the bottom, the Jordan River that connects them, and the Mediterranean Sea at the left). Suggested labels can be placed on slips of paper and attached to the map with removable tape. Supply atlases or Biblical maps to which students can refer.

When all are present, the teacher says:

Let us pray. (Use the Collect "First Sunday after the Epiphany," above, or a prayer of your choice.)

The chosen student lector reads from the class Bible:

A Reading from the Gospel of Matthew, chapter 3, verses 11 through 17.

(John said,) "I baptize you with water for repentance, but one who is more powerful than I is coming after me; I am not worthy to carry his sandals. He will baptize you with the Holy Spirit and fire. His winnowing fork is in his hand, and he will clear his threshing floor and will gather his wheat into the granary; but the chaff he will burn with unquenchable fire."

Then Jesus came from Galilee to John at the Jordan, to be baptized by him. John would have prevented him, saying, "I need to be baptized by you, and do you come to me?" But Jesus answered him, "Let it be so now; for it is proper for us in this way to fulfill all righteousness." Then he consented. And when Jesus had been baptized, just as he came up from the water, suddenly the heavens were opened to him and he saw the Spirit of God descending like a dove and alighting on him. And a voice from heaven said, "This is my Son, the Beloved, with whom I am well pleased."

Reader: The Word of the Lord.
Response: Thanks be to God.

INTRODUCING THE STORY
(Time: 10–20 minutes)

Tell in your own words the story of Jesus' baptism in the Jordan River. Refer to the story on the front page of the student newspaper, **Covenant Times** (Unit III, Issue 1) about the baptism. Point to the river on the map used at the Gathering (above), and add a label for it if the students have not already done so.

Include these elements of the scene as you tell the story:
• Jesus approaches and meets John the Baptist.
• The two men have a discussion, with John protesting and Jesus insisting. John agrees to baptize Jesus.
• They go into the river. John lowers Jesus into the water.
• As Jesus emerges, the Spirit of God descends like a dove lighting on his head.
• A voice from heaven says, "This is my Son, the Beloved, with whom I am well pleased."

Encourage the students to share mental pictures of the event. Then suggest the students to open their Bibles to *Mark 1:9-11*, *Luke 3:21-22*, and *John 1:29-34* to read the story in the other Gospels. How are the stories alike? What is different?

Ask for volunteers to role-play the scene. First decide which details to include and which version the group likes best.

After the students have had a chance to act out their versions of Jesus' baptism, display Poster No. 13 from the Teacher's Packet that shows an artist's concept of the event. Ask: How is this artist's painting similar to your ideas? How is it different?

EXPLORING
(Time: 15–20 minutes)

Option 1. Giant Dove

Cut a piece of cardboard in the shape of a large dove with wings outspread. Images of doves can be found on page 3 of the student newspaper and on Symbol Card No. 19. Attach white tissue so that the finished product will look like a fully-feathered descending bird. Use black or brown markers to draw on eyes and a beak.

As the students work, talk with them about the dove as a symbol for the Holy Spirit and the sacrament of baptism. Decide on a way to suspend the dove so that it can remain in the classroom, or another suitable area, throughout this Unit.

Option 2. Jesus Is Baptized

Supply art paper, paints, markers, and pencils. Encourage the students to paint or draw their own ideas about the baptism of Jesus by John the Baptist. Tell students that their images may be literal or abstract. Some may want to focus on the image of the dove or light.

Display Poster No. 13 and talk about ways their images differ from classical paintings.

Option 3. Word Puzzle

Turn in the student newspaper, *Covenant Times*, Unit III, Issue 1, to the word puzzle titled "Jesus' Baptism." Students may work individually, in pairs, or as a total group.

MUSIC
(Time: 10 minutes)

Listen to "When Jesus went to Jordan's stream" (*The Hymnal 1982*, 139) on the *Children Sing!* tape, especially the words of the first two stanzas. The hymn is a paraphrase of words written by Martin Luther to tell the story of Jesus' baptism.

CONNECTING/SPEAKING OUT
(Time: 15–20 minutes)

Option 1. Group Discussion

Direct the students to look again at the story of Jesus' baptism. Ask the group to name the "unusual" (or supernatural) elements in the Gospel account, and list these on a chalkboard or newsprint. Ask:

What happened when the "heavens were opened"?

Why does the Spirit of God "descend" on Jesus? What would a "voice from heaven" sound like?

Encourage the class members to describe the event in their own words. Share these concepts: The story reminds us that God is a part of our everyday world. Jesus Christ helps us to know and be close to God.

Option 2. Current Events

Jesus' baptism signaled the beginning of his ministry. From that point on, following his days alone in the wilderness, Jesus went about teaching, preaching, and healing.

Talk with the students about "beginnings" and "initiations" in their own lives. When have they experienced initiations, such as clubs, Scouts, teams, and other groups? Ask them to describe their experiences. How does it feel to start something new? How is Holy Baptism different from other types of initiation?

REFLECTING
(Time: 10 minutes)

In this Unit, suggestions are provided for guided meditations. While the teacher is the leader, students are encouraged to add their ideas. The aim is to encourage private and personal reflection. The students should be able to engage in quiet, inner conversation.

For this session, say: Imagine the River Jordan on the day Jesus was baptized, what kind of day was it? Who was there besides John and Jesus?

After the students have had a chance to think about these questions and share their thoughts, invite them to close their eyes and relax silently as you lead them in meditating. Speak slowly, with pauses between sentences to allow the class members to take in the images. Incorporate the students' contributions. Begin:

"It is a clear, pleasant day. The sun has come out from behind the clouds, and a gentle breeze is blowing. A few birds are drifting in the air overhead, and some are sitting on the branch of a willow tree.

"You look out over the River Jordan. It ripples with tiny waves. The riverside is covered with clean sand. You notice footprints in the sand, and you wonder about all the people who have walked here.

"You shade your eyes with your hands and look in all directions. It feels good to be here. Then you notice a man dressed in camel's hair and wearing a leather belt. He wades out into the water and turns. He looks directly at you and the other people on the shore. You wonder what he is going to say. Why is he there? What is he going to do?"

Allow a minute or so of silence, and then ask the students to open their eyes and share what it was like to be at the river. What were they expecting from John the Baptist?

LEARNING SKILLS
(Time: 10–15 minutes)

Option 1. Class Memory Challenge

The memory challenge for this Unit is The Baptismal Covenant (BCP, p. 304). The Covenant has been reproduced on Posters No. 16 and No. 17 in the Teacher's Packet. The first three questions on Poster No. 16 are drawn from the Apostles' Creed and could be called the "faith questions." They all begin with the words, "Do you believe . . . ?" Each one is answered with an "I believe . . ." statement.

The five questions on Poster No. 17 are often called "action questions," since they have to do with how we act out our faith in daily living. They all begin, "Will you . . . ?" Each has the same answer, "I will, with God's help."

Unit III. Baptism: New Life—Session 1
Shell Year Intermediate—Copyright © 2000 Virginia Theological Seminary and Morehouse Publishing

Practice saying to each other the first three questions and answers. Refer to the Memory Challenge block that appears in the student newspaper, *Covenant Times*.

Option 2. Learning Scripture

Invite the students to learn *Matthew 3:11, 16, or 17* before the next class session. See "Learning Scripture" in the student newspaper, *Covenant Times*.

To keep track of the students' progress in learning Scripture, prepare a large cardboard scallop shell, a symbol for Holy Baptism, such as the one on the front of this Teacher's Guide. Attach to the shell a series of long, colored ribbons—one for each Scripture verse memorized. Explain that each memorized verse will be written on a card and added to the end of a ribbon. Add a sticker or symbol for each student who memorizes a verse.

ONGOING PROJECT
(Time: 5–10 minutes)

Throughout this Unit, develop an exhibit entitled, "God's Baptized People" showing objects, symbols, facts, and images that are connected with the Sacrament of Holy Baptism. Students will create items to be included and may ask the whole congregation for contributions for a display that communicates the meaning of the sacrament. (Read the suggestions throughout the Unit for items that may be included.)

Locate a display space in the church building where the exhibit can remain as it grows. If this is not possible, collect and store items and display the exhibit at the end of the Unit. Spend time at each session to plan and prepare the exhibit.

At this session, describe the display and ask for the group's suggestions on how to make an exhibit the whole congregation can see and enjoy. Ask the students to plan the lettering that will go with exhibit. Some possible ideas: colored markers for hand printing, computer-generated headings, paper or plastic cutout letters.

SYMBOL CARD and TREASUREBOOK

Card 19 contains a picture of a descending dove, a Scripture verse, and an explanation on the back.

Ask the students to read about New Testament baptism in the *Shell Year Treasurebook*, Part III, Section 1. How did baptism begin? Why?

GOING FORTH

Gather the group for the dismissal. The teacher or a student will say the following, pausing for the students' response of "Lord, have mercy":

> For our Bishop, and for all the clergy and people, let us pray to the Lord.
> *Lord, have mercy.*
>
> For this city (town, village, __), for every city and community, and for those who live in them, let us pray to the Lord.
> *Lord, have mercy.*
>
> That we may end our lives in faith and hope, without suffering and without reproach, let us pray to the Lord.
> *Lord, have mercy.*
>
> For _____ [learners may add their own petitions], let us pray to the Lord.
> *Lord, have mercy.*
> From The Prayers of the People
> *The Book of Common Prayer*, pp. 384-385

Teacher: Let us go forth in the name of Christ.
Students: Thanks be to God.

TEACHER'S ASSESSMENT

As you reflect on this first session on Holy Baptism, what did you observe about the students' concepts of new beginnings, initiation, and belonging? How well do the class members articulate a sense of the church as a community of the baptized?

LOOKING AHEAD

The next session is the first of two studies on The Baptismal Covenant, *The Book of Common Prayer*, p. 304. The focus will be on baptism and beliefs contained in the Apostles' Creed. Think about your own baptism and reflect on the Creed. How have they affected your life?

BAPTISM: NEW LIFE
SESSION 2
BAPTISM AND OUR BELIEFS

FOCUS

At each celebration of Holy Baptism, the church's people renew their baptismal covenant, a series of questions on Christian faith and action (BCP, p. 304). The students should be able to say the Apostles' Creed and identify two or more traditional symbols for the Trinity.

GETTING READY

From the beginning, Christians have been baptized using the words " . . . in the name of the Father, and of the Son, and of the Holy Spirit (Ghost)." See *Matthew 28:19-20*. In ancient tradition, the person being baptized was immersed in water three times following a personal confession of faith in the Trinity—Father, Son, and Holy Spirit. This is called the trinitarian formula.

The Church's creeds began with the words used during baptism.

The first American Prayer Book (1789), following the form of the 1552 *Book of Common Prayer*, asked just one question: "Dost thou believe all the Articles of the Christian Faith, as contained in the Apostles' Creed?"

The 1979 Prayer Book's Service of Holy Baptism restored a traditional threefold affirmation of faith, using the words of the Apostles' Creed. The five questions that follow have to do with the way in which we live out our confession in daily life.

Intermediate-age students who were baptized as infants may not be fully aware of the significance of this sacrament in their spiritual journey. For that reason, two sessions will focus on the questions and responses of The Baptismal Covenant, which is renewed by all persons present at every baptism.

Almighty God, by our baptism into the death and resurrection of your Son Jesus Christ, you turn us from the old life of sin: Grant that we, being reborn to new life in him, may live in righteousness and holiness all our days; through Jesus Christ our Lord, who lives and reigns with you and the Holy Spirit, one God, now and for ever. Amen.

At Baptism
The Book of Common Prayer, p. 254

TEACHING TIP

All of us go through "stages of involvement" during worship, such as reciting the Apostles' Creed. Sometimes we say the words in rote fashion without thinking of their meaning. At other times we are deeply sensitive to the words and are challenged by their truth. Sometimes, we may be skeptical. Respect each student's questions, and avoid making judgments about those who may seem indifferent or disinterested in formal expressions of faith.

GATHERING

On the back of a display board or easel in an out-of-the-way area, mount Poster No. 7 from the Teacher's Packet that shows four examples of geometric symbols for the Trinity. Turn the board or cover it so that it cannot be seen as class members arrive. Ask the students to form pairs as they enter the classroom.

One member of each pair will go to the display board and quickly memorize the shapes of the symbols. The second member of each pair is given paper and a pencil. Ask the students who saw the symbols to describe them clearly to their partners. The listeners will try drawing the shapes, relying only on what they have heard. When everyone is finished, share the poster with everyone.

When everyone is present, say:

Let us pray. (Use the Collect "At Baptism," above, or a prayer of your own choosing.)

The chosen student lector reads from the class Bible:

A Reading from the Gospel of Matthew, chapter 28, verses 16 through 20.

Now the eleven disciples went to Galilee, to the mountain to which Jesus had directed them. When they saw him, they worshiped him; but some doubted. And Jesus came and said to them, "All authority in heaven and on earth has been given to me. Go therefore and make disciples of all nations, baptizing them in the name of the Father and of the Son and of the Holy Spirit, and teaching them to obey everything that I have commanded you. And remember, I am with you always, to the end of the age."

Reader: The Word of the Lord.
Response: Thanks be to God.

INTRODUCING THE STORY
(Time: 10–20 minutes)

Ahead of time, copy *Matthew 28:19* on a chalkboard or newsprint chart. With this verse on display, ask the students to look at Poster No. 16 from the Teacher's Packet that contains the first three questions and answers from The Baptismal Covenant (BCP, p. 304).

Ask: What do these questions in the Covenant have in common with the verse from Matthew's Gospel (above)?

Assist the class members in linking the questions to the persons of the Trinity—God the Father, God the Son, and God the Holy Spirit. Every baptism follows the "formula" provided in Jesus' words to the apostles at the end of Matthew's Gospel. For many centuries of the Church's history, the Apostles' Creed has been said in connection with baptisms.

Tell the story from the student newspaper, **Covenant Times** (Unit III, Issue 2) about a baptism in the first century. It describes the preparation the people went through and the dangers of joining the Church at that time. They answered the same basic questions asked at our baptisms today.

Ask the students to work alone or in pairs to locate at least two of the following examples of other baptisms in the early Church, as described in *Acts 2:38-41; 8:12-16; 10:47-48; 16:15;* and *19:3-5.* As passages are found, call for reports on the stories they tell.

Remind the students of the importance of the word "covenant" in the Bible and in the story of God's people. Discuss briefly the concept of a covenant as a binding agreement. When we reaffirm our Baptismal Covenant, we are saying over again that we are bound together by our common belief in God the Father, God the Son, and God the Holy Spirit. The words of the Creed spell out what we believe about each of these persons of the Trinity.

EXPLORING
(Time: 15–20 minutes)

Option 1. Trinity Banner

Ask the class members to choose a favorite symbol for the Trinity (possibly from the poster used at the Gathering). Supply a large piece of felt or burlap to serve as background for a banner. Invite the group to design and produce a banner to use in the classroom or in worship processions. As the students work, talk about the link between the symbol and the first three questions of The Baptismal Covenant (God the Father, God the Son, and God the Holy Spirit).

Option 2. Fill in the Blank

Use the puzzle from the *Covenant Times* or make your own on newsprint by writing the first three questions of the Apostles' Creed, deleting key words or phrases (*The Book of Common Prayer*, p. 304). Cover this with a blank piece of paper.

Divide the group into two teams to play a game based on the television show *Family Feud*. Ask a volunteer from each group to come forward and stand next to a bell or whistle. Explain that a portion of the Creed will be uncovered. The first volunteer to ring the bell or blow the whistle gets a chance to fill in the blank. Other team members cannot help at this point.

If the answer is correct, that person's team gets a point. If it is incorrect, the other person can confer with his or her team and give the answer for one point. If it is still incorrect, the first team gets another chance. Continue the game with two new volunteers and by uncovering the next part of the Creed. Game ends when all the blanks have been correctly filled in.

MUSIC
(Time: 10 minutes)

Listen on the *Children Sing!* tape to "Holy, holy, holy! Lord God Almighty!" (*The Hymnal 1982*, 362), a hymn of praise to the Trinity. See if the class can find three qualities of God in Stanza 3. (Look in the final line: "perfect in *power,* in *love,* and *purity.*")

CONNECTING/SPEAKING OUT
(Time: 15–20 minutes)

Option 1. Group Discussion

Suggest that the class members make a list of the *verbs* in the answer to the Baptismal Covenant question, "Do you believe in Jesus Christ, the Son of God?"

The verbs are: conceived, born, suffered, crucified, died, was buried, descended, rose, ascended, seated, come, judge. Ask: What does the list tell us about Jesus' life and what he came to do? What is left out? (His own baptism is not mentioned. Also, his work as teacher, preacher, and healer are omitted.)

Ask the students to look up the actual words used as a person is being baptized on page 307 of the *The Book of Common Prayer*. Encourage the students to consider what John said when he baptized Jesus.

Option 2. Current Events

Tell the students to imagine they have just invited a friend to join them at their church for a service where the people join in repeating the Apostles' Creed (Morning Prayer, Evening Prayer, or Holy Baptism). The friend has never been to church before and wonders what it means. Ask the class members: How would you explain the Apostles' Creed to your friend? Why do we say it? How important is it?

Remind them that the Creed is a statement of essential beliefs about the Christian faith that describes the way Christians should live each day.

REFLECTING
(Time: 10 minutes)

Review the description of the guided meditation process given in Session 1. For this session, solicit students' responses to these questions: When are baptisms likely to occur in your church? Where is the font located? Where do the people gather? Who leads the service?

If possible, go to the worship space in your church where baptisms occur. Invite students to touch the baptismal font and the chrism container (which holds consecrated oil used during the service). Ask a volunteer to describe a recent baptism he or she saw. Who came to the baptism? Why?

Have the group sit quietly with their eyes closed. Ask them to remember a baptism they attended or think about the one described. Then tell them to put themselves in the scene. Where did you stand? What role did you play? In closing, turn to page 304-305 in *The Book of Common Prayer* and read together the Baptismal Covenant.

LEARNING SKILLS
(Time: 10–15 minutes)

Option 1. Class Memory Challenge

Invite the students to practice memorizing the first three questions and answers of The Baptismal Covenant.

Refer to Poster No. 16 from the Teacher's Packet and to the Memory Challenge block in the student newspaper, *Covenant Times*.

Option 2. Learning Scripture

If students have learned verses given in the previous session, add ribbons, cards, and student symbols to the shell described in Session 1.

Invite the class members to memorize *Matthew 28:19* or *Acts 1:8* before the next session. See "Learning Scripture" in the student newspaper, *Covenant Times*.

ONGOING PROJECT
(Time: 5–10 minutes)

See Session 1 for a description of how to begin and develop this ongoing project. At this session, encourage the students to prepare an attractive illustrated chart labeled "Service of Holy Baptism." Include under this title at least the following headings from *The Book of Common Prayer,* pp. 301-308:

Presentation and Examination
The Baptismal Covenant
Prayers
Thanksgiving Over the Water
The Baptism

If possible, add to the chart some dates of recent or future celebrations of baptism in your congregation. (If service bulletins are available, copies could be included in the exhibit.)

SYMBOL CARD and TREASUREBOOK

Card 20 has an illustration of the Trinity, a Scripture verse, and an explanation on the back.

Ask the students to read Section III, Part 1 of the *Shell Year Treasurebook*, Part III, about preparations required for baptism. In the early Church, what were new followers of Jesus called? How long were they in training for baptism?

GOING FORTH

Gather the group for the dismissal. The teacher or a student will say the following, pausing for the students' response of "Lord, have mercy":

For our Bishop, and for all the clergy and people, let us pray to the Lord.
Lord, have mercy.

For this city (town, village, __), for every city and community, and for those who live in them, let us pray to the Lord.
Lord, have mercy.

That we may end our lives in faith and hope, without suffering and without reproach, let us pray to the Lord.
Lord, have mercy.

For _____ [learners may add their own petitions], let us pray to the Lord.
Lord, have mercy.

From The Prayers of the People
The Book of Common Prayer, pp. 384-385

Teacher: Let us go forth in the name of Christ.
Students: Thanks be to God.

TEACHER'S ASSESSMENT

From your observations, what are the students' viewpoints about the Apostles' Creed? Would they be able to say it from memory? What kinds of questions do they raise about the sections of the Creed? Encourage class members to continue thinking about creeds as summaries of Christian belief.

LOOKING AHEAD

The next session, "Baptism and Our Living," focuses on the last five questions of the Baptismal Covenant. Those questions ask us to look at how the Church's people demonstrate their faith in Christ as they go about their daily tasks. Read over the five questions, and look for evidence of Christian commitment among the people you encounter in your daily life.

BAPTISM: NEW LIFE

SESSION 3
BAPTISM AND OUR LIVING

FOCUS

The latter half of The Baptismal Covenant (Questions 4-8) relates to the way in which Christians promise to live as Christ's people in the world. The students should be able to outline the content of these questions and locate *Psalm 121* as a Scriptural basis for the response, "I will, with God's help."

GETTING READY

Older versions of *The Book of Common Prayer* asked this question in the service of Holy Baptism: "Wilt thou obediently keep God's holy will and commandments, and walk in the same all the days of thy life?"

Our Prayer Book replaces that one question with five questions that spell out what is needed to "keep God's holy will and commandments." The questions begin with *community life,* which includes teaching and fellowship, Eucharist, and prayers. Then there must be *resistance to evil* and a desire to repent and return to the Lord when we have sinned. Also important is a *life of witness* to the Good News of Christ by both word and example. A *life of service* helps us seek and serve Christ in all persons. And, finally, a *commitment to work for justice and peace* among all people encourages us to respect the dignity of every person.

In short, it is not enough to make the affirmation of faith required by the first three questions of The Baptismal Covenant. The Christian life requires an active effort to live out our faith in our daily experiences; Christian faith produces Christian action. We must also recognize and confess our sins against God and our neighbor. Through our repentance and God's redemption, we are able to "return to the Lord."

The response, "I will, with God's help," acknowledges our dependence upon God alone for any success we may have in keeping these solemn promises. We recall *Psalm 121:1a-2,* "From whence does my help come? My help comes from the Lord, who made heaven and earth."

Intermediate-age students are at a developmental stage in which they can make a serious commitment. Their loyalties to clubs, teams, and other groups involve promise-keeping. This is a good time for them to consider what Christians promise at Holy Baptism.

> Heavenly Father, we thank you that by water and the Holy Spirit you have bestowed upon these your servants the forgiveness of sin, and have raised them to the new life of grace. Sustain them, O Lord, in your Holy Spirit. Give them an inquiring and discerning heart, the courage to will and to persevere, a spirit to know and to love you, and the gift of joy and wonder in all your works. *Amen.*
> Holy Baptism
> *The Book of Common Prayer,* p. 308

TEACHING TIP

Intermediate-age students will throw themselves energetically into projects and assignments. They work hard and play hard. Be alert to finding ways of harnessing the class members' energy in productive activities. Consider how to involve the students in service projects in your church, challenging them to devote time and effort to helping others.

GATHERING

Prepare a "vine" for display in the classroom. It can be an actual vine or tree limb, or it could be made from sticks or strips of paper. Make a pile of "branches"—sturdy twigs or strips of paper, and provide a way for these to be labeled with markers, using stick-on notes or cards and tape.

As students arrive, direct their attention to the vine. Ask each one to choose a branch and write his or her name on the cards or post-its. Use string or tape to attach the branches to the vine.

When everyone is present, say:

Let us pray. (Use the prayer from the service of Holy Baptism, above, or a prayer of your own choosing.)

The chosen student lector reads from the class Bible (NRSV):

A Reading from the Gospel of John, chapter 15, verses 1 through 5 and 9 through 11:

(Jesus said), "I am the true vine, and my Father is the vinegrower. He removes every branch in me that bears no fruit. Every branch that bears fruit he prunes to make it bear more fruit. You have already been cleansed by the word that I have spoken to you. Abide in me as I abide in you. Just as the branch cannot bear fruit by itself unless it abides in the vine, neither can you unless you abide in me. I am the vine, you are the branches. Those who abide in me and I in them bear much fruit, because apart from me you can do nothing. . . . As the Father has loved me, so I have loved you; abide in my love. If you keep my commandments, you will abide in my love, just as I have kept my Father's commandments and abide in his love. I have said these things to you so that my joy may be in you, and that your joy may be complete."

Reader: The Word of the Lord.
Response: Thanks be to God.

INTRODUCING THE STORY
(Time: 10–20 minutes)

Begin by asking the students to turn in *The Book of Common Prayer* to Psalm 121, p. 779. Divide into two groups, and ask them to read the psalm antiphonally by half-verse. That is, one group reads to the asterisk (*), and the second group reads the rest of the verse.

Point out that the psalm is about relying on God for help. We can trust God to keep us and be with us.

Direct the class members' attention to Poster No. 17 from the Teacher's Packet showing the five action questions from The Baptismal Covenant (BCP, p. 304). Focus on the response, "I will, with God's help."

Choose one of the five questions to explain in your own words. Share what it means to you.

For example, Question 7 asks, "Will you seek and serve Christ in all persons, loving your neighbor as yourself?" When I mistreat a friend, I am not loving that person as I love myself. I know I must ask God to help me apologize when I am wrong—and to do my best not to mistreat my friend again.

When the students have had a chance to think about your explanation of a question, assign the other questions to groups or individuals. Ask them to develop similar explanations for these in their own words. For other ideas from a student's perspective, suggest they read the front page story of the student newspaper, ***Covenant Times*** (Unit III, Issue 3). Ask them to write their ideas on sheets of newsprint or choose one person to share the group's thoughts.

Invite the students to look up the following passages from New Testament epistles: *Ephesians 4:25-32; Ephesians 6:1-4; Colossians 4:2-6.* Suggest that the class members make a list of the advice given in these verses. Which question(s) in The Baptismal Covenant would they link with each passage?

EXPLORING
(Time: 15–20 minutes)

Option 1. Illustrating the Action Questions

Divide the class members into teams or pairs. Assign one or more of the five action questions from The Baptismal Covenant (BCP, pp. 304-305) to each team. Ask the students to decide on a creative way to illustrate the questions. Supply newsprint sheets, markers, and crayons.

When all the illustrations have been completed, post them around the classroom in order. Call on the teams to describe their illustrations. At the end of each explanation, ask the class members to join in saying, "I will, with God's help."

Option 2. Vine-and-Branch Hanging

Supply small clipped sections from a tree or bush, or actual vine clippings. Ask each student to choose one of these to serve as a personal "vine." Offer sheets of sturdy green paper in a size proportional to the vines. Attach the clippings to the paper.

Next to each "branch" or leaf, ask them to write one thing they could do this week to live out the promises from the action questions in the Baptismal Covenant. As the students work, talk to them about Jesus Christ as the Vine and his followers as branches. (See *John*, chapter 5.)

Option 3. Word Chain

Turn in the student newspaper, *Covenant Times*, Unit III, Issue 3, to the word chain titled "Christian Living." Students may work individually, in pairs, or as a total group.

MUSIC
(Time: 10 minutes)

Sing with the *Children Sing!* tape the hymn "Lord, you give the great commission" (*The Hymnal 1982*, 528). Focus especially on Stanzas 1, 2, and 4. Ask: Do these stanzas remind you of the promises in The Baptismal Covenant?

CONNECTING/SPEAKING OUT
(Time: 15–20 minutes)

Option 1. Group Discussion

Jesus used the image of a vine with branches to describe the relationship between himself and his followers. Invite the students to think about the display created at the Gathering (above), and to consider how they could be productive branches attached to the vine of Christ.

Ask: How can our answers to the questions of The Baptismal Covenant help us to be better "branches"? Encourage the students to think of the five questions as a challenge to stay close to Jesus Christ and be active Christians in our work and play.

Option 2. Current Events

Look together at the five action questions from The Baptismal Covenant on Poster No. 17 from the Teacher's Packet. Take time to consider how each question relates to our daily life in the world. Bring in local news sections of a daily newspaper. Ask students to look for examples of promises kept and promises broken. Ask: Why do people have trouble keeping their promises to do what is right and good?

Discuss with the students how they would handle a situation in which they broke a promise to others or to God. Stress the importance of confession and the assurance of forgiveness.

REFLECTING
(Time: 10 minutes)

A description of the guided meditation process is given under Reflecting in Session 1 of this Unit. For this session, lead the students in a meditation about the life of a Christian.

If you used the Current Events option during the lesson, refer back to the stories the group found and the promises they may have broken, or introduce the topic by asking the following questions: How important are promises? Why do we make promises? Can you think of a situation in your community or some other place where promises were made?

Use the responses from the group with the following ideas for a brief meditation. Ask them to close their eyes and be silent. Pause between sentences to give them time to think.

Think about a promise you made recently to your parents, a sibling, or a friend. Why did you make the promise? Did you intend to keep it? If you kept the promise, how did you feel? If you broke it, even a little bit, how did you feel about yourself?

Now think about a promise someone made to you at school, at home, or at church. Was the promise important to you? Did the person keep the promise? How do you feel when someone breaks a promise to you?

Finally, think about the promises we make to God. Have you kept your promises? How does God feel when we keep our promises?

Ask the group to open their eyes and read the last five questions of the Baptismal Covenant found on Poster No. 17. Encourage them to think about promises they make to God and how they can keep them.

LEARNING SKILLS
(Time: 10–15 minutes)

Option 1. Class Memory Challenge

Divide the class members into teams. Give each team large sheets of newsprint and markers, and ask the teams to reproduce the first three questions and answers of The Baptismal Covenant without consulting the poster in the Teacher's Packet, the Prayer Book, or the student newspaper, *Covenant Times*. (The teams might want to put questions in one color and answers in another.)

When the work is completed, post the sheets and compare the text. Do they all agree?

The students can check their final versions by looking at the text.

Option 2. Learning Scripture

If class members have memorized verses suggested in previous sessions, add ribbons, cards, and student symbols to the shell described in Session 1. Remind the students that any verse cited during this Unit may be memorized at any time; the complete list of passages for the Unit appears in the student newspaper, *Covenant Times*.

Invite the members of the group to memorize *Psalm 121:2, John 8:12,* or *Acts 2:42.*

ONGOING PROJECT
(Time: 5-10 minutes)

See Session 1 for a description of this ongoing project. At this session, add pictures of persons of all ages to represent God's baptized people. Consider these possibilities:

The pictures could be taken from old magazines and made into a montage on poster board. Students could create drawings of people and scenes showing baptism. The class members could use instant cameras to take pictures of themselves or others in the church. Before the next session, the group could solicit pictures from others in the congregation.

Invite the students to create their own captions for the assembled pictures (such as "All people can be baptized," or "It is never too late to be baptized").

SYMBOL CARD and TREASUREBOOK

Card 21 has a picture of a Paschal Candle, a Scripture verse, and an explanation on the back.

Ask the class members to read in the *Shell Year Treasurebook,* Part III, Section 3, about the life that baptized people are called to. How is passing the peace during Eucharist related to the last five questions of the Baptismal Covenant?

GOING FORTH

Gather the group for the dismissal. The teacher or a student will say the following, pausing for the students' response of "Lord, have mercy":

For our Bishop, and for all the clergy and people, let us pray to the Lord.
Lord, have mercy.

For this city (town, village, __), for every city and community, and for those who live in them, let us pray to the Lord.
Lord, have mercy.

That we may end our lives in faith and hope, without suffering and without reproach, let us pray to the Lord.
Lord, have mercy.

For _____ [learners may add their own petitions], let us pray to the Lord.
Lord, have mercy.
From The Prayers of the People
The Book of Common Prayer, pp. 384-385

Teacher: Let us go forth in the name of Christ.
Students: Thanks be to God.

TEACHER'S ASSESSMENT

As you think about the session and its emphasis on Christian living, which activities or elements of discussion seemed most important to the class members? How did the students react to the content of the action questions in The Baptismal Covenant? What may be needed to help them consider these questions more fully?

LOOKING AHEAD

The next session, titled "Baptized by Water and the Spirit," focuses on the prayer of Thanksgiving over the water (BCP, p. 306). Read the prayer several times. Consider also the symbolism of water. What roles has water played in your own life? When have you been thankful for it? When have you been afraid of it?

BAPTISM: NEW LIFE
SESSION 4
BAPTIZED BY WATER AND THE SPIRIT

FOCUS

At Holy Baptism, the celebrant leads a prayer of thanksgiving over the water. The prayer relates baptism to the Creation, the Exodus, the baptism of Jesus, his resurrection, and our own rebirth. The students should be able to locate this prayer in *The Book of Common Prayer* (p. 306) and identify the shell as a symbol for Holy Baptism.

GETTING READY

The act of immersing or sprinkling with water has been practiced in various religions. For example, in ancient times Gentile converts to Judaism would bathe to signify their new faith. But the initiation rite of baptism is an action with unique meaning for Christians. The word itself is from a Greek verb meaning "to immerse in or wash with water."

Early Church leaders suggested that all water had been made holy by the fact that Jesus submitted to John's baptism in the River Jordan. But by the third century BCE, special prayers were said over the water to be used in the rite of Holy Baptism. These prayers referred to Biblical stories in which water played an important part, such as the Creation itself, the rivers of Paradise, water that came from the rock when it was struck by Moses' rod, and the wedding feast at Cana.

The Book of Common Prayer introduces a prayer that comes from ancient tradition. In "Thanksgiving over the Water," notice the references to Creation, the crossing of the Red Sea, and Jesus' own baptism. Observe the words that introduce God's powerful presence in relation to water: "over it," "through it," "in it," and "by it."

It has been pointed out that this prayer touches on the act of bathing (being washed clean from sin), birth (entry into a new life in Christ), and the hope of resurrection (being raised up from death).

The intermediate age level is an ideal time to introduce students to the symbolism of the act of baptizing.

O God, whose wonderful deeds of old shine forth even to our own day, you once delivered by the power of your mighty arm your chosen people from slavery under Pharaoh, to be a sign for us of the salvation of all nations by the water of Baptism: Grant that all the peoples of the earth may be numbered among the offspring of Abraham, and rejoice in the inheritance of Israel; through Jesus Christ our Lord. Amen.
Easter Vigil
The Book of Common Prayer, p. 289

TEACHING TIP

Intermediate-age students enjoy making things and playing games, both in groups and individually. They also appreciate being challenged to think and to share their thoughts aloud. Because they are just beginning to understand symbols and metaphors, they may have trouble with some of the symbolic meanings of Holy Baptism. Encourage students to talk about what they are thinking and feeling.

GATHERING

Arrange on a table a pitcher of water and a large shell. The pitcher can be pottery, silver or pewter, or glass. If a real shell is unavailable, use a shell-shaped dish. Put the display near a chalkboard or posted sheets of newsprint.

As the students arrive, encourage them to look at the items on the table and write down words, phrases, or short sentences that relate to the items.

When everyone is present, say:

Let us pray. (Use the prayer from the Easter Vigil, above, or a prayer of your own choosing.)

The chosen student lector reads from the class Bible:

A reading from The Acts of the Apostles, chapter 2, verses 38 through 41.

Peter said to them, "Repent, and be baptized every one of you in the name of Jesus Christ so that your sins may be forgiven; and you will receive the gift of the Holy Spirit. For the promise is for you, and for your children, and for all who are far away, everyone whom the Lord our God calls to him." And he testified with many other arguments and exhorted them, saying, "Save yourselves from this corrupt generation." So those who welcomed his message were baptized, and that day about three thousand persons were added.

Reader: The Word of the Lord.
Response: Thanks be to God.

INTRODUCING THE STORY
(Time: 10–20 minutes)

In your own words tell a story about baptism from your own experience. For ideas, read the student newspaper, **Covenant Times** (Unit III, Issue 4) for a story about an Episcopal baptism, and imaginary interviews with a priest, parents, godparents, and an adult who was baptized recently.

Then write the words "water" and "baptism" on a piece of newsprint. Ask the students to name Bible stories from both the Old and New Testaments that talk about water in some way. (For example, Moses in the bulrushes and Jonah's time in the sea monster.)

Or, photocopy the references to baptism from a Bible concordance. Share copies with all the students, and invite them to work individually or in teams to look up three or more of the verses (such as *Mark 1:4, Acts 19:4,* and *Colossians 2:12*).

Introduce the prayer, "Thanksgiving over the Water," from *The Book of Common Prayer,* pp. 306-307. Read it together. Ask the group to list on a second piece of newsprint the Bible stories in the prayer that relate to water. They are:

• The Creation (*Genesis 1:1-2*)

• The Exodus from Egypt across the Red Sea (*Exodus 14:21-29*)

• The baptism of Jesus by John in the River Jordan (*Matthew 3:13-17*)

Reread the last part beginning on page 306. Describe a baptism by immersion practiced by many Christians. Persons being baptized are lowered into the water as if being drowned. Then they are raised up from the water as if being resurrected from the dead. Baptism is like death and resurrection. (Even though baptism is seldom by immersion in the Episcopal tradition, the symbolism is clear. By being baptized, we gain a new identity as a person who belongs to Jesus Christ.)

This baptism prayer helps us remember important stories, images, and symbols. We remember that we belong to Jesus Christ who died and rose again to save us from our sin.

EXPLORING
(Time: 15–20 minutes)

Option 1. River of Memory

Develop a five-paneled depiction of the prayer of thanksgiving over the water, from the Service of Holy Baptism (BCP, p. 306).

Prepare a large sheet of butcher paper to attach to a wall (five to ten feet in length). Letter a heading, "Thanksgiving over the Water at Holy Baptism." Make lines or folds to divide the sheet into five blank panels.

First, create a "river of life" from joined pieces of construction or tissue paper in several shades of blue and green. The paper river, varying in width and shape along its shorelines, should run at a slight angle across the whole distance of the butcher paper across all five panels. Glue the river onto the background.

Invite the students to create a scene within the surrounding area of each panel. The scenes should illustrate these five events, in order: the story of Creation; the Exodus from Egypt under Moses' leadership; Jesus' baptism in the River Jordan; Jesus appearing to the women in the garden (near the tomb); and a baptism in your own church. These illustrations may be drawn directly onto the paper, or they may be produced separately, cut out, and glued on.

When the panels are finished, read the prayer aloud in unison.

Option 2. Water and Shell Relay

Divide into teams of two or more for a water relay. If possible go outside for this activity. At one end of the room or open area, for each team set out a bucket of water, a shell, and an empty bucket. Ask each team to line up one behind another across from the buckets. When you say go, the first person will run to the buckets, scoop up a shell full of water, and pour it into the empty bucket. That person runs back to his or her team and taps the next person, who repeats the action. The game is over when you blow a whistle or everyone has had a turn. Measure the amounts of water to see which team has been most successful in scooping water with its shell.

Afterwards, talk about the use of a shell to dip water from the font at baptism.

Option 3. Word Search

Turn in the student newspaper, *Covenant Times*, Unit III, Issue 4, to the word search titled "Baptism." Students may work individually, in pairs, or as a total group.

MUSIC
(Time: 10 minutes)

Listen to "Baptized in water" *(The Hymnal 1982, 294)* on the *Children Sing!* tape. This hymn can be chanted or sung. Notice that the words link baptism with death and resurrection.

CONNECTING/SPEAKING OUT
(Time: 15–20 minutes)

Option 1. Group Discussion

In the story of Creation *(Genesis 1:1)*, the "Spirit of God moved" over the waters that covered the earth. In the New Revised Standard Version of the Bible, this clause is translated "a wind from God swept over the face of the waters." The same word in Hebrew is translated spirit, wind, or breath. At Holy Baptism we give thanks that we are "reborn by the Holy Spirit."

When someone comes near us, we are aware that they are breathing. That is how we know that people are truly alive—when we are sure they can breathe. Suggest that baptism is a time when God breathes nearby, and we know that we are received into God's presence.

Ask the students to share their own ways of thinking about the Holy Spirit at baptism. What does God offer to us in this service? How does sin separate us from God? What does forgiveness of all our sins mean? How can we show God that we are thankful?

Option 2. Current Events

Spend some time discussing the many forms, uses, and meanings of water.

- Water comes as dew, rain, sleet, and snow. It gathers in rivers, ponds, lakes, and seas.
- Water is used to cleanse and purify. It is used for blessing and consecrating. We drink it, and we include it in our food preparation.
- Water can be a symbol of danger and death, as in the cold depth of the sea or the roaring fury of a rainstorm or flood. But it is also a symbol for life and growth, since we cannot live without it. When we *baptize*, we stress *newness of life* that is associated with water.

Talk with the students about contemporary issues involving water, such as conservation, irrigation, water pollution, water treatment, drought, and recreation. Share recent news stories or published reports on these topics.

REFLECTING
(Time: 10 minutes)

For the group meditation in this session, consider playing a recording of music suggesting water, such as "Water Music," by George Frederick Handel; "Reflections in the Water," by Claude Debussy; or a tape of natural water sounds from the ocean, a rainstorm, or running brook.

Ask the students to listen quietly, with their eyes closed. When the recording ends, encourage individuals to describe the images that came to mind as they listened. Ask: How can these images help us remember Holy Baptism?

LEARNING SKILLS
(Time: 10–15 minutes)

Option 1. Class Memory Challenge

Begin working on the five questions that form the second half of The Baptismal Covenant. For this session, concentrate on Question 4, "Will you continue in the apostles' teaching and fellowship, in the breaking of bread, and in the prayers?" (This is the first question on Poster No. 17 in the Teacher's Packet. See "Class Memory Challenge," Session 1.)

Students may work in pairs or teams to memorize the question and its answer.

Refer to the Memory Challenge block in the student newspaper, *Covenant Times.*

Option 2. Learning Scripture

Add ribbons, cards, and symbols to the shell prepared for this Unit for those who have memorized a verse.

Remind the class members that any verse cited during the Unit may be memorized at any time. The complete list of verses for the Unit appears under the heading, "Learning Scripture," in the student newspaper, *Covenant Times.*

Invite the students to choose either of the following to be learned before the next session: *Acts 2:38* or *Ephesians 4:4-6.*

ONGOING PROJECT
(Time: 5–10 minutes)

For this ongoing project (described in Session 1), prepare a full-size, colored drawing of the baptismal font used in your congregation. The class members could take measurements and make preliminary sketches, then work out a cooperative way to produce the finished drawing to be included in the exhibit.

The label card could include any interesting facts the group may discover about your church's font (its age, where it came from, and the meaning of symbols in its design).

SYMBOL CARD and TREASUREBOOK

Card 22 has a picture of a shell with drops of water, a Scripture verse, and an explanation on the back.

Ask the students to read in the *Shell Year Treasurebook,* Part III, Section 4, the descriptions of baptismal symbols. What symbolizes light in the baptismal service?

GOING FORTH

Gather the group for the dismissal. The teacher or a student will say the following, pausing for the students' response of "Lord, have mercy":

For our Bishop, and for all the clergy and people, let us pray to the Lord.
Lord, have mercy.

For this city (town, village, __), for every city and community, and for those who live in them, let us pray to the Lord.
Lord, have mercy.

That we may end our lives in faith and hope, without suffering and without reproach, let us pray to the Lord.
Lord, have mercy.

For _____ [learners may add their own petitions], let us pray to the Lord.
Lord, have mercy.
　From The Prayers of the People
　The Book of Common Prayer, pp. 384-385

Teacher: Let us go forth in the name of Christ.
Students: Thanks be to God.

TEACHER'S ASSESSMENT

This session, like the previous ones in this Unit, includes several themes about the sacrament of baptism. Which aspect of the sacrament seems most important to your students? What kinds of questions do they ask? Make notes of topics to pursue at a later time.

LOOKING AHEAD

The focus of the next session, "Receiving the Newly Baptized," is about welcoming and being hospitable to persons who receive the sacrament of Holy Baptism. Think about your own experiences as someone being welcomed and as someone who reaches out to welcome others.

BAPTISM: NEW LIFE
SESSION 5
RECEIVING THE NEWLY BAPTIZED

FOCUS

At the conclusion of a baptism, the Celebrant says, "Let us welcome the newly baptized." This is followed by a statement in which the congregation joins: "We receive you . . . ." The baptized persons are told to confess Christ, proclaim the resurrection, and share in Christ's work. The students should be able to explain the significance of this act of welcoming and receiving, and describe ways in which they can do so.

GETTING READY

The service of Holy Baptism includes an act of welcoming (BCP, p. 308). The Celebrant says, "Let us welcome the newly baptized." The congregation responds, "We receive you into the household of God." The baptized are urged to confess their faith in Christ, proclaim the news of his resurrection, and share with all Christians in the work of Christ.

The welcome is followed by the passing of the Peace.

The New Testament contains hints that the first Christians exchanged greetings of peace. See, for example, *I Corinthians 16:20, Philippians 4:21,* and *I Thessalonians 5:26.* But the first solid evidence of the passing of the Peace appears in the texts of ancient Church liturgies. Persons who had not yet been baptized and were receiving instruction, called catechumens, were dismissed from services just before the Peace. When they were baptized, these persons were welcomed by the exchange of the Peace. That tradition is part of our baptismal and eucharistic celebrations.

It is important for the Church's people of all ages to reflect on the concrete ways in which newly received members can be welcomed and fully incorporated into the community of faith. Intermediate-age students can take part in acts of hospitality and inclusion.

Heavenly Father, you sent your own Son into this world. We thank you for the life of those entrusted to our care. Help us to remember that we are all your children, and so to love and nurture all, that they may attain to that full stature intended for them in your eternal kingdom; for the sake of your dear Son, Jesus Christ our Lord. *Amen.*
For the Gift of a Child (alt.)
The Book of Common Prayer, p. 841

TEACHING TIP

At the intermediate-age level, students form attachments to clubs and groups and may be reluctant to admit new members into their circles. It is important that they be encouraged to think about hospitality and a welcoming spirit in all aspects of their lives. Challenge the class members to describe their own feelings when they are the ones being welcomed. Encourage them to reciprocate by reaching out warmly to others.

GATHERING

Display Poster No. 14 from the Teacher's Packet showing five images associated with Holy Baptism (a baptismal font, a shell with water drops, a Trinity symbol, a cross, and a dove). As the students arrive, encourage them to think back over previous sessions and connect the images with the main ideas that have been discussed. Ask: Which symbol means the most to you?

When everyone is present, say:

Let us pray. (Use the prayer "For the Gift of a

Child," above, or a prayer of your own choosing.)

The chosen student lector reads from the class Bible:

A Reading from the Letter of Paul to the Romans, chapter 15, verses 5 through 7.

May the God of steadfastness and encouragement grant you to live in harmony with one another, in accordance with Christ Jesus, so that together you may with one voice glorify the God and Father of our Lord Jesus Christ.

Welcome one another, therefore, just as Christ has welcomed you, for the glory of God.

Reader: The Word of the Lord.
Response: Thanks be to God.

INTRODUCING THE STORY
(Time: 10–20 minutes)

Begin by placing the word "welcome" on a chalkboard or newsprint. Ask the students to define the word in their own way, and to give examples of times when they have been welcomed. (You may want to refer to "welcome mats" and other symbols of welcome, such as the pineapple.)

Focus on the welcome given to newly-baptized persons at a Service of Holy Baptism (BCP, p. 308). Share the fact that the welcome is linked to the exchange of the Peace (see Getting Ready, above).

Share a story from your own experience about welcoming the newly baptized or relate information from the article in the student newspaper, **Covenant Times** (Unit III, Issue 5) about a church celebrating baptism with a party. The community decorated the parish hall with balloons, ribbons, doves, and fresh-cut flowers. The families of the candidates knew about the party ahead of time, but it was kept secret from the newly baptized persons.

Brainstorm ways that Christian people can reach out to new members in their churches to assure them they are welcome and to offer opportunities for joining activities. List the ideas on a piece of newsprint. (Ideas might include greeting new members after a baptism service, providing refreshments after a baptism service, or passing out information about church activities and committees.)

Ask the group if they have ever done anything at church to welcome new members or visitors. Look back at the list the group made and circle the ideas that this group could do. Identify one or two ideas the group would like to carry out. Talk to your clergy about involving the class in welcoming new members at the next baptism service or on a typical Sunday.

Ask the students to turn in their Bibles to *Romans 15:7*. Suggest that the class members work individually or in teams to answer these questions: Who is writing these words? To whom is this written? What is meant by living "in harmony"?

EXPLORING
(Time: 15–20 minutes)

Option 1. Hands of Welcome

Distribute sheets of white construction paper, and encourage the students to make pairs of hand prints that suggest welcome from one person to another, as in the passing of the Peace. These may be made by tracing the shapes of hands with a pencil or pen and adding color with markers.

Another idea is to provide shallow dishes of finger paint or to make stamp pads created from diluted tempera poured onto felt or thicknesses of paper towel. Students cover the palms of their hands with paint and "stamp" them on the paper.

A third idea is to invite class members to pose their hands in welcoming gestures and make photographs with an instant camera. Use the prints as a border in the classroom.

Option 2. Baptismal Candles

Using plain white candles (10-12 inch tapers), make baptismal candles for the students to use at their own baptisms or to take home and use on the anniversary of their baptisms. Invite students to decorate the candles with symbols of baptism or the Trinity. Use colored wax or paper symbols, warmed and attached to the candles. The finished candles can be dipped in an outer coat of wax to secure the design.

Option 3. Crossword Puzzle

Turn in the student newspaper, **Covenant Times,** Unit III, Issue 5, to the crossword puzzle titled "One Baptism." Students may work individually, in pairs, or as a total group.

MUSIC
(Time: 10 minutes)

Sing again "Baptized with water" (*The Hymnal 1982*, 294) with the *Children Sing!* tape. Notice especially the final stanza, and consider the meaning it would have for a newly baptized person who is being welcomed into the church.

CONNECTING/SPEAKING OUT
(Time: 15–20 minutes)

Option 1. Group Discussion

Talk with the students about the ways in which they welcome new members of groups to which they belong. Ask: In what ways do you help new persons to feel at home in your group? at school? at church? Have you ever felt you were not welcome? Why? Encourage the students to make several specific suggestions for welcoming others.

Write on a chalkboard or newsprint *Romans 15:7*: "Welcome one another, therefore, as Christ has welcomed you, for the glory of God." Ask: How are Christians supposed to welcome each other? Who is our model? Talk about how we have all been welcomed by Jesus Christ whose welcome to us is wholehearted and unreserved. Christians are asked to exhibit that kind of welcome to other people.

Option 2. Current Events

Ask the students to look at instructions related to the service of Holy Baptism, in *The Book of Common Prayer*, p. 298, "Concerning the Service," and pp. 312-314, "Additional Directions." Call the students' attention to the heading, "Emergency Baptism," noting that any baptized person may administer Baptism in a real emergency when life is at stake. An article in the student newspaper also describes how to do emergency baptisms. When might someone need to do this? (Examples: nurses/doctors in a hospital, a member of the Armed Forces in wartime, or someone present at a serious accident.)

Ask: What would you do if someone needed to be baptized in an emergency situation? According to the instructions on page 314 of the Prayer Book, what else would you need to do?

REFLECTING
(Time: 10 minutes)

Lead a guided meditation about welcoming a new person at school. Before you begin, encourage students to describe the places where students congregate before school begins, during lunch, or after school.

Suggest the students close their eyes and sit quietly as you say something like the following:

"You have just entered the lunchroom with your class. This is your favorite time of day. You hope your mom or dad has packed something special in your lunch or that the cafeteria has one of your favorite meals.

"You also enjoy talking to your friends during lunch. Even though you have to sit with people in your class, you enjoy being with the people at your table.

"Today, just as you are about to sit down, the teacher walks up with a new student. The lunchroom is crowded, but she asks everyone to make space for the new person. The conversation, which had been lively, suddenly stops as everyone stares at the new person. What do you do?"

Allow a moment of silence. Ask: What did you do? Did you welcome the new person? How would you have felt if you had been that person?

LEARNING SKILLS
(Time: 10–15 minutes)

Option 1. Class Memory Challenge

Review the portion of The Baptismal Covenant already committed to memory (Questions 1-4). Ask the learners to work in pairs or teams to learn Question 5, "Will you persevere in resisting evil, and, whenever you fall into sin, repent and return to the Lord?" and the response, "I will, with God's help."

Refer to Poster No. 17 in the Teacher's Packet and to the Memory Challenge block in the student newspaper, *Covenant Times*.

Option 2. Learning Scripture

Call on any students who have memorized verses suggested in the previous session to say them, either individually or as a group. Place ribbons, cards, and student symbols on the shell.

Ask students to memorize *Romans 15:5* or *7* before the next class session. See "Learning Scripture" in the student newspaper, *Covenant Times*.

ONGOING PROJECT
(Time: 5–10 minutes)

As the class members continue their work on this project (described in Session 1), suggest that they devise a way to label and add to the exhibit the kinds of items that might be gifts to a newly baptized person (such as baptismal candles and small crosses for infants and children, or Bibles and Prayer Books for older persons). Such items may be brought to the session ahead of time by teachers or students, or they may be available in the church building.

SYMBOL CARD and TREASUREBOOK

Card 23 pictures a baptismal font and includes a Scripture verse, along with an explanation on the back.

Ask the students to read Part III, Section 5, in the *Shell Year Treasurebook* about welcoming newly baptized members of the Church. Who are the ministers in the church?

GOING FORTH

Gather the group for the dismissal. The teacher or a student will say the following, pausing for the students' response of "Lord, have mercy":

> For our Bishop, and for all the clergy and people, let us pray to the Lord.
> *Lord, have mercy.*
>
> For this city (town, village, __), for every city and community, and for those who live in them, let us pray to the Lord.
> *Lord, have mercy.*
>
> That we may end our lives in faith and hope, without suffering and without reproach, let us pray to the Lord.
> *Lord, have mercy.*
>
> For _____ [learners may add their own petitions], let us pray to the Lord.
> *Lord, have mercy.*
> From The Prayers of the People
> *The Book of Common Prayer,* pp. 384-385

Teacher: Let us go forth in the name of Christ.
Students: Thanks be to God.

TEACHER'S ASSESSMENT

How would you evaluate the students' understanding of what it means to be warmly welcomed? Can they list ways they can welcome others into the church? What clues did you pick up that would help you foster a welcoming spirit among the class members?

LOOKING AHEAD

The remainder of this Unit focuses on themes from Lent, Holy Week, and Easter. The next session is titled "Jesus Is Servant." As you prepare, think about persons who have served you in some way during your lifetime. How would you describe their personalities? What is their attitude toward others?

BAPTISM: NEW LIFE

SESSION 6

JESUS IS SERVANT

FOCUS

At the Last Supper, Jesus washed the feet of his disciples in an act of humble service. He asked them to become servants, following his example. The students should be able to retell the story of the footwashing, explain what it means to engage in service today (citing one or more significant examples), and identify the towel and basin as a symbol of Christian humility.

GETTING READY

This is the first of four sessions related to events of Holy Week. We have not, however, left the sacrament of Holy Baptism behind. Jesus' passion and resurrection are at the heart of what baptism signifies for Christians.

In the *Gospel of John* (chapter 13:1-15), the story of the Last Supper does not include Jesus' words about the bread and the wine and the New Covenant established in him. Instead, the writer focuses on the footwashing before the meal—a story not found in the Gospels of *Matthew, Mark,* and *Luke.*

During the meal, Jesus startled his disciples by getting up from the table, removing his outer robe, and putting a towel around himself. He poured water in a basin and began to wash his friends' feet.

It was Jesus' way of dramatizing the importance of being a servant to others. He told his disciples that they were right to call him Teacher and Lord. But he wanted to set an example of serving with humility. Jesus charged the disciples to follow his example.

The word "servant" in this story has the literal meaning of "slave"—a person who has an obligation to a master. Since the disciples are to become apostles (that is, persons sent out under the commission of their Lord), it is important that they conform as nearly as possible to the character of the One who sent them. The disciples are to be like Jesus, willing to perform servant-like tasks of hospitality and courtesy to other people.

The intermediate age level is an ideal period for helping young persons to value all forms of service.

> The Lord Jesus, after he had supped with his disciples and had washed their feet, said to them, "Do you know what I, your Lord and Master, have done to you? I have given you an example, that you should do as I have done."
> Maundy Thursday
> *The Book of Common Prayer,* p. 274

TEACHING TIP

Students at this age level may find the washing of another person's feet funny or strange. Explain that in Jesus' day, servants washed the feet of visitors because most people wore only sandals on the dusty or muddy roads. The washing of feet was important for keeping the home clean. While we no longer do this today, the symbol remains in the Church to represent to role of a servant to God.

GATHERING

Ahead of time, place the following agree/disagree statements on a chalkboard or sheet of newsprint, with lines and space below each one, as follows:

Jesus was a king who deserved special privileges.

Disagree	Not Sure	Agree

Unit III. Baptism: New Life—Session 6
Shell Year Intermediate—Copyright © 2000 Virginia Theological Seminary and Morehouse Publishing

Jesus expected his followers to rule over others.

Disagree   Not Sure   Agree
_____

As the students arrive, ask them to study the statements and put their initials on the lines at the points that come nearest to their own reactions. Do they agree? disagree? Are they unsure?

When everyone is present, say:

Let us pray. (Use the prayer from the Maundy Thursday service, above, or a prayer of your own choosing.)

The chosen student lector reads from the class Bible:

A Reading from the Gospel of John, chapter 13, verses 1 through 9.

Now before the festival of the Passover, Jesus knew that his hour had come to depart from this world and go to the Father. Having loved his own who were in the world, he loved them to the end. The devil had already put it into the heart of Judas son of Simon Iscariot to betray him. And during supper Jesus, knowing that the Father had given all things into his hands, and that he had come from God and was going to God, got up from the table, took off his outer robe, and tied a towel around himself. Then he poured water into a basin and began to wash the disciples' feet and to wipe them with the towel that was tied around him. He came to Simon Peter, who said to him, "Lord, are you going to wash my feet?" Jesus answered, "You do not know now what I am doing, but later you will understand." Peter said to him, "You will never wash my feet." Jesus answered, "Unless I wash you, you have no share with me." Simon Peter said to him, "Lord, not my feet only but also my hands and my head!"

Reader: The Word of the Lord.
Response: Thanks be to God.

INTRODUCING THE STORY
(Time: 10–20 minutes)

Begin by placing on a chalkboard or posted newsprint these two words: "service" and "humility." Challenge the students to describe what images or descriptions each word brings to mind.

In your own words, tell the story of the footwashing, from *John 13:1-15*. Use the story from page 1 of the student newspaper, **Covenant Times** (Unit III, Issue 6) as a guide. Stress the ideas included under Getting Ready (above).

Explain that the Passover was a Jewish feast to celebrate the freeing of the Hebrew people from slavery in Egypt. Now Jesus was showing his disciples a new way of freedom through the events of Holy Week. The footwashing was an introduction to the sacrifice that Jesus was now ready to make. He would give his own life for others and set them free from the power of sin and death.

Ask the students to find the following in their Bibles: *John 13:14* and *13:34-35*. How would they explain the connection between these passages?

You may want to share with the class members the meaning of Maundy Thursday. "Maundy" is an old English word for the Latin "mandatum" (mandate, or commandment). We use this term for Thursday in Holy Week because after the Last Supper, Jesus said, "I give you a new commandment, that you love one another. Just as I have loved you, you also should love one another" *(John 13:34)*. Encourage the students to read about Maundy Thursday services in the student newspaper, *Covenant Times*.

Return to the words on the board and and the statements from the Gathering exercise. Ask the class members whether they have new ideas about humility and service. Would they still put their initials on the lines in the same place?

EXPLORING
(Time: 15–20 minutes)

Option 1. Servant Card Game

Prepare a deck of 30 oversize game cards containing these words: humble, loving, servant, Jesus, serving, others, Christians, following, Christ's example, Maundy, Thursday, Service, washing, disciples', feet. (Repeat each of the 15 items for a total of 30.)

Shuffle the cards and place them face down in a stack. Invite the students to draw one card at a time, in turn, until they are able to collect three-card "suits" that form a meaningful phrase. The suits are separated by semicolons in the list above.

No one may keep more than three cards at a time, and each player must discard cards that do not fit with others.

Option 2. Silhouettes

Supply sheets of dark construction paper, pencils, scissors, and glue. Ask the students to sketch their own simple images of a foot, a basin, and a towel. Simple drawings of these images can be found on page 2 of the student newspaper, *Covenant Times*, and Symbol Card No. 24. Cut out each drawing and attach it to a white paper background to form silhouettes.

Individuals may want to design decorative borders and add a printed heading: Serving.

Option 3. Crossword Puzzle

Turn in the student newspaper, *Covenant Times*, Unit III, Issue 6, to the crossword puzzle titled "Holy Week." Students may work individually, in pairs, or as a total group.

MUSIC
(Time: 10 minutes)

The hymn "There is a green hill far away" (*The Hymnal 1982*, 167; *We Sing of God*, 31) will be used in Sessions 6-7. Listen to it on the *Children Sing!* tape.

This Holy Week hymn is part of a series written by Cecil Frances Alexander for a Sunday School class to teach the meaning of the Apostles' Creed. It explains the words, "suffered under Pontius Pilate."

CONNECTING/SPEAKING OUT
(Time: 15–20 minutes)

Option 1. Group Discussion

Jesus presented himself as a servant when he washed the feet of his disciples at the Last Supper (*John 13:1*). He told his disciples that he came "not to be served but to serve" (*Mark 10:45*).

Ask the group to think about their responses to the agree/disagree statements used at the Gathering (above). How would they rewrite the statements so that everyone could agree? Ask: What does it mean for us to be servants? Is it possible to do what Jesus asks us to do? Why or why not?

Invite the students to look up "humble" in a dictionary. Look for these definitions: not proud; not self-assertive; modest; low in condition, rank, or position; unimportant. Ask: Why would we use the word humble to describe Jesus and his followers? Who are the humble servants you know in your family, at school, and in the community?

Option 2. Current Events

Consider inviting a member of the congregation or someone from the larger community to visit the class and share information about church groups or local service organizations that provide meals for shut-ins, assist in shelters or soup kitchens, visit the prisons, or provide other services for people in need.

Ask the visitor: What led you to this service? Why do you do it? Brainstorm types of service that class members could undertake, such as making cards for shut-ins or visiting a nursing home. Select one idea and find a way to do it.

REFLECTING
(Time: 10 minutes)

Prepare a guided meditation on the scene in the Upper Room as Jesus washed the disciples' feet.

Before you begin, let the group experience a foot washing. Bring in one or more basins of warm water and towel. Ask students to remove their shoes and sit in chairs in a circle. Go around the room asking each person to dip his or her feet in the basin. You then dry the feet with a towel. (Several foot washers may be needed if the group is large.) Be prepared for students to laugh during this activity.

Afterwards, reread the scripture passage from *John* while the group sits in silence. Ask them to imagine themselves as disciples. The disciples felt as uncomfortable having their feet washed as the group did.

Allow a moment of silence. Ask: What would you have said to Jesus? Would you have said something like Peter said? What would Jesus have said to you?

LEARNING SKILLS
(Time: 10–15 minutes)

Option 1. Class Memory Challenge

Ask the students to memorize Question 6 of The Baptismal Covenant, "Will you proclaim by word and example the Good News of God in Christ?"

Invite the students to sit in a tight circle where they can easily hear one another. Explain that they are going to "round-robin" saying the words of The Baptismal Covenant that have been memorized so far. Ask each person to contribute a phrase, in order and from memory. For example: Student 1 says, *Do you believe;* Student 2 says, *in God the father?;* Student 3 says, *I believe in God,* and the process continues around the circle.

If there is interest, suggest that the round-robin be repeated. Note that a phrase of the Covenant will vary in length from two to five words. Refer to the Teacher's Packet poster and to the Memory Challenge block in the student newspaper, *Covenant Times*.

Option 2. Learning Scripture

Add ribbons, cards, and student symbols to the shell for any verses students have learned from suggestions offered in previous sessions.

Invite the class members to choose one or both of the following verses to be committed to memory before the next class session: *Matthew 20:28* or *John 13:15*. See "Learning Scripture" in the student newspaper, *Covenant Times*.

ONGOING PROJECT
(Time: 5–10 minutes)

Continue working on the exhibit described in Session 1. For this session, make a large cardboard figure of a priest in your church—possibly proportional in size to the font created earlier. Then add the vestments used at Holy Baptism in your church (made from paper or fabric scraps). If a special baptismal stole is used, the students can copy its design for use in this display.

Make arrangements for the class members to see the actual vestments before they begin this task. Prepare a label on a large card.

SYMBOL CARD and TREASUREBOOK

Card 24 shows a basin, towel, and pitcher for a footwashing, along with a Scripture verse and an explanation on the back.

Ask the students to look again at *Shell Year Treasurebook*, Part III, Section 3. Which question(s) in The Baptismal Covenant remind us of Jesus' command that we serve one another?

GOING FORTH

Gather the group for the dismissal. The teacher or a student will say the following, pausing for the students' response of "Lord, have mercy":

For our Bishop, and for all the clergy and people, let us pray to the Lord.
Lord, have mercy.

For this city (town, village, __), for every city and community, and for those who live in them, let us pray to the Lord.
Lord, have mercy.

That we may end our lives in faith and hope, without suffering and without reproach, let us pray to the Lord.
Lord, have mercy.

For _____[learners may add their own petitions], let us pray to the Lord.
Lord, have mercy.
 From The Prayers of the People
 The Book of Common Prayer, pp. 384-385

Teacher: Let us go forth in the name of Christ.
Students: Thanks be to God.

TEACHER'S ASSESSMENT

Christians refer to themselves as servants of God and servants for Christ. How do the students seem to picture Jesus? How did they respond to the idea of being servants? Do they have a sense of how they serve others?

LOOKING AHEAD

The next session focuses on the crucifixion of Jesus. Consider the sacrifice Jesus made in order to present us with the gift of salvation. How would you describe this gift of Christ in your own life?

BAPTISM: NEW LIFE
SESSION 7
JESUS WAS CRUCIFIED

FOCUS

The *Gospel of John* (chapters 18-19) describes the events of Holy Thursday (following the Last Supper) and Good Friday. The students should be able to outline and share in their own words the events of these two days.

GETTING READY

The four Gospels together provide a detailed narrative of Jesus' passion. In the *Book of John*, the account begins at chapter 18, following Jesus' farewell address to his disciples and a long prayer to God the Father.

Jesus and the disciples went to a garden in the Kidron valley near Jerusalem. Here he was arrested by both Roman soldiers and "police from the chief priests and the Pharisees."

Peter reacted angrily, cutting off the ear of Malchus, a slave of the chief priest. But Jesus told Peter to put his sword back in its sheath. (John says nothing about Jesus' healing of the ear; this is found only in *Luke 22:51*.)

From the garden Jesus was led to Annas and Caiaphas for formal trial before the Sanhedrin and later to Pilate, the Roman procurator of Judea. Jesus was accused of making himself a king. Pilate relented to the demands of a hostile crowd and handed Jesus over to death by crucifixion.

Jesus' hours on the cross ended with his final words, "It is finished" *(John 19:30)*.

Intermediate-age students are better able to handle the details of the crucifixion story than younger learners. They can read and analyze it for themselves. Even so, it is important to emphasize the link between the Good Friday events and the good news of Christ's resurrection.

Lord Jesus Christ, you stretched out your arms of love on the hard wood of the cross that everyone might come within the reach of your saving embrace: So clothe us in your Spirit that we, reaching forth our hands in love, may bring those who do not know you to the knowledge and love of you; for the honor of your Name. Amen.
Morning Prayer
The Book of Common Prayer, p.101

TEACHING TIP

Crucifixion is a horrible form of execution. Even so, many intermediate-age students will want to know details of Jesus' death on the cross, including the nails, the pain, and the thirst. While such curiosity and questioning is normal, it may be very uncomfortable for some. In teaching about Good Friday, convey objective information while avoiding over-dramatizing the agony of the story.

GATHERING

Display Poster No. 15 from the Teacher's Packet of a painting of Judas betraying Jesus with a kiss. As the students arrive, ask them to observe the details of the picture. What is happening? Who are the people in the painting? Do they know what will come next?

When everyone is present, say:

Let us pray. (Use the Collect from Morning Prayer, above, or a prayer of your own choosing.)

The chosen student lector reads from the class Bible:

A Reading from the Gospel of John, chapter 18, verses 1b through 8.

(Jesus) went out with his disciples across the Kidron valley to a place where there was a garden, which he and his disciples entered. Now Judas, who betrayed him, also knew the place, because Jesus often met there with his disciples. So Judas brought a detachment of soldiers together with police from the chief priests and the Pharisees, and they came there with lanterns and torches and weapons. Then Jesus, knowing all that was to happen to him, came forward and asked them, "Whom are you looking for?" They answered, "Jesus of Nazareth." Jesus replied, "I am he." Judas, who betrayed him, was standing with them. When Jesus said to them, "I am he," they stepped back and fell to the ground. Again he asked them, "Whom are you looking for?" And they said, "Jesus of Nazareth." Jesus answered, "I told you I am he. So if you are looking for me, let these men go."

Reader: The Word of the Lord.
Response: Thanks be to God.

INTRODUCING THE STORY
(Time: 10–20 minutes)

Begin with a detailed examination of *John 18-19*. Invite the students to work individually, in pairs, or in teams to read and report on sections of the story. After you assign the passages, encourage students to refer to the story in the student newspaper, ***Covenant Times*** (Unit III, Issue 7) to put their passage in context. Some may also want to consult *Matthew 26:47-27:61, Mark 14:43-15:47,* or *Luke 22:47-23:56* to compare details in the Passion stories in the other Gospel accounts..

The list below is based on the New Revised Standard Version. Asterisks (*) indicate shorter passages that could be combined:
- Betrayal and arrest *(John 18:1-11)*
- Jesus before the high priest *(John 18:12-14)**
- Peter denies Jesus *(John 18:15-18)**
- High priest questions Jesus *(John 18:19-24)**
- Peter denies Jesus again *(John 18:25-27)**
- Jesus before Pilate *(John 18:28-38a)*
- Jesus sentenced *(John 18:38b-40; 19:1-16a)*
- The crucifixion *(John 19:16b-30)*
- Piercing Jesus' side *(John 19:31-37)**
- Burial of Jesus *(John 19:38-42)**

As the students complete their summaries in order, list the headings on the board or newsprint. Between the sections on Jesus' sentencing and crucifixion, look at the map on page 2 of the student newspaper, *Covenant Times*. Use it to trace the way of the cross from the prison to Golgotha. Look at the passages in *John 18-19* that describe the events of the two days. Locate the places mentioned in the passage on the map. What happened at each place during the last hours of Jesus' life?

EXPLORING
(Time: 15–20 minutes)

Option 1. Contrasts

The story of Jesus' passion in John's Gospel contains both negative and positive images. Some words and phrases also suggest "darkness and death." Others can be associated with "light and life."

On a chalkboard or newsprint, write these contrasting terms as headings for two columns. Ask the students to open their Bibles and follow along as you read slowly *John 18-19*. Pause frequently to allow the students to call out any words or phrases to place under either heading. (Ask for a volunteer to do the writing.) Several examples are listed below.

Darkness/death	**Light/life**
Judas	valley
betrayed	garden
weapons	Jesus
sword	disciples

When the story is completed, ask the group to look again at the lists. Even in the midst of the tragic story of the cross, signs of life are present.

Option 2. Live, from Jerusalem

Prepare a news report about the passion of Jesus similar to segments shown on television news shows such as *20/20* or *60 Minutes*. Decide who will be the anchor and the director. Others in the class will play the roles described in the *Gospel of John* or be other journalists. Use the headings from Introducing the Story to help you decide which scenes to include. It may be necessary for some actors to play several parts.

Decide whether you want to use interviews only, or if you want to reenact some of the scenes. If possible bring in costumes (robes and towels for head pieces) and a video camera to tape the interviews or depictions.

After editing your report, share it with another group in the church or show it at an appropriate church gathering.

Option 3. Word Scramble

Turn in the student newspaper, *Covenant Times*, Unit III, Issue 7, to the word scramble titled "Good Friday." Students may work individually, in pairs, or as a total group.

MUSIC
(Time: 10 minutes)

Listen again to "There is a green hill far away" (*The Hymnal 1982*, 167; *We Sing of God*, 31) on the *Children Sing!* tape. Suggest that the students listen with their eyes closed. What images do they visualize? Why is the hymn associated with Holy Week?

CONNECTING/SPEAKING OUT
(Time: 15–20 minutes)

Option 1. Group Discussion

The account of Jesus' arrest and crucifixion in John's Gospel is filled with dialogue and details that make us curious. Invite the students to share any questions they wish to raise. Some possible areas to explore are:

Why would Judas decide to betray his beloved Teacher? How would he feel after he had done it?

After the Last Supper, Jesus had said Peter would deny him three times before the cock crowed the next morning. (See *John 13:36-38*.) How did Peter feel when he realized he had done just what Jesus predicted?

When Pilate saw no real reason to punish Jesus, why do you think he listened to the crowd's demands?

What do you imagine Jesus' mother was thinking on Good Friday?

Option 2. Current Events

During Jesus' last days, he heard people saying things about him that clearly showed they did not understand him and did not know why God had sent him. It must have been heartbreaking for him to listen to their misconceptions.

Similarly, intermediate-age students sometimes experience being misunderstood by friends, parents, and teachers. Students say, "You just don't understand!"

Encourage the students to list examples of people misunderstanding others. They may share their own stories or cite stories about people in the community or other places in the world. Ask: How can we deal with misunderstandings? What is the wisest thing to do?

REFLECTING
(Time: 10 minutes)

It is sometimes easy to keep the story of Jesus' death in the past. We would like to think that we would not have been in the crowd who demanded that Pilate crucify Jesus. And we cannot imagine being the Roman guard who nailed his body to the cross.

Use a meditation to help your students be a part of the passion so they can better understand that Jesus died for each of them. (You will need enough large nails for each student and a metal container.)

Before you begin reading, give the students the following instructions. When you clap your hands, they should jump up and yell, "Crucify him! Crucify him!" as loudly as possible. (You may want to practice this a few times.)

Ask the group to close their eyes and listen quietly as you read *John 18:29-19:6*. You may want to read it dramatically or with little emotion. When you come to *John 19:6b*, clap your hands after reading "they shouted." Motion the group to be seated and finish reading verse 6.

After a moment of silence, continue reading *John 19:16b-18a*. Ask the students to think about something they have done or said that has hurt someone else. When they have thought of something, ask them to come up to the front of the room one at a time, pick up a nail from the table, and drop it into the container. Tell them that the sound should remind them of the nails of the cross and Christ's sacrifice as well as the forgiveness of our sins.

End the meditation with a prayer.

LEARNING SKILLS
(Time: 10–15 minutes)

Option 1. Class Memory Challenge

Encourage the students to memorize Question 7 of The Baptismal Covenant, "Will you seek and serve Christ in all persons, loving your neighbor as yourself?" and the answer, "I will, with God's help."

Ask the class members to sit in a semi-circle,

facing a chalkboard or easel. Supply a piece of chalk or marker. Let the first student write the word "will". The marker is passed to the next person who writes "you", and the process continues, a word at a time through "help" (the last word of the answer).

If the students enjoy this exercise, they can return to earlier Covenant questions and write a word at a time in the same way.

The students may wish to consult the Memory Challenge block in the student newspaper, *Covenant Times*.

Option 2. Learning Scripture

Add ribbons, cards, and student symbols to the shell for students who have memorized verses.

Suggest that the students choose one of the following verses to memorize before the next session: *John 14:1, 6* or *15:13*. See "Learning Scripture" in the student newspaper, *Covenant Times.*

ONGOING PROJECT
(Time: 5–10 minutes)

For this ongoing project (described in Session 1), obtain a blank copy of a typical baptismal certificate. Make enough photocopies for everyone in the class to have one. Suggest that the students fill in the certificates with information about their own baptisms. These certificates can be assembled attractively as an addition to the exhibit. Add an appropriate label. Class members may want to take the blanks home to copy information from the certificates received at their own baptisms.

SYMBOL CARD and TREASUREBOOK

Card 25 has a picture of a crucifix, a Scripture verse, and an explanation on the back.

Ask the students to read again in the *Shell Year Treasurebook,* Part III, Section 4, the comments about water. How is Holy Baptism related to what happened on Good Friday?

GOING FORTH

Gather the group for the dismissal. The teacher or a student will say the following, pausing for the students' response of "Lord, have mercy":

For our Bishop, and for all the clergy and people, let us pray to the Lord.
Lord, have mercy.

For this city (town, village, __), for every city and community, and for those who live in them, let us pray to the Lord.
Lord, have mercy.

That we may end our lives in faith and hope, without suffering and without reproach, let us pray to the Lord.
Lord, have mercy.

For _____ [learners may add their own petitions], let us pray to the Lord.
Lord, have mercy.

From The Prayers of the People
The Book of Common Prayer, pp. 384-385

Teacher: Let us go forth in the name of Christ.
Students: Thanks be to God.

TEACHER'S ASSESSMENT

Appreciating the significance of what happened on Good Friday is the work of a lifetime. We struggle to express the deep meaning of the cross of Christ. As you worked with the students in this session, what were their most pressing concerns? How do you think they interpret Good Friday at this time in their lives?

LOOKING AHEAD

The next session focuses on the resurrection of Jesus Christ. Read *John 20*. What does the joy of Easter mean in your own life? Think about the Easter Vigil as it is described in *The Book of Common Prayer,* pp. 284-295.

BAPTISM: NEW LIFE

SESSION 8
JESUS WAS RAISED FROM THE DEAD

FOCUS

John's account of the resurrection of Jesus is a series of episodes involving Mary Magdalene, Peter and an unnamed apostle, and Thomas and the other ten apostles. The students should be able to describe the first Easter from the point of view of these witnesses and two or more traditional symbols of the resurrection.

GETTING READY

The resurrection account in *John 20:1-29* offers an intimate view of the participants' struggle to overcome their disbelief and accept the news that Jesus Christ had risen from the dead.

Mary Magdalene discovered Jesus' empty tomb "early on the first day of the week" following the crucifixion (verses 1-2). She ran quickly to tell Peter and "the other disciple, the one whom Jesus loved." We assume the unnamed disciple is John.

Mary saw the stone that had been removed. Peter saw the burial clothes and head wrapping. The other disciple, who had reached the tomb first, was the last to enter it. He was the one who "saw and believed" (verse 8).

In the next scene (verses 11-18), Mary was weeping outside the tomb. Then two angels asked her why she was crying. At that moment, the risen Lord himself spoke to her. She became the very first person to see him after his resurrection. He told her not to hold on to him and that his presence was temporary. He would ascend to his Father in heaven.

On that same day, in the evening, ten of the apostles were together in a locked room when Jesus appeared to convince them that he had indeed risen. He breathed on them, imparting the Holy Spirit. (The Greek word, *pneuma,* is translated both "breath" and "spirit.") In this episode (verses 19-23), the disciples move from fear to joy.

In a final scene, Thomas is convinced that Jesus is living. He had been absent when the other disciples saw their Lord. Jesus told Thomas to touch him (verses 24-29).

The experiences of these first witnesses are our only evidence that the resurrection occurred. Jesus spoke not only to the apostles but also to us when he said, "Blessed are those who have not seen and yet believe." (See *John 20:29*.)

O God, who for our redemption gave your only-begotten Son to the death of the cross, and by his glorious resurrection delivered us from the power of our enemy: Grant us so to die daily to sin, that we may evermore live with him in the joy of his resurrection; through Jesus Christ your Son our Lord, who lives and reigns with you and the Holy Spirit, one God, now and for ever. *Amen.*
Easter Day
The Book of Common Prayer, p. 222

TEACHING TIP

Intermediate-age students may be taking part in Easter celebrations as acolytes, choir members, or ushers. Their experiences in worship services will give them an opportunity to think about the meaning of the services. As you talk about resurrection, draw on the language of the Prayer Book. Invite the class members to share their insights about the drama of Holy Week and Easter.

GATHERING

Devise a way to make a colorful display of the Easter symbols of a lamb, pomegranate, butterfly, peacock, lily, and phoenix found in the student newspaper, *Covenant Times* (Unit III, Issue 8). You may want to enlarge the pictures and mount them on background sheets of paper or poster board.

As the students arrive, invite them to inspect the symbols and talk with one another about what each one might stand for.

When everyone is present, say:

Let us pray. (Use the Collect "Easter Day," above, or a prayer of your own choosing.)

The chosen student lector reads from the class Bible:

A Reading from the Gospel of John, chapter 20, verses 1 through 10.

Early on the first day of the week, while it was still dark, Mary Magdalene came to the tomb and saw that the stone had been removed from the tomb. So she ran and went to Simon Peter and the other disciple, the one whom Jesus loved, and said to them, "They have taken the Lord out of the tomb, and we do not know where they have laid him." Then Peter and the other disciple set out and went toward the tomb. The two were running together, but the other disciple outran Peter and reached the tomb first. He bent down to look in and saw the linen wrappings lying there, but he did not go in. Then Simon Peter came, following him, and went into the tomb. He saw the linen wrappings lying there, and the cloth that had been on Jesus' head, not lying with the linen wrappings but rolled up in a place by itself. Then the other disciple, who reached the tomb first, also went in, and he saw and believed; for as yet they did not understand the scripture, that he must rise from the dead. Then the disciples returned to their homes.

Reader: The Word of the Lord.
Response: Thanks be to God.

INTRODUCING THE STORY
(Time: 10–20 minutes)

Depending on the time available, decide whether to tell the story of Jesus' resurrection in your own words or to involve the class members in dramatizing the scenes in *John 20:1-29*.

You might select one of the characters (Mary Magdalene, the angels, Peter, Thomas, or another disciple) and share the account from that figure's point of view. A simple costume would add a heightened dimension to the telling. The story on page 1 of the student newspaper, *Covenant Times*, is from Mary Magdalene's point of view.

Another idea is to assign the following sections to teams of students and to ask them to dramatize the actions. Narrators could read the passages as actors mime the roles:

• The empty tomb is discovered by Mary, Peter, and another disciple (verses 1-10).
• Jesus appears to Mary Magdalene (verses 11-18).
• Jesus appears to ten disciples (verses 19-23).
• Jesus convinces the disciple Thomas (verses 24-29).

When everyone has had a chance to prepare, ask the teams to present the scenes in order without interruption.

Afterwards, suggest that students look for resurrection stories in the other three gospels (*Mark:16:1-8; Matthew 28:1-10; Luke 24:1-43*) to compare the accounts with the *Gospel of John*.

EXPLORING
(Time: 15–20 minutes)

Option 1. Easter Symbols

Look at the symbols used during the Gathering (above). For a complete description of each symbol, read the story on page 2 of the student newspaper, *Covenant Times*:

• Because of its three stages of life as a caterpillar, chrysalis, and winged insect, the *butterfly* is a symbol of life, death, and resurrection.
• The *lily* bulb, which has been dormant and appears dead, springs to life in a flower.
• A *lamb* standing represents the risen Lord.
• The *pomegranate* is full of seeds that burst forth when the fruit is opened.
• The *peacock* loses its feathers only to grow new ones that are even more splendid, just as our lives in Christ are more glorious than before.
• The *phoenix* is a mythical bird that is said to live 500 years, and at its death, be consumed by fire. It arises again out of its own ashes, more beautiful than before.

Ask each person to select one of the symbols that has the most meaning for him or her. Ask students to draw pictures or write brief poems about the symbols they have selected. Display the drawings or poems somewhere in your church.

Option 2. Easter Garden Dioramas

Collect small boxes, miniature rocks, pebbles, sand, plants, and small flowers—enough to permit each class member to construct a diorama of an Easter morning scene. The students may use their imaginations and fashion scenes that include an empty tomb in the midst of a pleasant garden setting.

Option 3. Word Puzzle

Turn in the student newspaper, *Covenant Times*, Unit III, Issue 8, to the word puzzle titled "Easter Message." Students may work individually, in pairs, or as a total group.

MUSIC
(Time: 10 minutes)

Listen to the well-known Easter hymn, "Come, ye faithful, raise the strain" (*The Hymnal 1982*, 199) on the *Children Sing!* tape.

The first stanza refers to the story in *Exodus 15*. The other stanzas describe Jesus' resurrection, using the imagery of springtime.

CONNECTING/SPEAKING OUT
(Time: 15–20 minutes)

Option 1. Group Discussion

Ask the students to consider again the different reactions of three witnesses to Jesus' resurrection—Mary Magdalene, Peter, and Thomas. Place the following sentences on a chalkboard or newsprint, without the names in parentheses:

I am overjoyed that I heard and saw the Lord. (Mary Magdalene)

I can only believe if I see and touch for myself. (Thomas)

I am both puzzled and amazed at the empty tomb. (Peter)

Ask: Which statement would you match with each of the three witnesses? Why did they react differently? How do your own reactions to Easter compare with theirs?

Option 2. Current Events

Invite the students to compare the commercial activities of the secular Easter with the Church's symbols of the resurrection. Look in newspapers for advertising and pictures that illustrate the Easter season as viewed by merchants and others.

Ask: What are the signs in the stores that Easter is coming? (Bunnies, eggs, candy, greeting cards, new spring clothing.) What do these things seem to represent? (They stand for springtime, growth of plants and animals, and family togetherness.)

How do the secular signs differ from Easter symbols in the Church? (List the empty cross, lilies, butterflies, and other familiar symbols for the resurrection. They stand for new life in Christ and God's victory over sin and death.) How are the signs and symbols similar? (New life, hope, sharing.)

REFLECTING
(Time: 10 minutes)

We often associate light with the resurrection. In traditional Easter Vigil service, the worship space is often darkened at the beginning of the service, then slowly illuminated with candlelight.

Use light and darkness to help your students think about that first Easter. If possible meet in a room that can be darkened. Separate chairs so that they are evenly spaced throughout the room facing toward the center. Ask the students to be silent and refrain from talking.

Using a small flashlight, read the scripture passage from *John 20:1-10*. (Or you could maintain the total darkness by telling the story in your own words.) When you come to the description of Peter and the other disciple reaching the tomb, light a large candle in the center of the room. After each following phrase, light a smaller candle and hand it to a different person. By the end of the passage, the room should be filled with light.

Before you extinguish the candles, ask each person to think of one way he or she could bring light into someone's life. Encourage the group to ask God to help them do this as they blow out their candles.

LEARNING SKILLS
(Time: 10–15 minutes)

Option 1. Class Memory Challenge

Ask the students to memorize Question 8 of The Baptismal Covenant, "Will you strive for justice and peace among all people, and respect the dignity of every human being?" and the response, "I will, with God's help."

After the group has had time to master this final question, try a review of Questions 4-8 (the "action" questions) and the common answer. A student begins with a spoken clue consisting of the *first three words* of each question, "Will you (continue . . . , persevere . . . , proclaim . . . , seek . . . , strive . . .)." Individuals can volunteer to complete the questions, or the class members can respond in unison.

Refer to the Memory Challenge block in the student newspaper, *Covenant Times*.

Option 2. Learning Scripture

Add ribbons, cards, and student symbols to the shell for any verses learned throughout this Unit.

For the next session, ask class members to learn *John 20:29b, I Corinthians 15:21* or *II Corinthians 5:17*. See "Learning Scripture" in the student newspaper, *Covenant Times*.

ONGOING PROJECT
(Time: 5–10 minutes)

As another feature of the exhibit (described in Session 1), add labeled samples or drawings of baptismal garments. In modern baptisms, people wear a wide variety of clothes in any color. The students will be interested in the fact that the traditional baptismal garment is white. When priests wear albs (white vestments used at Baptism and Holy Communion), these are symbols of the white garment for a newly baptized person in ancient times.

Many families have treasured baptismal dresses for infants, passed down for several generations. If someone in your congregation could visit the class and show one of these to the class members, the group could make an instant photograph to be labeled and added to the exhibit.

SYMBOL CARD and TREASUREBOOK

Card 26 depicts an Easter cross, and has a Scripture verse and an explanation on the back.

Ask the students to go through *Shell Year Treasurebook*, Parts II and III, to find all the references to Jesus' resurrection. What is the sacrament of the resurrection?

GOING FORTH

Gather the group for the dismissal. The teacher or a student will say the following, pausing for the students' response of "Lord, have mercy":

For our Bishop, and for all the clergy and people, let us pray to the Lord.
Lord, have mercy.

For this city (town, village, __), for every city and community, and for those who live in them, let us pray to the Lord.
Lord, have mercy.

That we may end our lives in faith and hope, without suffering and without reproach, let us pray to the Lord.
Lord, have mercy.

For _____[learners may add their own petitions], let us pray to the Lord.
Lord, have mercy.
 From The Prayers of the People
 The Book of Common Prayer, pp. 384-385

Teacher: Let us go forth in the name of Christ.
Students: Thanks be to God.

TEACHER'S ASSESSMENT

How well do the students grasp the importance of Easter for all Christians? As they took part in this session's activities, what was their general mood? Was there a significant contrast between the previous sessions and this one?

LOOKING AHEAD

The last session in this Unit is entitled "Jesus Offers New Life." Its aim is to help students understand that Holy Baptism is a sacrament that is directly related to the good news of Jesus' resurrection. In what ways have you experienced "new life" for yourself? Once more, prayerfully consider the promises made in The Baptismal Covenant.

BAPTISM: NEW LIFE
SESSION 9
JESUS OFFERS NEW LIFE

FOCUS

In the season of Easter, we recall the sacrament of baptism as a symbol of resurrection for all Christ's people. In baptism, we are buried into death and raised up to new life. The students should be able to state the relationship between the Easter story and Holy Baptism and what they believe "newness of life" means.

GETTING READY

The apostle Paul explains in *Romans 6:3-4* that Christians are intimately united with Christ through their baptism. As Christ has died, so also the Christian dies to sin. As Christ was raised from the dead and enjoys a new relationship with God the Father, so also the Christian now has a share in this "newness of life."

Throughout the Easter season, we reflect on Jesus' resurrection. A walk through the service of the Easter Vigil in *The Book of Common Prayer* leads us again and again to the theme of his triumph over the grave.

In the opening address at the Vigil, the Celebrant reminds us that "we share in his (Christ's) victory over death" (BCP, p. 285).

In the prayer on pages 286-287 of the Prayer Book, we pray, "This is the night, when Christ broke the bonds of death and hell, and rose victorious from the grave."

Baptism is preceded by an address in which the Celebrant says, "Through the Paschal mystery, dear friends, we are buried with Christ by Baptism into his death, and raised with him to newness of life" (p. 292).

And finally, at the Eucharist, the Collect includes direct references to the resurrection. For example, see this petition in the first Collect on page 295: "Grant us so to die daily to sin, that we may evermore live with him (Christ) in the joy of his resurrection."

This session provides an opportunity for reflecting on the compelling imagery of death being overcome by eternal life—the essence of the Christian faith.

Almighty and everlasting God, who in the Paschal mystery established the new covenant of reconciliation: Grant that all who have been reborn into the fellowship of Christ's Body may show forth in their lives what they profess by their faith; through Jesus Christ our Lord, who lives and reigns with you and the Holy Spirit, one God, for ever and ever. *Amen.*
Second Sunday of Easter
The Book of Common Prayer, p. 224

TEACHING TIP

Christians are an Easter people. The sense of joy associated with Easter lasts for more than one day, or even the fifty days of the Easter season. It is the reason we are Christians. Help the students experience this joy in their own lives. Remind the class members that each time we repeat the words of the Baptismal Covenant, we are affirming our belief in the good news of new life in Jesus Christ.

GATHERING

Display again Posters No. 16 and No. 17 from the Teacher's Packet that show The Baptismal Covenant. Alongside these, place Poster No. 18 of Holy Week symbols, also found in the packet. On a separate board or sheet of newsprint, list these words:

Unit III. Baptism: New Life—Session 9
Shell Year Intermediate—Copyright © 2000 Virginia Theological Seminary and Morehouse Publishing

servant, crucifixion, resurrection, and new life.

As the students arrive, ask them to talk about the connections they see among the four items on display. How would they link them all together?

When everyone is present, say:

Let us pray. (Use the Collect "Second Sunday of Easter," above, or a prayer of your own choosing.)

The chosen student lector reads from the class Bible:

A Reading from the Letter of Paul to the Romans, chapter 6, verses 3 and 4.

Do you not know that all of us who have been baptized into Christ Jesus were baptized into his death? Therefore we have been buried with him by baptism into death, so that, just as Christ was raised from the dead by the glory of the Father, so we too might walk in newness of life.

Reader: The Word of the Lord.
Response: Thanks be to God.

INTRODUCING THE STORY
(Time: 10–20 minutes)

Ask the students to recall some of the things they remember best about Holy Baptism and the events of Holy Week and Easter. Jot down key words and phrases on a chalkboard or newsprint. (Teachers may wish to reread the Unit letter.)

Remind the class members that Easter has always been a time when the Church welcomes newly baptized people.

Describe again early Christian baptisms, which were probably like that of Jesus. A person being baptized was immersed—that is, lowered into a river or stream and completely covered with water. Then the newly baptized individual was raised up out of the water to celebrate a new beginning as a member of the Way (the Christian community of professed believers).

The first-century Christians came to think of baptism as a kind of temporary "burial"—not in a tomb but in water. No one stayed immersed, for all were raised up from the water to give thanks to God for their new life together. Thus they compared baptism to Jesus' death and resurrection.

When the apostle Paul wrote a letter to Christians in Rome, he spoke about baptism as dying to sin and being raised up to live in a new way as Christ's people. Ask the students to look up *Romans 6:1-12*. What mental pictures do they see as they read these lines by the apostle Paul?

You may want to cite the passages from the Easter Vigil service in *The Book of Common Prayer* that are mentioned in Getting Ready (above).

Ask the students to describe their favorite part of Easter at their church. Do you like the music? What is your favorite hymn? Did the service make you feel joyful? Do you feel that joy at other times of the year? What would help you keep that Easter joy?

EXPLORING
(Time: 15–20 minutes)

Option 1. New Life Collage

Distribute scissors, glue, a large sheet of poster board, and a generous supply of old magazines. Ask the students to work together as a group to create a collage that suggests the "new life" of Easter and of Holy Baptism. They may clip out pictures, words and phrases from headlines and advertising, and any other items that suggest the main topic. Encourage the group to talk about the theme as they work.

Option 2. New Life Abstract

Provide a variety of art materials, glue, and pieces of poster board approximately 9 x 12 inches in size. Invite the students to create their own abstract interpretations of the concept of "new life." Explain that they can rely on colors and shapes and rich, impressionistic designs. They do not have to draw realistic images. The end effect of their work should convey both newness and a sense of life and growth.

When everyone is finished, hang the abstracts around the room. Ask volunteers to talk about their interpretations. What color suggests new life for you? What else do you associate with new life?

Option 3. Acrostic

Turn in the student newspaper, *Covenant Times*, Unit III, Issue 9, to the acrostic titled "New Life." Students may work individually, in pairs, or as a total group.

MUSIC
(Time: 10 minutes)

Listen on the *Children Sing!* tape to "We know that Christ is raised and dies no more" (*The Hymnal 1982*, 296). Call attention to the way in which this modern hymn connects Holy Baptism with the good news of Easter.

CONNECTING/SPEAKING OUT
(Time: 15–20 minutes)

Option 1. Group Discussion

Ask the students to turn in *The Book of Common Prayer*, p. 15, to the second paragraph to discover how the Church determines the date of Easter Day each year. Note that it cannot be earlier than March 22 nor later than April 25.

Point out that Easter is a "moveable feast" that occurs on different days each year, in contrast to Christmas Day, for example. (See the story on page 3 of the student newspaper.) Then ask the class members to turn to the table on page 882. Here we can find the dates for Easter Day from 1900 through 2051. Knowing that date for any given year makes it possible to use the next table on pages 884-885. If we find the day for Easter, we can move back to find Ash Wednesday and forward to find Ascension Day and Pentecost.

Easter in most parts of the United States corresponds with the season of spring. How does this affect the way we feel at Easter? What if the season were different?

Option 2. Current Events

Talk with the class members about anyone they know who has experienced newness of life—who has been given a "second chance," who has "turned over a new leaf," or who has gained "a new lease on life."

Ask the students to look through several issues of newspapers and news magazines for stories about individuals or groups who have had the opportunity to start over in their lives. Look for articles about persons who have recovered from injuries, who have overcome handicaps, or who have been chosen for special tasks.

Cut out the articles or pictures you find and ask the students to mount them on poster board or put them in a pile at a central place in the room. At the dismissal, ask the group to help you pray for each person in the collection. Include a request that God will help us find new life.

REFLECTING
(Time: 10 minutes)

Go outside on the church grounds or to a nearby park. Ask the students to go off individually or in pairs to look for signs of new life. Give them paper and pencil to write down descriptions of their discoveries. Remind them that they are to enjoy the things they find, but to leave them for others. If weather does not permit outside activities, ask students to list from memory things they believe symbolize new life.

After about five or ten minutes, ring a bell or blow a whistle to bring them back together. Either go back inside or sit in a circle outside. Ask each person to share the new life he or she found.

When everyone has had an opportunity to talk, ask the group to be silent while you share a brief meditation such as the following:

"It is several days since we celebrated Easter Day. But the good news of Easter lasts through our whole lives. Every Sunday is a little Easter Day when we come together to celebrate what God has done for us in Jesus Christ.

"Our lives are made new at baptism. The dawning of each new day reminds us that God is forever giving us new life. Whenever you see new life around you in nature, think about God's gift."

After a brief silence, ask the students, "What symbol or part of nature reminds you most of the Easter message? Does it also make you think of baptism and the gift of new life?"

LEARNING SKILLS
(Time: 10–15 minutes)

Option 1. Class Memory Challenge

Conduct a final review of all the questions from The Baptismal Covenant. Use Posters No. 16 and No. 17 provided in the Teacher's Packet. Refer also to the Memory Challenge block in the student newspaper, *Covenant Times*.

Encourage the students to return often to the words of the Covenant so that they will be able to respond comfortably when baptisms occur at your church.

Option 2. Learning Scripture

Add ribbons, cards, and student symbols to the shell described in Session 1 and used throughout this Unit, for those who have memorized verses. See

Unit III. Baptism: New Life—Session 9
Shell Year Intermediate—Copyright © 2000 Virginia Theological Seminary and Morehouse Publishing

"Learning Scripture" in the student newspaper, *Covenant Times.*

Talk with the group about what to do with the shell and its ribbons. Perhaps it could be put on display where others in the congregation would see it.

In Unit IV, another group of verses will be introduced, along with a different procedure for recording what has been memorized.

ONGOING PROJECT
(Time: 5–10 minutes)

As a final addition for this project described in Session 1, prepare a sheet of poster board labeled "We Are Baptized." Think of ways the class members could solicit signatures (autographs) of baptized people in your church. The names could be collected on separate, smaller sheets of paper and added to the board. The project could be announced in a church bulletin and newsletter, with students posted at various locations to collect signatures. People may wish to add the dates of their baptisms, or other information.

If this project has not been a continuing display with additions at each session, assemble all the items prepared throughout the Unit. Set up the exhibit in a prominent place for everyone in the church to enjoy. Suggest that the class members stand back and look at all the items and their labels. Does the exhibit tell the story of baptism? Would additional labels and descriptions be helpful?

SYMBOL CARD and TREASUREBOOK

Card 27 contains a picture of a butterfly, a Scripture verse, and an explanation on the back.

Ask the students to look through *Shell Year Treasurebook,* Part III, and choose a favorite sentence or paragraph they might copy for a greeting card to be given to someone who is being baptized.

GOING FORTH

Gather the group for the dismissal. The teacher or a student will say the following, pausing for the students' response of "Lord, have mercy":

For our Bishop, and for all the clergy and people, let us pray to the Lord.
Lord, have mercy.

For this city (town, village, __), for every city and community, and for those who live in them, let us pray to the Lord.
Lord, have mercy.

That we may end our lives in faith and hope, without suffering and without reproach, let us pray to the Lord.
Lord, have mercy.

For ____ [learners may add their own petitions], let us pray to the Lord.
Lord, have mercy.
   From The Prayers of the People
   The Book of Common Prayer, pp. 384-385

Teacher: Let us go forth in the name of Christ.
Students: Thanks be to God.

TEACHER'S ASSESSMENT

As this Unit concludes, how would you describe the students' point of view about Holy Baptism and Easter? Do you detect signs that they are thinking more deeply about the meaning of the new life God grants us through the resurrection of Christ?

Note: The following letter is for teachers and parents of children in the Intermediate level of church school. These two pages can be reproduced or used as a model for a personalized letter.

Episcopal Children's Curriculum
Unit IV: THE APOSTLE PAUL

Dear Parents and Guardians,

In the final Unit for the Shell year, we will be introducing the students to the apostle Paul. We will be looking at the book of *The Acts of the Apostles* and Paul's own writings.

When we promise in the Baptismal Covenant to "continue in the apostles' teaching," we join countless Christians before us who owe a great debt to Paul. If it had not been for his life and ministry, we would know little about what the apostles taught. The history of the Church would certainly have been very different without him.

We will not be able to share all the details of his adventure-filled days or all the elements of his theology. We will provide "snapshots" of Paul and help him to come alive as a real human being. He was a pioneer and innovator who worked tirelessly and fearlessly to share the gospel of Jesus Christ.

We encourage you to talk to your student about what he or she is learning. You can do this by reading the Scripture passages cited below, discussing the **Symbol Cards** and ***Covenant Times*** sent home each week, and by exploring Part IV of the ***Shell Year Treasurebook***, which includes information about Paul's work and beliefs.

Following are summaries of the Unit IV sessions:

Session 1: "Paul the Hebrew" is about the religious background of Paul, his place of birth, his education, and his early attitude toward the Followers of the Way (as the early Christians were called). The session will leave students wondering what happened to this Saul of Tarsus, the devout "Hebrew of Hebrews" who was so dead set on opposing those who believed that Jesus was the Christ or Messiah. (*Acts 22:3-5*)

Session 2: "Paul the Convert" shares the story of what happened on the road to Damascus. This dramatic incident turns Paul from a persecutor to an ardent disciple. Throughout his life, Paul insisted that he met Jesus when he was blinded and heard a voice from Heaven speaking. From Paul's point of view, the episode was a direct revelation from God. It is important for young people to grasp the concept of conversion and what it can mean as a life-changing experience. (*Acts 9:1-9*)

Session 3: "Paul the Apostle" introduces the meaning of apostleship—being sent out as an ambassador for Jesus Christ. By definition, an apostle was someone who had actually been a disciple of Jesus before his death and resurrection. Paul never saw Jesus in the flesh, but he insisted that he was just as much an apostle as the Twelve. The revelation from the risen Lord and his certainty that he had been called to preach the gospel to Gentiles (people who were not of the Jewish faith) qualified him to use the title "Apostle." (*Romans 1:1-6*)

Session 4: "Paul the Traveler" explores the wide-ranging journeys of the apostle. Map study and other activities, along with stories related to Paul's travel experiences, will give students a glimpse of Paul's remarkable devotion to sharing the gospel throughout the Mediterranean region. The three journeys are more than just lines on a map; they are lively encounters between a determined preacher and teacher of Christ and the people in cities, towns, and countryside. Paul endured great danger and hardship on his travels. (*II Corinthians 11:24-28*)

Session 5: "Paul the Missionary" focuses attention on the apostle's work in shaping the common life of the churches he founded and visited. We read his advice to church leaders with the benefit of hundreds of years of experience in communities of faith. Paul formed these groups of believers without any models to guide him. He had to instruct and guide the Gentile communities about how to live and worship as Christ's people in the world. (*Philippians 1:3-11*)

Session 6: "Paul the Writer" gives a taste of the many-faceted letters written by Paul to churches and individuals. Of the thirteen letters that bear his name, nine are believed to be authentically from Paul's hand. For various reasons, scholars believe the other four are probably the work of later authors. All the letters are valued by the Church and are part of Holy Scripture for Christians. (*I Corinthians 1:3, 15:3-10*)

Session 7: "Paul the Leader" encourages students to think about the way Christians should confront moral and ethical issues and how to deal with conflict among the Church's own people. In his letters, Paul addressed these matters openly. Some of his strongest advice is directed at those who profess faith in Christ but whose lives do not reflect their commitment to Christian values. Paul felt his task was speaking the truth in love, and he did not shrink from saying what he believed God wanted him to say. (*Ephesians 1:1-2, 4:1-7*)

Session 8: "Paul the Pastor" is the last in this series. Students will discover the kind, compassionate Paul in his personal letter to Philemon concerning the runaway slave, Onesimus. This letter is a "book" of only one page and can be read quickly. Students will wonder how the story ended. They will also consider the work of present-day people who help individuals and congregations meet troubles and crises. (*II Timothy 3:14-17*)

Session 9: "Pentecost: Festival of the Spirit" is to be used on or near the Day of Pentecost. Students can now enter fully into the church's celebration of this Principal Feast and enjoy the symbolism and excitement of the day. We will look back over the entire year's work and recognize the value of the themes that have been studied from Scripture and the liturgical life of the Church. At Pentecost, we can greet one another with the apostle Paul's words, "The grace of the Lord Jesus Christ be with you." (*Acts 2:1-4*)

Yours in Christ,

Church School Teachers

THE APOSTLE PAUL
SESSION 1
PAUL THE HEBREW

FOCUS

Saul of Tarsus was a Roman citizen who was well-educated in the Hebrew Scriptures and opposed to Christian believers. He had great ability as a scholar and administrator, and practiced the trade of tent-making. The students should be able to describe Paul's background.

GETTING READY

The apostle Paul was born in the city of Tarsus, which was the capital of Cilicia and an important center of coastal trade. His family was possibly well-to-do, and it was probably from his father that he learned tent-making and leather-working. As a member of a Greek-speaking, Jewish family, he was a Roman citizen by birth. His name was originally Saul, and he changed it to Paul following his conversion.

Outside the Bible, we have no biographical data on Paul. Josephus, the famous Jewish historian, does not mention him. It is only from Luke's writing in *The Acts of the Apostles* and from Paul's own letters written to churches that we are able to piece together the following information: He was a member of the Pharisees *(Philippians 3:5)*. According to *Acts 22:3*, he was educated in Jerusalem "at the feet of Gamaliel," a teacher highly honored among the Pharisees.

No doubt enraged by the Followers of the Way who identified the crucified Jesus as the Christ (Messiah), Paul became a zealous persecutor of Christians. He favored getting rid of this new sect because he had been taught to expect a triumphant Messiah, not someone who would bear the curse of the cross *(Galatians 3:13)*.

As an educated person of his time, Paul would have been familiar with the classical culture of Greece and Rome in addition to the Hebrew Scriptures. His knowledge of the world was a significant advantage as he became Christianity's first theologian and leading missionary.

O God, because without you we are not able to please you, mercifully grant that your Holy Spirit may in all things direct and rule our hearts; through Jesus Christ our Lord, who lives and reigns with you and the Holy Spirit, one God, now and for ever. *Amen.*
Proper 19
The Book of Common Prayer, p. 233

TEACHING TIP

Paul is an important figure in the New Testament. Much of Christian thought and language is based on his writing. Because of this, it is important to see Paul as a pioneer and innovator. He led a fascinating life as a "man of many parts," totally dedicated to Jesus Christ. Help the students form their own portraits of a very real person whose life continues to affect everyone in the Church today.

GATHERING

Ahead of time, on a sheet of newsprint or a chalkboard, draw a simple outline of a human figure with this question above it: Who am I?

Scattered around the figure, include statements like these:

I wrote part of the New Testament.
I am a Hebrew and a Roman citizen.
I survived three shipwrecks.
I have been stoned and sent to jail.

As the students arrive, invite them to speculate on the identity of this person. Who do they think it is? (If the group guesses accurately that it is the apostle Paul, challenge them to write some additional statements about him.)

When everyone is present, the teacher says:

Let us pray. (Use Proper 19 above, or a prayer of your own choosing.)

The chosen student lector reads from the class Bible:

A Reading from The Acts of the Apostles, chapter 22, verses 3 through 5.

(Paul said), "I am a Jew, born in Tarsus in Cilicia, but brought up in this city at the feet of Gamaliel, educated strictly according to our ancestral law, being zealous for God, just as all of you are today. I persecuted this Way up to the point of death by binding both men and women and putting them in prison, as the high priest and the whole council of elders can testify about me. From them I also received letters to the brothers in Damascus, and I went there in order to bind those who were there and to bring them back to Jerusalem for punishment.

Reader: The Word of the Lord.
Response: Thanks be to God.

INTRODUCING THE STORY
(Time: 10–20 minutes)

Display Poster No. 19 from the Teacher's Packet of a statue of the apostle Paul from the front of the National Cathedral in Washington, D.C.

Begin by announcing that this Unit is devoted to the life and writings of a man who did more than anyone else in the first century to assure the spread of the good news of Jesus Christ. He is known as the apostle Paul.

Ask the students to find *Galatians 1:13-14* in their Bibles and compare these verses with *Acts 22:3-5*. How are they similar? What are the differences? Who is speaking in both passages?

Then, on a chalkboard or newsprint, write the following headings. Add all the information the class members can find in these passages concerning Paul:
- his religious background
- his place of birth
- his education
- his early attitude toward Christ's followers

In your own words, share the additional information provided in Getting Ready (above) and the story about Paul in the student newspaper, *Covenant Times* (Unit IV, Issue 1). Include information from other stories in the newspaper about Hebrew schooling and Roman citizenship.

EXPLORING
(Time: 15–20 minutes)

Option 1. Making a Tent

Obtain a supply of sturdy fabric pieces, cut into odd and varied sizes. Remind the students that Paul's chosen trade would have involved sewing such pieces together to form the large sheets needed to make a tent. Other information about tent-making can be found in the student newspaper, *Covenant Times*.

Invite the group to work together to construct a table-top tent from the fabric on hand. They may use needles and thread or glue, to join the pieces. Decide how to use sticks or dowels to serve as the tent frame.

As the class members work, talk about life in the time of the apostle Paul. Tell them that Paul might also have been a leather worker who made beds, cushions, or harnesses for horses and chariots.

Option 2. Clay Sculptures

Suggest that the students use modeling clay or play dough to make their own sculptures of the apostle Paul. These could be either busts or full figures. Poster No. 19 from the Teacher's Packet, showing the statue at the National Cathedral in Washington, D.C., may be helpful as a model.

Option 3. Word Search

Turn in the student newspaper, *Covenant Times*, Unit IV, Issue 1, to the word search titled "Paul's Early Life." Students may work individually, in pairs, or as a total group.

MUSIC
(Time: 10 minutes)

Listen on the *Children Sing!* tape to "The Church's one foundation" (*The Hymnal 1982*, 525). Call attention to the second line which describes the Church as a new creation of Jesus Christ, "by water and the word." Ask: What do you think the hymn writer means by this expression? (Describe the Church as a community of the baptized.) In the second stanza, the words "one Lord, one faith, one birth." Point out that this expression comes from the apostle Paul in his letter to the Ephesians (*Ephesians 4:4*). The hymn substitutes "birth" for baptism.

CONNECTING/SPEAKING OUT
(Time: 15–20 minutes)

Option 1. Group Discussion

The apostle Paul was a well-educated man who came from Tarsus, a city outside Palestine. Invite students to discuss how his preparation for serving Jesus Christ differed from the background of the other apostles.

Ask: What did Peter, James, John, and the other apostles share that was not available to Paul? (Encourage the students to think about the experiences of Jesus' disciples who were actually with him through his three years of ministry. Paul only experienced the risen Jesus

What did Paul have that was not available to the others? Stress his knowledge, including Greek philosophy and culture, and tell about his studies with the famous teacher, Gamaliel. The disciples of Jesus were not men of great learning. The student newspaper has more information about the schooling Paul might have had.

Option 2. Current Events

Paul had a broad knowledge of the world of his time. He knew the geography of the empire and moved freely among all sorts and conditions of people. He spoke fluent Greek as well as Aramaic (a dialect of Hebrew), and he read the Hebrew Scriptures.

Look at a globe or a world map. Ask the group to find places outside the United States they have visited, from which they have relatives, or have studied in school. How are those places similar to or different from our country?

Ask: Why would it be important for the Church's members to understand the people, culture, and languages of other nations? What can we learn from one another across the boundaries of languages and customs? What, specifically, would you most like to know about people in another country? Why?

REFLECTING
(Time: 10 minutes)

For this Unit's reflections, invite the learners to prepare a series of letters to the apostle Paul. These are to be private notes, saved and taped together in a scroll.

At this first session, use construction paper or pieces of fabric to make individual "scroll covers," approximately 7 x 9 inches in size. Supply sturdy ribbon or yarn for use in tying the covers around the scrolls, and markers for adding students' names.

A scroll can be fashioned from 8 1/2 x 11-inch sheets of paper, with a new sheet attached at each session.

For this session, suggest that the class members reflect on their own life stories. Invite them to write letters to Paul about their personal backgrounds, including their beliefs about God and the Christian faith.

When students have finished writing, ask them to roll up their letters, enclose them in the scroll covers, and tie them securely. Keep the scrolls in a large shopping bag and redistribute them at each succeeding session.

LEARNING SKILLS
(Time: 10–15 minutes)

Option 1. Class Memory Challenge

Begin to memorize the books of the New Testament, in order. To assist with this task, a special chart has been included in the student newspaper, *Covenant Times*, Unit IV, Issues 1-9.

Many students will probably know the four Gospels in the first box. The second box includes the next four books: *Acts, Romans, I* and *II Corinthians*. Say the names over together several times in unison. (To assist in remembering them, it may be helpful to notice that the first letters spell ARC, with an extra C added.)

NOTE: The newspaper chart includes an asterisk (*) after all the letters attributed to the apostle Paul. Call this fact to the attention of the students.

Option 2. Learning Scripture

In this Unit, a selection of verses from Paul's writings have been chosen to memorize. To keep a record of the students' progress, prepare a large outline drawing of a church building. The students can indicate that they have learned verses by taping individual paper stones (or bricks) to the outline—one stone per student for each verse.

At this session, the class members may assist in producing the church outline (on a large sheet of butcher paper or poster board). They can also cut out an ample supply of paper stones to be saved in a basket or other container for use at succeeding sessions.

The teacher will write the Scripture citations on individual stones, adding each one to the outline when the first student reports having learned it. As other students continue to accomplish each memory task, they can add other blank stones at random, one for each verse learned. By the end of the Unit, the outline should be brimming with taped-on stones.

Encourage the students to memorize before the next session *Romans 1:16* or *5:1*. See "Learning Scripture" in the student newspaper, *Covenant Times.*

ONGOING PROJECT
(Time: 10 minutes)

Tarsus

A possible project to be continued throughout the Unit would be the production of a series of travel posters for cities connected with the apostle Paul. Large sheets of posterboard or butcher paper may be used, along with construction paper, markers, crayons, and other art supplies. Plan how to arrange a grand display of the travel posters at the end of the Unit.

The posters may include illustrations (drawings) and printed slogans or sentences. Encourage the students to use their imaginations and to parcel out tasks among teams as they produce creative advertisements for the various cities.

For this first session, the poster should be about Tarsus. Share the following information:

Tarsus was the capital city of Cilicia, built on a river bank. It was about 30 miles from the Taurus (Silver) Mountains. Lead and silver were found there in abundance. Cold water from the mountain range flowed down to the plain where Tarsus was located. Excellent Roman highways went through the city. In about 1000 BCE, a great wall was cut through heavy rock to form a pass into the uplands. Tarsus had a university supported by the state and the people placed high value on education. Paul learned the trade of tent-making. Tarsus became a headquarters city for the Roman government, so all its inhabitants were granted Roman citizenship.

SYMBOL CARD and TREASUREBOOK

Card 28 shows Paul's symbol of a sword through a scroll, along with a Scripture verse and an explanation on the back.

Ask the students to read in the *Shell Year Treasurebook,* Part IV, Section 1, about Paul's background. Why was Paul an opponent of Christians?

GOING FORTH

Gather the group for dismissal. The teacher or a student will say:

I ask your prayers for peace; for goodwill among nations; and for the well-being of all people.
Pray for justice and peace.
Silence

I ask your prayers for the poor, the sick, the hungry, the oppressed, and those in prison.
Pray for those in any need or trouble.
Silence

[Learners may add their petitions.]

I ask your prayers for all who seek God, or a deeper knowledge of him.
Pray that they may find and be found by him.
From The Prayers of the People
The Book of Common Prayer, p. 386

Teacher: Let us go forth in the name of Christ.
Students: Thanks be to God.

TEACHER'S ASSESSMENT

During this first session, what evidence did you gather about the students' present knowledge of the life and work of Paul? What do they seem to be curious about?

LOOKING AHEAD

The next session is based on the story of Paul's conversion on the road to Damascus. He was converted and transformed by a dramatic encounter with the risen Lord Jesus. In your own life, have you had experiences that proved to be transforming? What does "conversion" mean for you?

THE APOSTLE PAUL
SESSION 2
PAUL THE CONVERT

FOCUS

On the road to Damascus, while seeking out Christians he intended to take as prisoners, Saul underwent a dramatic conversion. He heard the voice of Jesus. The students should be able to describe Paul's conversion and contrast his new life with his former way of living.

GETTING READY

Very soon after Jesus' resurrection and the apostles' Pentecost experience, the Followers of the Way—as the first Christians were called—were faced with an issue that divided them.

Some spoke Aramaic and continued to be very loyal to their Jewish heritage. They kept the Law and remained faithful to Jewish custom, including worship in the temple at Jerusalem. As "Hebrew" Christians, they wanted any new followers of Christ to become good Jews as well.

Other followers of the risen Lord spoke Greek and had far less zeal for the Hebrew tradition. They were the "Hellenists." For them, the reality of the empty tomb and the resurrection appearances of Jesus came to be a sufficient basis for their faith. They believed that the good news of Christ was to be shared with Gentiles (people who are not of the Jewish faith) as well as the Jews.

The conversion of Saul of Tarsus happened in the context of this division between Hebrews and Hellenists in the early Christian movement. As a Pharisee and devout Jew, Saul hated the Hellenistic tendency in particular, and he saw no need for any path to salvation other than strict obedience to the Law of Moses. For him, the works of righteousness under law were the way to obtain the favor of God. He could conceive of no other way for people to be related to the Lord of heaven and earth.

Hence, Saul's "conversion" was not a change of heart on the part of a repentant sinner. On the contrary, it was a sudden invasion of his whole being by the living Lord Jesus Christ. He was on his way to Damascus with authority to seize members of the Way and persecute them when he was overcome by a blinding light. He heard words spoken directly to him, and it was plainly the voice of the very One whose followers he was attacking!

In the dramatic account found in *Acts 9:3-19,* Saul the persecutor is changed into an apostle of the Christian faith and he receives his call to preach the gospel to the world beyond Israel.

Intermediate-age students can understand the surprise about the suddenness of this change in Saul. It is a wonderful work of God in the life of a gifted human being.

> O God, you led your holy apostles to ordain ministers in every place: Grant that your Church, under the guidance of the Holy Spirit, may choose suitable persons for the ministry of Word and Sacrament, and may uphold them in their work for the extension of your kingdom; through him who is the Shepherd and Bishop of our souls, Jesus Christ our Lord, who lives and reigns with you and the Holy Spirit, one God, for ever and ever. Amen.
>
> For the choice of fit persons for the ministry
> *The Book of Common Prayer,* p. 256

TEACHING TIP

Intermediate-age students have accumulated enough life experience to be able to look back over their lives and identify ways they "used to think" and "used to be." They will be able to recognize Paul's conversion as an example of a changed life. Be specific in affirming the students' own experiences of change and transformation. Assure them that it is right to let go of the past and move on to the future.

GATHERING

Ahead of time on a chalkboard or large sheet of paper, write the words "The Way We Were." As students arrive, invite them to take pencils and 3 x 5 cards and describe a belief or idea that they had as a child that they no longer have. Descriptions can be serious or silly. For example, a student may have thought mom or dad could fix anything, or that rabbits hide eggs at Easter.

Provide loops of tape so that all the cards can be attached to the paper or chalkboard.

When everyone is present, the teacher says:

Let us pray. (Use the Collect "For the choice of fit persons for the ministry," above, or a prayer of your own choosing.)

The chosen student lector reads from the class Bible:

A Reading from The Acts of the Apostles, chapter 9, verses 1 through 9.

Meanwhile Saul, still breathing threats and murder against the disciples of the Lord, went to the high priest and asked him for letters to the synagogues at Damascus, so that if he found any who belonged to the Way, men or women, he might bring them bound to Jerusalem. Now as he was going along and approaching Damascus, suddenly a light from heaven flashed around him. He fell to the ground and heard a voice saying to him, "Saul, Saul, why do you persecute me?" He asked, "Who are you, Lord?" The reply came, "I am Jesus, whom you are persecuting. But get up and enter the city, and you will be told what you are to do." The men who were traveling with him stood speechless because they heard the voice but saw no one. Saul got up from the ground, and though his eyes were open, he could see nothing; so they led him by the hand and brought him into Damascus. For three days he was without sight, and neither ate nor drank.

Reader: The Word of the Lord.
Response: Thanks be to God.

INTRODUCING THE STORY
(Time: 10–20 minutes)

Begin by reading some of the cards written for the Gathering exercise. Ask students to talk about the entries on the cards. Then ask: Have you ever known someone who changed greatly in the way he or she believed and acted? (Allow time for thought, but do not press the students to share aloud.)

Announce that Saul of Tarsus was such a person. He started toward Damascus with authority to capture followers of the risen Christ and see that they were punished severely. As he traveled, he had an experience that changed him forever.

In your own words, tell the story of Paul's conversion as it appears in *Acts 9:3-19*. Display Poster No. 20 in the Teacher's Packet of this scene. For storytelling ideas, read the article about Paul in the student newspaper, ***Covenant Times*** (Unit IV, Issue 2).

Explain that Paul believed he had been doing the right thing in bringing Christians to judgment. He was a good man, a devout and faithful follower of God's Law. He simply had not understood what God was doing through the life, death, and resurrection of Jesus. On the road to Damascus, he was blinded by the truth. He met Jesus Christ for himself and was changed into a believer and follower.

We call what happened to Saul a "conversion." He was converted (changed) from a life devoted to stamping out Christianity. He became a Christian himself and changed his name to Paul.

The history of the whole world was affected by Paul's conversion. His preaching and writing have caused many other people through the centuries to embrace the Christian faith.

Invite the students to look in their Bibles at *Acts 9:10-19*. Ask: What did Ananias say to Saul when he called him "brother"? What happened next? When Paul's sight was restored, what did he do? (Note that he was baptized even before he took food.)

EXPLORING
(Time: 15–20 minutes)

Option 1. Mime: Paul's Conversion

Suggest that the students dramatize Paul's conversion on the road to Damascus without using their voices. Assign roles of Paul, Ananias, Paul's companions, and Christians in Damascus.

Talk through possible ways to mime the following: Paul's firm intention to move on to Damascus and arrest Christians there; his experience of hearing the voice of the risen Jesus; his blindness; friends leading him into the city; his inability to eat anything; Ananias having a vision and going to meet Paul; Paul's baptism; and his first preaching about what had happened in his life.

Note that actions need to be exaggerated in order to convey what is being expressed.

Option 2. Conversion Silhouettes

Give each class member a sheet of dark construction paper, folded in half. Demonstrate how to outline and cut a pair of profiled faces that look in opposite directions (left and right). Begin at the top of the fold and draw the top of a head, slant downward to create a forehead, then do the nose, mouth, and chin, sweeping down and back to form the neck.

Use glue to attach the finished two-faced silhouette to a light background sheet of paper. Label the left side, "Saul of Tarsus," and the right side, "the apostle Paul."

Listed below are words and phrases related to *Acts 9:3-19* and *22:3-5*. As a group, decide which picture to put them under. The items (separated by the semicolons) are in random order:

Damascus; knew Jewish law; lived in Jerusalem; fasted for three days; tent maker; filled with the Holy Spirit; prayed to God; voice from heaven; received authority from priests; Ananias; persecuted the Way; chosen instrument; regained sight; letters from the brethren; scholar; studied with Gamaliel; blinding light; arrested believers; baptized; devout Jew; missionary to Gentiles. Remind students that Gentiles are people who are not of the Jewish faith.

(The students may debate about some of the items. In several cases, they may decide to place items under both pictures.)

Option 3. Word Puzzle

Turn in the student newspaper, *Covenant Times*, Unit IV, Issue 2, to the word puzzle titled "Conversion." Students may work individually, in pairs, or as a total group.

MUSIC
(Time: 10 minutes)

Use "We sing the glorious conquest" (*The Hymnal 1982*, 255) for Sessions 2-4. Begin by listening to it on the *Children Sing!* tape. To introduce the hymn, call the students' attention to the designation line at the bottom, *Conversion of Saint Paul* (January 25). This hymn celebrates what happened to change Saul from a persecutor to a Christian.

You may want to look together at the following words: "conquest," the act of conquering or winning; "Damascus," the city to which Paul was traveling when he was converted to the Christian faith; "spoiler," one who plunders or robs; "zealot," one who is fiercely devoted to a viewpoint; and "reproving," correcting.

CONNECTING/SPEAKING OUT
(Time: 15–20 minutes)

Option 1. Group Discussion

Refer to the descriptions written at the Gathering (above). Would the students like to add to anything they wrote? What would Paul have written on his card?

Lead the students in a discussion of what is meant by "conversion." Why do people change? What makes you change your beliefs or ideas? How are you different now than you were before? Did the changes in you take place suddenly or was it a gradual process?

Are you glad you changed as you grew older? Who helped you understand things better? How would you describe the way Paul changed? Who helped Paul become a new person?

Option 2. Current Events

Almost every day the media includes stories of marked changes in individuals, groups, or nations. Cite some current examples, such as athletes who overcome obstacles or a politician who changes his or her mind. In each case, ask: Who changed? What caused the change to come about? In which cases did people or groups refer to God?

Invite students to tell about anyone they know who has undergone a transformation in views and behavior.

REFLECTING
(Time: 10 minutes)

Use the process of reflecting outlined in Session 1, with students adding letters to Paul on individual scrolls. (Note: Students can make scroll covers and begin writing letters at any session.)

Distribute the stored scrolls and invite the students to untie them and prepare another letter addressed to the apostle. For this session, encourage the students to reflect on Paul's experience of being changed dramatically on the road to Damascus. Suggest that they write letters to him about times when *they* have had a change of heart, including any new beliefs or feelings about Jesus Christ.

When the writing is completed, ask the students to tape the letters to the scrolls and tie the covers. Store them in a safe place.

LEARNING SKILLS
(Time: 10–15 minutes)

Option 1. Class Memory Challenge

Review the names of the first eight books of the New Testament (*Matthew, Mark, Luke, John, Acts, Romans, I and II Corinthians*). Refer to the chart in the student newspaper, *Covenant Times,* Unit IV, Issue 2, for the next four books. They appear in the third box at the top: *Galatians, Ephesians, Philippians,* and *Colossians.*

These letters of Paul form a pleasant chant, since each one has three syllables. All end in "ians." Say the names together several times. The initial letters, GEPC, are also easy to remember in order; they all have the long "e" sound.

Option 2. Learning Scripture

Ask students to add stones to the church outline (as described in Session 1)—one stone with the verse citations written on it, and additional blank stones from all students who have memorized each verse.

Encourage the students to memorize, before the next session, *Galatians 2:20a, Ephesians 2:8a,* or *Philippians 3:13-14.* See "Learning Scripture" in the student newspaper, *Covenant Times.*

ONGOING PROJECT
(Time: 5–10 minutes)

Damascus

Continue or begin this ongoing project. Supply materials for developing a travel poster devoted to the city of Damascus. (See Session 1 for details on the process.) Share this information about the city:

The city was located in an area crisscrossed by streams. Damascus was famous for its water. Gardens and orchards were abundant. To the west was snow-capped Mount Hermon; to the east, a string of marshes and lakes. The city was at the end of three caravan routes, making it a popular place for traders. It was a very old city. King Ahaz of Judah once saw a great altar in Damascus, and he had a copy of it made for the temple in Jerusalem.

SYMBOL CARD and TREASUREBOOK

Card 29 illustrates the shield for Saint Peter and Saint Paul. There is a Scripture verse and an explanation on the back.

Ask the students to read in the *Shell Year Treasurebook,* Part IV, Section 1, about Paul's conversion. After his conversion, why was Paul caught in an awkward position?

GOING FORTH

Gather the group for dismissal. The teacher or a student will say:

I ask your prayers for peace; for goodwill among nations; and for the well-being of all people.
Pray for justice and peace.
Silence

I ask your prayers for the poor, the sick, the hungry, the oppressed, and those in prison.
Pray for those in any need or trouble.
Silence

[Learners may add their petitions.]

I ask your prayers for all who seek God, or a deeper knowledge of him.
Pray that they may find and be found by him.
From The Prayers of the People
The Book of Common Prayer, p. 386

Teacher: Let us go forth in the name of Christ.
Students: Thanks be to God.

TEACHER'S ASSESSMENT

What were the reactions of students to the story of Paul's conversion? Are they able to articulate the idea of change and transformation in people's lives as they turn from one way of believing and acting to another?

LOOKING AHEAD

The next session focuses on Paul as an apostle of Jesus Christ—one sent forth in his name, like an ambassador or envoy. What experiences have you had in representing another person, group, or idea? Think about the responsibilities of such a role, and in particular what it would be like to carry the gospel of Christ to others.

THE APOSTLE PAUL
SESSION 3
PAUL THE APOSTLE

FOCUS

Paul became a chief evangelist to the non-Jewish world of his time. The students should be able to define the word "apostle," and explain how Paul could refer to himself as one.

GETTING READY

The word "apostle" comes from Greek, and it means "one who is sent forth" with a message of importance. Another word for apostle is "herald," one who announces striking news. Used more often in Scripture than in other writings of the time, "apostle" came to mean a person who had received a personal command from Jesus Christ to be his messenger to the world.

The New Testament does not present a consistent view of who could be called an apostle. The eleven faithful disciples who had been with Jesus in his ministry—together with Matthias, who was chosen to replace Judas—are named as apostolic leaders in the Church. But the title is also used for Paul and Barnabas (Acts 14:4, 14), Andronicus and Junia (Romans 16:7), and James, the brother of the Lord (Galatians 1:19).

A warning against "false" apostles (II Corinthians 11:13) suggests that the title was also used by people of questionable faith and credentials.

For Paul, who believed his conversion to be a result of Christ's direct revelation, there was never any doubt that he should be numbered with the original company of apostles. He believed himself to have received a commission from the Lord to preach the gospel to the Gentiles, non-Jewish people.

See *Galatians 1:1-2* for Paul's spirited defense of his apostleship. He did not believe he had been sent out by "human" commission and authority. His call came "through Jesus Christ and God the Father." Even though he and Barnabas had been set apart by prayer and the laying on of hands by Christian prophets and teachers *(Acts 13:1-4)*, Paul did not think of this act of the Church's leaders as his certification to be an apostle. He needed no other justification for his ministry than the fact that he had met the Lord in his dramatic conversion.

After Paul's time, the Church restricted the use of the title "apostle" to the Twelve and Paul. Paul's role is considered exceptional.

> Almighty God, whose blessed apostles Peter and Paul glorified you by their martyrdom: Grant that your Church, instructed by their teaching and example, and knit together in unity by your Spirit, may ever stand firm upon the one foundation, which is Jesus Christ our Lord; who lives and reigns with you, in the unity of the Holy Spirit, one God, now and for ever. Amen.
> Saint Peter and Saint Paul
> *The Book of Common Prayer,* p. 241

TEACHING TIP

Intermediate-age students can be totally involved in their interests, such as computer games, sports, music, and other activities. It should not be difficult for the students to identify with the single-mindedness and zeal the apostle Paul brought to his work as a Christian evangelist. Point to Paul's intensity of purpose as similar, in some ways, to their own natural enthusiasms.

GATHERING

Display Poster No. 19 from the Teacher's Packet showing the apostles Paul and Peter. As the students arrive, invite them to study the picture. Ask: What are the two men doing? What do you know about them?

When everyone is present, the teacher says:

Let us pray. (Use the Collect "Saint Peter and Saint Paul," above, or a prayer of your own choosing.)

The chosen student lector reads from the class Bible:

A Reading from the Letter of Paul to the Romans, chapter 1, verses 1 through 6.

Paul, a servant of Jesus Christ, called to be an apostle, set apart for the gospel of God, which he promised beforehand through his prophets in the holy scriptures, the gospel concerning his Son, who was descended from David according to the flesh and was declared to be Son of God with power according to the spirit of holiness by resurrection from the dead, Jesus Christ our Lord, through whom we have received grace and apostleship to bring about the obedience of faith among all the Gentiles for the sake of his name, including yourselves who are called to belong to Jesus Christ . . . .

Reader: The Word of the Lord.
Response: Thanks be to God.

INTRODUCING THE STORY
(Time: 10–15 minutes)

Ask the students to turn in their Bibles to *Romans 11:13-16*. Suggest that they work individually or in teams to discover how Paul described his ministry in these verses. What does he call himself? Where did he get his authority?

Write the word "apostle" on a chalkboard or newsprint. Ask the class members how they would define the word. Tell them that an apostle is "one sent forth" to bear a message or announce important news. Ask: Whose name(s) would you associate with this term?

In your own words, tell the story of Paul's apostleship using Getting Ready (above) and two stories in the student newspaper, ***Covenant Times*** (Unit IV, Issue 3). Focus especially on Paul's insistence that he had truly been called by Jesus Christ. He was converted from being a persecutor of Christians to being a commissioned messenger of the risen Lord. He was very sure that he had been given the task of preaching the Christian gospel to the Gentile, or non-Jewish, world.

You may want to point out that the Church regards its bishops as successors to the apostles. That is, they carry on the work begun by the Holy Spirit at Pentecost.

From generation to generation, through prayer and the laying on of hands, bishops are set apart to be pastors to the people of God. From New Testament times until now, God has provided direction and leadership for the Church through these appointed servants. Like Paul and the faithful disciples of Jesus who were with him in his ministry, they bear the message of Jesus Christ, risen from the dead. They are heralds of the good news.

EXPLORING
(Time: 15–20 minutes)

Option 1. Introducing Paul

Divide the class members into small groups or teams. Suggest that each group is composed of several friends in a New Testament community. They have learned that Paul, the traveling evangelist for Jesus Christ, is coming to their area. He is their friend, and they want to introduce him to their neighbors who are not Christians. What will they say about him? How will they introduce him?

Allow time for the groups to work out their introductions and decide on spokespersons. Appoint a member of the class to play the role of the apostle Paul. Ask him to visit each small group. As he arrives, he will be introduced to the others.

When all the introductions have been completed, ask: What did the statements have in common? What might be added?

Option 2. False Apostles

Make a list of statements about Paul and the other apostles from information in the Getting Ready section and the *Covenant Times*. Change key words in about half of the statements that result in "false" information. For example, Paul did not feel he was an apostle since he had not seen Jesus.

Divide the group into two teams. Read aloud the first statement to Team 1. Let the group discuss it and decide if it is true or false. If they answer correctly they get one point. Then read the second statement to Team 2 and give them a chance to answer. The other team can offer advice to confuse the issue. Continue until all the statements have been considered.

Option 3. Word Puzzle

Turn in the student newspaper, *Covenant Times*, Unit IV, Issue 3, to the word puzzle titled "Called to Be an Apostle." Students may work individually, in pairs, or as a total group.

MUSIC
(Time: 10 minutes)

Listen again to "We sing the glorious conquest" (*The Hymnal 1982*, 255) on the *Children Sing!* tape. In stanza 2, the hymn speaks of Paul as "a prisoner of his Lord." Ask: What does the hymn writer mean by this expression?

CONNECTING/SPEAKING OUT
(Time: 15–20 minutes)

Option 1. Group Discussion

Paul insisted that he deserved the title of "apostle" along with the Twelve who were witnesses to the resurrection and who had received the Holy Spirit at Pentecost. Ask: Why did Paul feel so strongly about this? Why was it important to him?

Encourage the class members to assist in making a chalkboard list of the Twelve (the eleven faithful disciples of Jesus, plus Matthias who took Judas' place). Add Paul's name. Ask: What are some words or phrases you would use to describe these persons? Why are they remembered by the Church?

Option 2. Current Events

Talk with the students about people in the church who carry the gospel message to others. Examples include people who have served as missionaries or who are involved in outreach projects. Ask students to share stories about family members or friends who carry the gospel message by the work they do.

REFLECTING
(Time: 10 minutes)

Distribute the students' covered scrolls and invite them to continue writing to the apostle Paul. (See Session 1 for a description of this process of reflecting, which can be started at any session.)

Encourage the class members to think about Paul who was "sent forth" to share the good news of Jesus Christ with others. Suggest that they write to Paul about times when they have talked with someone else about God and their faith. What did they share? Did they feel like "apostles"?

When the writing is completed, ask the students to cover and tie their scrolls. Put them in a place for safekeeping.

LEARNING SKILLS
(Time: 10–15 minutes)

Option 1. Class Memory Challenge

Continue working on the memorization of the books of the New Testament. Ask the students to assemble in teams to recite what has been learned thus far: the four Gospels, *Acts*, and five of Paul's letters (*Romans* through *Colossians*).

Refer to the chart in the student newspaper, *Covenant Times*, Unit IV, Issue 3, for the next four books: *I and II Thessalonians* and *I and II Timothy*. These four letters of Paul are an easy group to recall, since they all begin with the letter "T." Encourage the group to say the names aloud several times.

Option 2. Learning Scripture

For each new verse that students learn, write the appropriate citations on a paper stone and tape it to the church outline (as described in Session 1). Individual students may add blank stones, at random, for each verse they have just memorized.

Invite the students to learn, before the next session, *Romans* 10:9, *I Corinthians* 15:10a, or *Ephesians* 2:19-20. See "Learning Scripture" in the student newspaper, *Covenant Times*.

ONGOING PROJECT
(Time: 5–10 minutes)

Antioch in Syria

Continue this ongoing project as described in Session 1. (Note: This project can be started at any session.) Distribute supplies for making a travel poster on the city of Antioch in Syria.

You will need to share the following information to spur the students' imagination:

Antioch was twenty miles from the Mediterranean Sea, and about 300 miles north of Jerusalem. It had streets with columns and lamps on either side, and many fine buildings. The city included waterfalls, groves of cypress trees, and lovely public gardens.

Paul began his three missionary journeys from Antioch. It was an important center for early Christianity. Barnabas was the first leader of the church there.

SYMBOL CARD and TREASUREBOOK

Card 30 shows the outline of a fish and has a Scripture verse and an explanation on the back.

Suggest that the students read, in *Shell Year Treasurebook,* Part IV, Section 1, about Paul's insistence on being called an apostle. Also look at "Paul Traveled Widely" in Section 2. What forms of transportation were available to him?

GOING FORTH

Gather the group for dismissal. The teacher or a student will say:
I ask your prayers for peace; for goodwill among nations; and for the well-being of all people.
Pray for justice and peace.
Silence

I ask your prayers for the poor, the sick, the hungry, the oppressed, and those in prison.
Pray for those in any need or trouble.
Silence

[Learners may add their petitions.]

I ask your prayers for all who seek God, or a deeper knowledge of him.
Pray that they may find and be found by him.
From The Prayers of the People
The Book of Common Prayer, p. 386

Teacher: Let us go forth in the name of Christ.
Students: Thanks be to God.

TEACHER'S ASSESSMENT

How well do the students sense the connection and continuity between the Twelve apostles, Paul, and the Church they know today? Is there evidence that they have a deepening appreciation for Paul's contribution to the history of the Christian faith?

LOOKING AHEAD

The next session is on the travels of Paul. Consider what it might have been like for him to be "on the road" for such long periods. What would be his source of strength? Think about people of today who spend much time traveling. How do they cope with the feelings of being away from their homes and families?

THE APOSTLE PAUL
SESSION 4
PAUL THE TRAVELER

FOCUS

Paul traveled widely on three major journeys to preach and establish Christian congregations. The students should be able to explain why Paul's travel was important to the expansion of the Christian faith, to locate on a map major centers where he visited, and to describe how his travels affected him personally.

GETTING READY

The apostle Paul became the early Church's most effective voice. He was a pioneer in spreading the Christian faith.

At first, the gospel of Christ was shared with people largely through casual contacts on the streets, in marketplaces, in synagogues, and on the highways. A trip deliberately planned and undertaken to preach and evangelize the Greek and Roman world was a novel idea. Certainly it entailed hardship and danger. Travel over land and sea was hazardous at best, and Paul suffered illness, cruel punishment and imprisonment, and even shipwrecks.

The first journey began with Barnabas in charge. John Mark was with them. By the end of the trip, Paul was leader of the party. At Lystra, Paul was stoned by synagogue leaders who had come there from Antioch and Iconium. A witness to this episode was one of Paul's young converts—Timothy, who later became his faithful companion and secretary. (See *Acts 16:1-5* and *II Timothy 1:1-7*.)

On his second extended journey, Paul brought Christianity to Europe. In the city of Philippi, the first European to confess the faith and be baptized was Lydia, a business woman *(Acts 16:11-15)*. Paul and Silas were imprisoned in Philippi, and the result was the conversion of the jailer and his family *(Acts 16:16-40)*. Later, Paul visited Athens, where he impressed his hearers with his knowledge of philosophy, poetry, architecture, and religion. He spent eighteen months in Corinth.

The third journey took Paul through familiar regions of Asia Minor, Macedonia, and Greece, and back to Jerusalem. On this trip, the church at Ephesus was placed on a stronger footing as Paul preached and won converts there over a period of more than two years.

To symbolize the unity of Christians in all places, Paul promoted a collection of money to be sent to the church in Jerusalem. (See *Acts 20:35; Romans 15:26; I Corinthians 16:1*.)

From Paul's evangelistic enterprise stemmed the Church's organized approach to sharing the gospel with the whole world. Had he not initiated his habits of travel and correspondence, the Christian faith could not have grown as it did in the centuries following.

> O God, our heavenly Father, whose glory fills the whole creation, and whose presence we find wherever we go: Preserve those who travel; surround them with your loving care; protect them from every danger; and bring them in safety to their journey's end; through Jesus Christ our Lord. Amen.
>
> For Travelers
> *The Book of Common Prayer,* p. 831

TEACHING TIP

Geography and maps are a part of social studies classes for most intermediate-age students. Capitalize on this fact while exploring the journeys of Paul across the Mediterranean world. Encourage class members to trace Paul's journeys and correlate the areas Paul visited to present-day maps.

GATHERING

Arrange a display of Posters No. 20 and 22 from the Teacher's Packet—a picture of the embarkation of Paul and a map showing his missionary journeys.

As the students arrive, invite them to speculate on the scene in the picture. Where is it? Ask: What would you want to do if you were there? Why? What questions does the picture raise for you? How is the picture related to the map?

When everyone is present, the teacher says:

Let us pray. (Use the prayer "For Travelers," above, or a prayer of your own choosing.)

The chosen student lector reads from the class Bible:

A Reading from the Second Letter of Paul to the Corinthians, chapter 11, verses 24 through 28.

(Paul said) Five times I have received from the Jews the forty lashes minus one. Three times I was beaten with rods. Once I received a stoning. Three times I was shipwrecked; for a night and a day I was adrift at sea; on frequent journeys, in danger from rivers, danger from bandits, danger from my own people, danger from Gentiles, danger in the city, danger in the wilderness, danger at sea, danger from false brothers and sisters; in toil and hardship, through many a sleepless night, hungry and thirsty, often without food, cold and naked. And, besides other things, I am under daily pressure because of my anxiety for all the churches.

Reader: The Word of the Lord.
Response: Thanks be to God.

INTRODUCING THE STORY
(Time: 10–20 minutes)

Suggest that the students read a "sample" of Luke's account of Paul's many travels by turning to *Acts 21:1-6* in their Bibles. Ask: How many place names are found in these four verses? How many places can you find in the map used in the Gathering?

Talk about the importance of Paul's travels during the early history of the Christian movement. He went to many cities to preach the good news of Christ.

Look again at the map of Paul's journeys, on Poster No. 22 in the Teacher's Packet and in the student newspaper, **Covenant Times** (Unit IV, Issue 4). Invite the students to trace his route of travel during each journey.

Explain that Paul faced many dangers when he undertook these long trips over a period of about ten years. In the end, when he was imprisoned for his faith at Caesarea, he appealed his case to Rome and was sent there by ship. In *Acts 27:1-28:6*, we have one of the most exciting adventure stories to be found anywhere—Paul's experience with danger and shipwreck as he was being taken to Rome.

EXPLORING
(Time: 15–20 minutes)

Option 1. Journey Game

Ahead of time, prepare three sets of 3 x 5 journey cards, with a place name from a journey of Paul on each card:

Journey I—Antioch in Syria, Seleucia, Salamis, Paphos, Perga, Antioch of Pisidia, Iconium, Lystra, Derbe, Lystra, Iconium, Antioch of Pisidia, Perga, Attalia, Antioch in Syria.

Journey II—Antioch in Syria, Syria, Cilicia, Derbe, Lystra, Troas, Philippi, Thessalonica, Beroea, Athens, Corinth, Ephesus, Caesarea, Jerusalem, Antioch in Syria.

Journey III—Antioch in Syria, Galatia, Phrygia, Ephesus, Troas, Philippi, Thessalonica, Beroea, Corinth, Philippi, Troas, Miletus, Tyre, Caesarea, Jerusalem.

(Note: Each set has some duplicate cards because Paul went to the same place more than once, and Antioch in Syria is duplicated in the first two sets because the journey both began and ended there.)

Divide the class members into three small groups or teams. Deal a set of cards, at random, to members of each group. Their task is to study the map from the Teacher's Packet and work cooperatively to arrange their set of cards in the order of Paul's travels. If the class is small, the students can work with each set of cards in turn.

Option 2. Paul's Adventures

Invite the class members to turn to *Acts 27:1-28:6* in their Bibles and examine the details of Paul's adventures. In your own words, summarize *Acts*

27:1-26. Then divide the students into four small groups or teams, and distribute large sheets of white paper and markers. Ask the groups to draw simple illustrations showing what happened in these climactic sections of the story:

Acts 27:27-32—Midnight soundings, danger, and the sailors' attempted escape.

Acts 27:33-38—Paul urging the crew to eat and promising them safety.

Acts 27:39-44—Landing on a reef in a damaged ship and swimming to shore.

Acts 28:1-6—Kind natives on the island of Malta and Paul's brush with death from a poisonous snake.

When all the groups have finished, assemble the drawings like a comic strip, and ask each group to tell the story of their frame.

Option 3. Crossword

Turn in the student newspaper, *Covenant Times,* Unit IV, Issue 4, to the crossword puzzle titled "Paul the Traveler." Students may work individually, in pairs, or as a total group.

MUSIC
(Time: 10 minutes)

Sing with the *Children Sing!* tape the hymn "We sing the glorious conquest" *(The Hymnal 1982,* 255).

CONNECTING/SPEAKING OUT
(Time: 15–20 minutes)

Option 1. Group Discussion

Obtain an up-to-date map of the Mediterranean area. Place it alongside the map showing Paul's journeys. Invite the students to discover the names of countries and cities on the contemporary map that match the areas visited by the apostle. If possible, trace the journeys on the modern map.

Talk with the students about the effect of Paul's missionary travels on the early expansion of the Christian faith. Ask: What difference did it make that Paul reached out to people in so many different places and "planted" the Christian gospel in their hearts and minds?

What might have happened to the Church if it had remained open only to Jewish people in the region of Jerusalem?

Note also the problems of communication in New Testament times. Travel was slow and hazardous, and letters were few and far between. In spite of these facts, the good news of Jesus Christ spread to regions throughout the Roman empire. What obstacles do missionaries face today?

Option 2. Current Events

In parts of today's world, religious groups continue to be very hostile to one another. In some places it is dangerous for a Christian to travel. In other places, it is dangerous to be Jewish, Muslim, or a member of other faiths.

Ask the group to look through newsmagazines and newspapers to find stories about people who live in danger because of their faith. Locate the areas described in the stories on a globe or world map. Include the stories during the intercessory prayers at the dismissal, and ask the students to pray for the people in the stories throughout the coming week.

REFLECTING
(Time: 10 minutes)

Continue with (or arrange to begin) the method of reflecting suggested in Session 1. Distribute the scrolls to the class members and invite them to add another letter.

Ask the students to think about Paul's hazardous journeys, including shipwrecks. He continued his travel because he was on the all-important mission of sharing his faith in Christ.

Suggest that the group write letters to Paul describing their own travels. As they visited other places, did they worship at a Christian church? What would they like to tell the apostle about their experiences?

When the writing is completed, ask the students to add their letters to their scrolls, wrap them in the covers, and tie them securely.

LEARNING SKILLS
(Time: 10–15 minutes)

Option 1. Class Memory Challenge

Review the list of sixteen New Testament books that have been memorized in previous sessions. (See the chart in the student newspaper, *Covenant Times,* Unit IV, Issue 4.) Ask a volunteer to go to a chalkboard or newsprint easel to write, from memory, the initial letters of the books, *Matthew* through *II Timothy,* as they appear in the first four boxes of the chart. Then ask the class members to call out the names in unison as you point to each initial letter in turn. If the class is large, you may want to divide into teams for this exercise.

Note that the next box of the chart contains the names of three books. Say aloud, several times, the "triplet" of names: *Titus, Philemon, Hebrews*. (*Titus* and *Philemon*, marked with asterisks, are the final two letters of Paul.)

ONGOING PROJECT
(Time: 5–10 minutes)

Thessalonica

Continue this ongoing project as described in Session 1. Distribute supplies for making a travel poster on the city of Thessalonica. The earliest letter of Paul, in the New Testament, was written to Christians in Thessalonica, where Paul had helped to establish their community. (See *I Thessalonians*.)

Share the following information:

Land and sea connections made Thessalonica a very important trade center. The city was laid out along a gulf coast, and it looked like a giant amphitheater. In Paul's day, it was a strong naval base. It was called a "free" city and was allowed to manage its own government. Many wealthy and prominent people lived there.

Option 2. Learning Scripture

Add paper stones to the church outline, as described in Session 1. Use written citations on the first stone for each new verse that has been memorized. Encourage others who have just memorized any of the posted verses to add blank stones to the outline.

Challenge the class members to memorize, before the next session, *Romans 8:28* or *Philippians 4:13*.

See "Learning Scripture" in the student newspaper, *Covenant Times*.

SYMBOL CARD and TREASUREBOOK

Card 31 contains an illustration of a boat, a Scripture verse, and an explanation on the back.

Encourage the students to read in the *Shell Year Treasurebook*, Part IV, Section 3, "The Last Trip." Ask: What was Paul's destination? Why?

GOING FORTH

Gather the group for dismissal. The teacher or a student will say:

I ask your prayers for peace; for goodwill among nations; and for the well-being of all people.
Pray for justice and peace.
Silence

I ask your prayers for the poor, the sick, the hungry, the oppressed, and those in prison.
Pray for those in any need or trouble.
Silence

[Learners may add their petitions.]

I ask your prayers for all who seek God, or a deeper knowledge of him.
Pray that they may find and be found by him.

From The Prayers of the People
The Book of Common Prayer, p. 386

Teacher: Let us go forth in the name of Christ.
Students: Thanks be to God.

TEACHER'S ASSESSMENT

How well do the students grasp the significance of Paul's missionary journeys for the expansion of the Christian faith? What kinds of questions arose in connection with their map study?

LOOKING AHEAD

The next session is on Paul as a missionary. Be alert to the ways in which the Church's people use the words "mission" and "missionary" today. Which forms of Christian mission are most important to you?

THE APOSTLE PAUL
SESSION 5
PAUL THE MISSIONARY

FOCUS

Paul helped to form independent Christian communities throughout the Mediterranean area. We speak of him as the first missionary. He emphasized the local churches' common bonds in "the body of Christ" (the universal church). The students should be able to name one or more important New Testament churches that traced their beginning to the apostle Paul.

GETTING READY

Paul was dauntless in his approach to missionary work. He would arrive in a city, take up life with the people, and proceed to preach the good news of Christ. People, in varying numbers, would ask to be baptized. In some cases only a few souls became the nucleus of a new congregation of believers.

Clearly, Paul trusted the Holy Spirit to supply direction and strength for the fledgling congregations. He also had the dream of a world evangelized for the risen Lord.

On his several journeys, Paul was instrumental in establishing churches in at least the following places: Antioch of Pisidia, Iconium, Lystra, Philippi, Thessalonica, Beroea, Athens, Corinth, and Ephesus. We know that he visited churches in Syria and Cilicia, and he "strengthened" churches in Galatia and Phrygia.

At various other places Paul found disciples and believers, particularly in Caesarea, Tyre, and Ptolemais. In Salamis, he preached in synagogues; in Paphos, he converted the proconsul; in Derbe, he proclaimed the gospel.

So his story goes. From the time of his conversion until his death as a martyr in Rome, Paul was constantly on the move and dedicated to sharing the good news of the risen Christ. He followed no rigid time table. Sometimes he stayed in a place only a few days. He was in Ephesus for three years. At times he supported himself by working at his trade as a tent maker.

As he surveyed the world he knew and thought about the work of the Holy Spirit in his ministry, Paul came to think of Christian people—with all their gifts and abilities—as "the body of Christ," with each member fully engrafted into the whole. He wrote of this understanding in *I Corinthians*, chapter 12.

Almighty and everlasting God, we thank you for your servant Paul, whom you called to preach the Gospel to the people. Raise up in this and every land evangelists and heralds of your kingdom, that your Church may proclaim the unsearchable riches of our Savior Jesus Christ; who lives and reigns with you and the Holy Spirit, one God, now and for ever. *Amen.*

Of a Missionary
The Book of Common Prayer, p. 247

TEACHING TIP

Students are increasingly conscious that they are citizens of the world. Many have been exposed to languages and cultures of other lands, either first-hand or by way of television or the Internet. Through maps, stories, and recordings, help students become aware of the presence of the Christian Church worldwide.

GATHERING

From the Teacher's Packet, display Poster No. 21 of a picture of Paul preaching. Cut out circles of light-colored paper and tape them near the poster.

As the students arrive, encourage them to look at the picture. Supply markers, and ask the class members to write on the circles their ideas of what Paul might be saying.

When everyone is present, say:

Let us pray. (Use the Collect "Of a Missionary," above, or a prayer of your own choosing.)

The chosen student lector reads from the class Bible:

A Reading from the Letter of Paul to the Philippians, chapter 1, verses 3 through 11.

(Paul said) I thank my God every time I remember you, constantly praying with joy in every one of my prayers for all of you, because of your sharing in the gospel from the first day until now. I am confident of this, that the one who began good work among you will bring it to completion by the day of Jesus Christ. It is right for me to think this way about all of you because you hold me in your heart, for all of you share in God's grace with me, both in my imprisonment and in the defense and confirmation of the gospel. For God is my witness, how I long for all of you with the compassion of Christ Jesus. And this is my prayer, that your love may overflow more and more with knowledge and full insight to help you to determine what is best, so that in the day of Christ you may be pure and blameless, having produced the harvest of righteousness that comes through Jesus Christ for the glory and praise of God.

Reader: The Word of the Lord.
Response: Thanks be to God.

INTRODUCING THE STORY
(Time: 10–20 minutes)

Begin by writing the word "missionary" on a chalkboard or newsprint. Ask the class members to share their understanding of the words "mission" and "missionary."

Ask the students to find *Acts 13:47-49* in their Bibles. Paul and Barnabas spoke the words in verse 47, while on a mission at Antioch of Pisidia, where many people came to hear them preach. How did the Gentile (non-Jewish) listeners respond (verses 48-49)?

In your own words, tell the story from the student newspaper, **Covenant Times** (Unit IV, Issue 5), of Paul's visit to Philippi and the baptism of Lydia, a prominent business woman. Lydia owned a large house in the city where she invited Paul and his companion to stay during their visit. She became an important member of the new church in Philippi.

You may want to speak about various kinds of missions people pursue, such as a trip into outerspace or a journey to another country on behalf of their own nation or church.

Explain that the apostle Paul's missionary journeys were in pursuit of a very important goal: to establish new communities of Christian believers throughout the Gentile part of the Mediterranean area. Refer again to the map on Poster No. 22 in the Teacher's Packet, showing Paul's three journeys. Point out the locations of some of the important churches Paul founded, such as Philippi, Thessalonica, Corinth, and Ephesus.

Note that these cities and others Paul visited were along well-established trade routes. This was a good mission strategy because it meant that the early Christians would be in contact with travelers who passed through on route to other parts of the region. This offered the opportunity for them to share their faith more widely.

EXPLORING
(Time: 15–20 minutes)

Option 1. Missionary Journey

Invite the group to plan their own missionary journey. Bring in a map of your community. Ask the students to describe or name places where people congregate or pass through on their way to other places. For example, a local mall or shopping area, sporting field or arena, train station, or airport. Which places could they have the greatest impact on the most people?

Plot out your imaginary journey with lines drawn with a marker or by using colored yarn. Where should the journey begin? Where should it end? Is there anyone at my school or neighborhood to whom I could share the good news?

Option 2. Line Drawings

Supply paper and fine-point markers or soft pencils, preferably all black. Ask the students to picture mentally a new group of Christians gathered for worship in Paul's day. They could be inside a house or outdoors.

Suggest that the class members make simple line drawings of these early followers of Jesus Christ. Shading and details are omitted, like some print cartoons. For an example, look at the illustration on page 2 of the student newspaper, *Covenant Times*.

Option 3. Word Search

Turn in the student newspaper, *Covenant Times*, Unit IV, Issue 5, to the word search titled "Missionary." Students may work individually, in pairs, or as a total group.

MUSIC
(Time: 10 minutes)

Look at "Christ is made the sure foundation" (*The Hymnal 1982*, 518) for Sessions 5-8. Listen to it on the *Children Sing!* tape.

The hymn uses architectural imagery. Suggest that the students look for other architectural words in the hymn, such as cornerstone, foundation, city temple, and walls.

CONNECTING/SPEAKING OUT
(Time: 15–20 minutes)

Option 1. Group Discussion

Remind the students of this question from the Baptismal Covenant: Will you proclaim by word and example the Good News of God in Christ?

Ask: What does this promise have to do with being a "missionary"? Who are the Church's missionaries today? How does their work differ from that of Paul? What is the same? (Share briefly the fact that today's professional missionaries are usually trained in fields like medicine, agriculture, nutrition, or education. Not only do they share their Christian faith by preaching and teaching but they also offer concrete assistance to people.)

Ask the students to consider how they can help to share the message of Jesus Christ with other people through forms of service open to them, both in the congregation and in the wider community.

Option 2. Current Events

If possible, display a map of the world. Bring in newsmagazines and ask students to look for stories about different countries where there are active groups of Christians. Find the location of the stories on the map.

Ask: What are the stories about? How many stories deal with problems that Christians face? How many are about Christians helping others?

REFLECTING
(Time: 10 minutes)

Distribute the scrolls of letters to Paul. (See Session 1 for details on how to begin this activity.) Ask the students to untie the covers and prepare another message to the apostle.

Suggest that the group recall all that they have learned about Paul's patient and tireless ministry in the churches he visited across the Roman empire.

Invite the class members to think of themselves as modern Christian missionaries. Ask: What thoughts would you like to share in a letter to the apostle Paul? What have you done recently to help others? How does your church reach out to people in need in your community?

When the writing is completed, ask the students to add their letters to the scrolls, wrapping and tying them as usual. Keep them all together in a safe place.

LEARNING SKILLS
(Time: 10–15 minutes)

Option 1. Class Memory Challenge

Review briefly the nineteen books of the New Testament that have been learned thus far. Then introduce the second of the three "triplets" from the chart in the student newspaper, *Covenant Times*, Unit IV, Issue 5. The books are *James* and *I and II Peter*. Along with *Hebrews*, from the previous box, these are among "other letters" in the New Testament. Say them over aloud in unison several times. Then lead the group in reciting all the books, *Matthew* through *II Peter*.

Option 2. Learning Scripture

Ask students to share any verses they have memorized since the previous session. Prepare paper stones with the citations and add them to the church outline, as described in Session 1. Encourage students who have learned these and other verses to add blank stones to the outline.

Before the next session, the students may memorize one or both of the following: *Romans 10:13* or *I Corinthians 15:57*.

See "Learning Scripture" in the student newspaper, ***Covenant Times***.

Unit IV. The Apostle Paul—Session 5
Shell Year Intermediate—Copyright © 2000 Virginia Theological Seminary and Morehouse Publishing

ONGOING PROJECT
(Time: 5–10 minutes)

Philippi

Supply materials needed to permit the students to work in teams on another poster in this ongoing series. (See the description of the project in Session 1.)

Share the following information about Philippi:

Built on the spur of a mountain range, it was named for Philip of Macedon, in the fourth century BCE. A battle with the Romans occurred on the plain below the city, and the Romans were defeated. The church at Philippi was Paul's favorite. He returned to visit his friends there and they sent him gifts as he traveled on his journeys. Women were given more privileges in Philippi than in other parts of the world.

SYMBOL CARD and TREASUREBOOK

Card 32 has a beehive picture, a Scripture verse, and an explanation on the back.

Suggest that the students review *Shell Year Treasurebook,* Part IV, Section 2-3, for details about the outcome of Paul's missionary journeys. Why did Paul go to Caesarea?

GOING FORTH

Gather the group for dismissal. The teacher or a student will say:

I ask your prayers for peace; for goodwill among nations; and for the well-being of all people.
Pray for justice and peace.
Silence
I ask your prayers for the poor, the sick, the hungry, the oppressed, and those in prison.
Pray for those in any need or trouble.
Silence
[Learners may add their petitions.]
I ask your prayers for all who seek God, or a deeper knowledge of him.
Pray that they may find and be found by him.
From The Prayers of the People
The Book of Common Prayer, p. 386

Teacher: Let us go forth in the name of Christ.
Students: Thanks be to God.

TEACHER'S ASSESSMENT

How would you assess the students' concepts of a missionary's work? of a Christian mission? What would help them most to expand their understanding?

LOOKING AHEAD

The next session is about the New Testament letters attributed to the apostle Paul. The thirteen books begin with *Romans* and end with *Philemon.* Scan them, one by one, and notice how they begin and end.

THE APOSTLE PAUL

SESSION 6
PAUL THE WRITER

FOCUS

The New Testament contains thirteen letters traditionally attributed to the apostle Paul. These letters (epistles) are read aloud as part of the Church's Lectionary. The students should be able to identify the characteristics of an epistle, and to state why the Church values Paul's writings.

GETTING READY

About one-fifth of the New Testament is composed of letters that bear the name of the apostle Paul. They are treasured by the Church and read aloud as a part of the Lectionary. They are the oldest Christian documents, predating the Gospels, that have greatly influenced the nature of the Church's life.

Nine of the letters are addressed to churches: *Romans, I and II Corinthians, Galatians, Ephesians, Philippians, Colossians, I and II Thessalonians*. It is widely believed that these were meant to be read aloud and shared freely. *Ephesians*—which may not have been written by Paul—was probably intended for a group of Christian congregations.

Four letters are addressed to individuals: *I and II Timothy, Titus*, and *Philemon*. Authorship of the messages to Timothy and Titus is questioned; they may have been written by someone else after Paul's death. *Philemon* was written by Paul while he was under house arrest in Rome.

The form followed in composing these letters was the common usage of the day. The apostle added his own touches. For example, a typical letter in Greek would begin with the word "Greeting." Paul never used this word; instead, he employed both "grace" and "peace." (To this day, Jewish people greet one another with the word "shalom," which means peace.)

The opening line of a letter was followed by expressions of thanksgiving and various urgent appeals to the readers.

At the close, Paul would add greetings to readers (from himself and others with him), mentioning names. The final lines were a farewell or benediction.

No doubt the apostle would be very much surprised to discover these letters in Holy Scripture if he were to visit us today. Still, he would rejoice that his ministry as a servant of the living Lord is so greatly honored by the Church universal.

> Blessed Lord, who caused all the holy Scriptures to be written for our learning: Grant us so to hear them, read, mark, learn, and inwardly digest them, that we may embrace and ever hold fast the blessed hope of everlasting life, which you have given us in our Savior Jesus Christ; who lives and reigns with you and the Holy Spirit, one God, for ever and ever. *Amen.*
> Proper 28
> *The Book of Common Prayer*, p. 236

TEACHING TIP

Most intermediate-age students have experience writing letters and e-mails, thanking family members for gifts or people who have assisted in their classroom at school. Compare their letters to those of Paul in the New Testament. How do our letters usually begin? How did Paul begin? What kind of information do we include? How do we close our letters? How did Paul end his?

GATHERING

Display the two portraits on Poster No. 23 of Paul that are included in the Teacher's Packet. Both suggest that he was a writer.

As the students arrive, invite them to compare the two pictures. Which do they like? Why? Discuss the details in each portrait. Ask: If you were going to paint a picture of Paul, what would you include?

When everyone is present, the teacher says:

Let us pray. (Use Proper 28, above, or a prayer of your own choosing.)

The chosen student lector reads from the class Bible:

A Reading from the First Letter of Paul to the Corinthians, chapter 1, verse 3, and chapter 15, verses 3 through 10.

Grace to you and peace from God our Father and the Lord Jesus Christ. . . . For I handed on to you as of first importance what I in turn had received: that Christ died for our sins in accordance with the scriptures, and that he was buried, and that he was raised on the third day in accordance with the scriptures, and that he appeared to Cephas, then to the twelve. Then he appeared to more than five hundred brothers and sisters at one time, most of whom are still alive, though some have died. Then he appeared to James, then to all the apostles. Last of all, as to one untimely born, he appeared also to me. For I am the least of the apostles, unfit to be called an apostle, because I persecuted the church of God. But by the grace of God I am what I am, and his grace toward me has not been in vain. On the contrary, I worked harder than any of them—though it was not I, but the grace of God that is with me. Whether then it was I or they, so we proclaim and so you have come to believe.

Reader: The Word of the Lord.
Response: Thanks be to God.

INTRODUCING THE STORY
(Time: 10–20 minutes)

Select a letter Paul wrote to a church or individual that you are familiar with. Describe Paul and the people or person to whom he was writing. The student newspaper, **Covenant Times** (Unit IV, Issue 6), describes the letter Paul wrote to the Christian community in Thessalonica.

The article briefly tells about the community and the content of the letter. It mentions Timothy and Silvanus who also brought the gospel to the Thessalonians.

Next, write a list of Paul's letters on a chalkboard or newsprint. Explain that about one-fifth of the New Testament is composed of these writings from the apostle.

Point out the nine letters (epistles) that were written to churches or congregations. The other four letters are addressed to individuals. The messages to Timothy and Titus are called "pastoral letters" about the care of the church by its leaders. *Philemon* is the only private letter from Paul.

Ask the class members: Why do you think the early Church wanted to save these letters from Paul? Who reads them today? When? Where? (Explain that Paul's writing is the oldest part of the New Testament. His letters were written before the Gospels, and they give us a picture of how the Church should order its life and ministry.)

Ask the students to turn in *The Book of Common Prayer* to "The Lectionary" on pages 889-1001. Encourage them to examine the listings of readings for Sundays and at the Daily Office. Are all of Paul's letters included? When?

EXPLORING
(Time: 15–20 minutes)

Option 1. Letters from Paul

Play a game to help students remember the places Paul wrote letters to. Beforehand, get enough adhesive name tags for each student. On each one, write a name of a place Paul wrote a letter to, using the list from Introducing the Story. Also find several softballs that are easy to catch.

As a group, find the places Paul wrote letters to, using the map on Poster No. 22 from the Teacher's Packet.

Then pass out the name tags and ask students to put them on and stand in a circle. Begin the game by saying one of the places at the same time you gently toss the ball to the person wearing the tag with that place. That person continues by saying a new place while tossing the ball to another person.

After everyone has had the ball, repeat the process in the same order, only faster. The third time, start another ball about halfway through the order. Add new balls to add to the fun and confusion.

Option 2. Writing in New Testament Times

Invite the class members to try their hand at copying one of Paul's final greetings, in Greek. The student newspaper, *Covenant Times*, includes the farewell line from *I Thessalonians 5:28*: "The grace of our Lord Jesus Christ be with you." Underneath each Greek word is the English translation.

Note that the letters are all capitals, which was the custom in New Testament times. (If students wish to know the names of the letters, these may be found in many dictionaries, under "alphabet.")

To make the project especially interesting, you may be able to supply paper that has the appearance of parchment. Light tan construction paper would be a suitable substitute. The students may prefer to write lightly in pencil, then trace over the letters with a felt-tipped pen.

Option 3. Code Puzzle

Turn in the student newspaper, *Covenant Times*, Unit IV, Issue 6, to the code puzzle titled "Greetings from Paul." Students may work individually, in pairs, or as a total group.

MUSIC
(Time: 10 minutes)

Listen again to "Christ is made the sure foundation" (*The Hymnal 1982*, 518) on the *Children Sing!* tape. Suggest that the students look in their Bibles at *I Corinthians 3:11*, in which Paul speaks of Jesus Christ as the "foundation."

CONNECTING/SPEAKING OUT
(Time: 15–20 minutes)

Option 1. Group Discussion

Talk about the topics Paul discussed in his letters. He included teaching and interpretation of the Christian gospel, thanksgivings and special greetings, admonitions and warnings, and specific advice about appropriate behavior. If available, look at copies of Bibles that include sub-headings for the different parts of the letters. Scan one of the letters, such as *I Thessalonians*, to note the sections.

Ask: What do you think Paul hoped his readers would do with his letters? Who would read them? Where would they be kept? (Point out that the letters would be read aloud and possibly passed on to other churches.)

Option 2. Current Events

Introduce two Christian writers, C. S. Lewis and Madeleine L'Engle, who have written books and stories for young people. If possible, show a portion of the video based on Lewis' *The Lion, the Witch, and the Wardrobe* series. (This movie should be available from video rental outlets.) Another ideas is to read a portion of one of L'Engle's books written for young people, such as *A Wrinkle in Time*.

Talk about ways that we communicate today through publications, movies, and computers. You may want to play some contemporary music from Christian performers such as Jars of Clay or Amy Grant. How would Paul have used these media if they had been available? How would he have written to others by e-mail? What would Paul's website look like?

REFLECTING
(Time: 10 minutes)

Distribute the students' covered scrolls and invite them to continue writing to the apostle Paul. (See Session 1 for a description of this process of reflecting.)

To spark ideas for this session's letter, ask the students to think about Paul's writing. What would you like to say to Paul about his letters? Would you suggest ways he might reach young people through music or television? What would you write?

When this writing is completed, ask the students to cover and tie their scrolls. Put them in a place for safekeeping.

LEARNING SKILLS
(Time: 10–15 minutes)

Option 1. Class Memory Challenge

Review the books of the New Testament that have been learned thus far (*Matthew* through *II Peter*).

Refer to the chart in the student newspaper, *Covenant Times*, Unit IV, Issue 6. Notice that the final "triplet" of names (first box in the last row) is easy to remember: *I, II, and III John*. These are "other letters" in the New Testament—along with *Hebrews, James,* and *I and II Peter*. Include them in a final recitation (either as a total group or in teams).

Option 2. Learning Scripture

Suggest that the students memorize, before the next session, *I Corinthians 1:3* and *16:23*. These two similar lines, respectively, are a greeting and a farewell in this letter that the apostle Paul wrote. See "Learning Scripture" in the student newspaper, *Covenant Times.*

ONGOING PROJECT
(Time: 5–10 minutes)

Corinth

Continue this ongoing project as described in Session 1. Distribute supplies for making a travel poster for the city of Corinth.

Share the following information with the students as they prepare the next poster in the series:

Corinth was a commercial center located two miles inland from a gulf on an elevated terrace at the foot of a rocky hill. It was famous for pottery and bronze work, and its products were shipped to distant places. The city was surrounded by a wall six miles long. A large theater and a temple to the Greek god Apollo were located there. The marketplace was expansive. Near it was a white and marble platform that was used for public speaking. This was where the apostle Paul addressed the Corinthians.

SYMBOL CARD and TREASUREBOOK

Card 33 has a burning torch illustration, a Scripture verse, and an explanation on the back.

Ask the students to read *Shell Year Treasurebook,* Part IV, Section 4, about the letters of Paul. Do the letters of Paul appear in the Bible in the order in which they were written?

GOING FORTH

Gather the group for dismissal. The teacher or a student will say:

I ask your prayers for peace; for goodwill among nations; and for the well-being of all people.
Pray for justice and peace.
Silence
I ask your prayers for the poor, the sick, the hungry, the oppressed, and those in prison.
Pray for those in any need or trouble.
Silence
[Learners may add their petitions.]

I ask your prayers for all who seek God, or a deeper knowledge of him.
Pray that they may find and be found by him.
From The Prayers of the People
The Book of Common Prayer, p. 386

Teacher: Let us go forth in the name of Christ.
Students: Thanks be to God.

TEACHER'S ASSESSMENT

As a result of this survey of letters attributed to the apostle Paul, how do the students assess the value of these writings for the early Church? Were they aware of how many of the Epistle readings in weekly worship are from Paul?

LOOKING AHEAD

The next session focuses on Paul as a leader of the early Church. Think about the qualities that make for true spiritual leadership. What do you value most in a Christian leader? Who are the persons who have been especially important in your own life in the Church?

THE APOSTLE PAUL

SESSION 7
PAUL THE LEADER

FOCUS

From the letters of Paul, we learn about his role as leader, organizer, and shaper of Christian communities. When disputes arose or when questions were raised, it was Paul who wrote thoughtful and reconciling words. The students should be able to explain how today's Church continues to be guided by Paul's vision.

GETTING READY

Beyond a doubt, Paul was an organizing leader of the early Christian movement whose ministry shaped the character of the Church.

From the evidence within the letters Paul wrote to major churches, we can picture problems that arose. Sometimes these were simple human disputes among people who could not agree. At other times they were centered around important matters of belief and practice that could have threatened the Church's health and witness.

Paul, as missionary and founder, could best speak to these situations and issues. He rose to the occasion and provided counsel and direction that still guide Christians.

The Church in each generation honors Paul for articulating his vision of the Christian life. Following are some examples of his inspiring words:

I Corinthians 6:19-20—Christians at Corinth are advised that their very bodies are temples of the Holy Spirit. Paul appeals for wholesome behavior.

I Corinthians 11:23-28—When Paul learned that the Lord's Supper was being corrupted by drunkenness and unseemly behavior, he shared again the words of institution for the Eucharist. (These words form a part of the Church's Great Thanksgiving in the liturgy.)

Galatians 5:16-25—Paul appeals to Christians to be guided by the Spirit in their living, and lists the "fruit" of the Spirit.

Philippians 2:1-11—The apostle calls on Christ's people to allow their lives to be permeated with compassion, sympathy, love, and unity.

Ephesians 4:1-16—This passage presents a glorious image of Christian unity, with the many gifts of the Church's people.

O God, by your Holy Spirit you give to some the word of wisdom, to others the word of knowledge, and to others the word of faith: We praise your Name for the gifts of grace manifested in your servant Paul, and we pray that your Church may never be destitute of such gifts; through Jesus Christ our Lord, who with you and the Holy Spirit lives and reigns, one God, for ever and ever. Amen.

Of a Theologian and Teacher
The Book of Common Prayer, pp. 248-249

TEACHING TIP

Students at the intermediate-age level are learning skills for group living. Tendencies to form cliques or exclusive groupings, however, may appear at this stage in their development. The principles of cooperation and shared leadership need to be emphasized, along with the importance of including everyone. Look for opportunities to relate Paul's advice to our roles as leaders and followers today.

GATHERING

Ahead of time, arrange a display of the six pictures of Paul found in the Teacher's Packet on Posters No. 19, 21, and 23. All have been used at previous sessions: a statue, a scene showing Peter and Paul, Paul as a traveler and preacher, and two portraits of Paul alone. You may want to add any other pictures that are available in your church.

As the students arrive, encourage them to look again at all the posters and to reflect on why Paul occupies so prominent a place in the Church's life. Why is he regarded as a major leader?

When everyone is present, the teacher says:

Let us pray. (Use the Collect "Of a Theologian and Teacher," above, or a prayer of your own choosing.)

The chosen student lector reads from the class Bible (NRSV):

A Reading from the Letter of Paul to the Ephesians, chapter 1, verses 1 and 2, and chapter 4, verses 1 through 7.

Paul, an apostle of Christ Jesus by the will of God, To the saints who are in Ephesus and are faithful in Christ Jesus: Grace to you and peace from God our Father and the Lord Jesus Christ. . . . I therefore, the prisoner in the Lord, beg you to lead a life worthy of the calling to which you have been called, with all humility and gentleness, with patience, bearing with one another in love, making every effort to maintain the unity of the Spirit in the bond of peace. There is one body and one Spirit, just as you were called to the one hope of your calling, one Lord, one faith, one baptism, one God and Father of all, who is above all and through all and in all. But each of us was given grace according to the measure of Christ's gift.

Reader: The Word of the Lord.
Response: Thanks be to God.

INTRODUCING THE STORY
(Time; 10–20 minutes)

Most of Paul's letters were written when he was imprisoned. Tell the story of how Paul came to be in prison from the article on page 1 of the student newspaper, ***Covenant Times*** (Unit IV, Issue 7). It describes his appearance before Festus, the Roman Governor of Judea, and Agrippa, king of Judea.

Paul had already been in prison for two years when he went before Festus. He was accused of taking Gentiles into the temple, and he was beaten by the crowds. At that point, he declared his rights as a Roman citizen.

After a death threat, he was taken to Felix, then the Roman governor. Felix was sympathetic toward Paul, but frightened by the Jews. He chose to keep Paul in prison.

When Festus replaced Felix as governor, he met with the Jews who asked that Paul be brought to Jerusalem for trial. Paul then claimed his right to a hearing before the emperor in Rome. After consulting Agrippa, Festus sent Paul to Rome.

Talk about Paul's life as a prisoner and the importance of exercising leadership by keeping in touch with the new churches he had founded.

List the following on a chalkboard or newsprint:
• The life of a Christian *(Ephesians 4:1-3)*.
• The Church *(Ephesians 4:4-6)*.
• What Christians do in the Church *(Ephesians 4:7-13)*.

Explain that Paul played the leading role in helping the first Christians to form what we now call the Church. He gave broad outlines for its organization and described how its members should live out their commitment to Jesus Christ.

Suggest that the students open their Bibles to *Ephesians 4*, and look at the citations listed above. Ask:

What is said about the way Christians should live together?

How many times does the word "one" appear in verse 4? Why do you think the letter focuses on "oneness"?

Ask the students to find in their Bibles *Philippians 2:1-4*. How does Paul want the people at Philippi to live? In what way do these lines remind us of *Ephesians 4*?

EXPLORING
(Time: 15–20 minutes)

Option 1. Paul Mobile

Suggest that the group create a class mobile devoted to the apostle Paul. Prepare a large hoop or ring, and devise a way to use string or thin wire to suspend it from the ceiling.

Ask the students to prepare colorful shapes of paper or fabric suitable for attaching to the mobile with yarn, ribbon, or strands of embroidery floss. The items may include pictures, symbols, words, or phrases associated with the work of the apostle Paul.

Concentrate especially on his qualities as a leader of the early Church (bravery, determination, ability to persuade, and love for others).

Assemble the mobile. Make plans for exhibiting the mobile elsewhere in the church building so that others may enjoy it.

Option 2. Paul Puppets

Offer the students a choice of materials for creating simple puppets that can be constructed from two crossed sticks. Use glue to attach scraps of cloth, yarn, cotton, and other materials for dressing the figure. Make the face, hands, and feet from light cardboard, using markers to add facial features.

Use the puppets in telling the story of Paul's life to a younger group in your church. Think about the events you want to include, who will be the narrator, and which characters you need to tell Paul's story.

Option 3. Word Puzzle

Turn in the student newspaper, *Covenant Times,* Unit IV, Issue 7, to the word puzzle titled "Paul's Vision." Students may work individually, in pairs, or as a total group.

MUSIC
(Time: 10 minutes)

Sing with the *Children Sing!* tape the hymn, "Christ is made the sure foundation" (*The Hymnal 1982,* 518). Ask the class members to look in their Bibles for *Ephesians 2:20* in which Paul speaks of Jesus Christ as the "cornerstone."

CONNECTING/SPEAKING OUT
(Time: 15–20 minutes)

Option 1. Group Discussion

Talk with the students about Paul's practical advice to the Church's members concerning Christian behavior. For example, in *Ephesians 4:25,* Paul denounced falsehood and called for people to speak the truth. He went on to denounce stealing, dishonesty, and failure to share with the needy. In *Ephesians 5:4,* he told his readers to avoid "obscene, silly, and vulgar talk." He told them not to "get drunk with wine." Ask: Do we still need his advice today?

Paul also spoke about the relationship between parents and children. Read aloud *Ephesians 6:1-4.*

Ask: Why should children obey their parents? What did Paul say about the duty of fathers (and mothers)? How do you think people would react to Paul's advice today?

Option 2. Current Events

Ask the students to look up *Acts 20:36-38,* a description of Paul's farewell to the church at Ephesus where he had worked for many months. What did Paul do? How did the people react to Paul's departure? What does this glimpse of Paul reveal about his relationships with people?

Talk about clergy or people in your church that have moved to other places. How did the church react? How did the community say goodbye? How are they remembered?

REFLECTING
(Time: 10 minutes)

Continue with the method of reflecting suggested in Session 1. Hand out the covered scrolls to class members, and invite them to add another letter.

Ask the students to think about the apostle Paul as he faced many problems in the early Church. Refusing to be discouraged, he went on traveling, teaching, preaching, and writing letters. Even when he was in prison, he continued to give practical help and advice to the Christians. What would the students like to say to Paul about his work as a leader while he was in prison? What questions would they ask him?

When the writing is completed, ask the students to add their letters to their scrolls, wrap them in the covers, and tie them securely. Store in a safe place.

LEARNING SKILLS
(Time: 10–15 minutes)

Option 1. Class Memory Challenge

Review briefly the books of the New Testament that have been learned in previous sessions.

Refer to the chart in the student newspaper, *Covenant Times,* Unit IV, Issue 7, for the final box containing the last two books: *Jude* and *Revelation.* *Jude* is the last of the "other letters," and the *Book of Revelation* stands alone. Include these two names as you lead the class members in a group recitation of all twenty-seven books.

Option 2. Learning Scripture

Assign for the next session *Ephesians 4:7* and *I Timothy 4:14a.* Students may learn either or both of these passages. See "Learning Scripture" in the student newspaper, *Covenant Times*.

ONGOING PROJECT
(Time: 5–10 minutes)

Ephesus

Continue this ongoing project as described in Session 1. Distribute supplies for making a travel poster on the city of Ephesus.

Share the following information to help the students get started:

Ephesus was a large seaport city, center of commerce and religion. It had splendid harbors and good access to the inland valleys. The temple of the god Artemis was located there, containing pillars and oxen made of gold. The city had a stadium, a large library, beautiful gateways, and many fine statues of famous persons.

SYMBOL CARD and TREASUREBOOK

Card 34 has a picture of myrtle, a Scripture verse, and an explanation on the back.

Ask the students to read in the *Shell Year Treasurebook,* Part IV, Section 5, about Paul's ideas and his influence in the life of the Church. What is a theologian? Did you find other definitions that were new to you?

GOING FORTH

Gather the group for dismissal. The teacher or a student will say:

I ask your prayers for peace; for goodwill among nations; and for the well-being of all people.
Pray for justice and peace.
Silence

I ask your prayers for the poor, the sick, the hungry, the oppressed, and those in prison.
Pray for those in any need or trouble.
Silence

[Learners may add their petitions.]

I ask your prayers for all who seek God, or a deeper knowledge of him.
Pray that they may find and be found by him.
From The Prayers of the People
The Book of Common Prayer, p. 386

Teacher: Let us go forth in the name of Christ.
Students: Thanks be to God.

TEACHER'S ASSESSMENT

How have students been able to see Paul's leadership of the people of God? Is he still only an historical figure, or do they see Paul as a real person who had a great deal of influence on others?

LOOKING AHEAD

The next session focuses on Paul as a pastor. When you hear the word pastor, who comes to mind? What are the qualities you look for in a pastor? Who are some of the most effective pastors you have known?

THE APOSTLE PAUL

SESSION 8
PAUL THE PASTOR

FOCUS

Paul showed compassion and pastoral concern for individuals (such as his friends, Timothy and Titus, and the slave Onesimus). By example, he demonstrated the character of Christian ministry. The students should be able to describe Paul's concern for the welfare of others.

GETTING READY

Paul had a pastor's heart. Even though he could issue harsh warnings and at times seem impetuous, there is little doubt that he cared deeply about the people of the churches with whom he worked. He also showed loving concern for the persons who accompanied and assisted him.

The pastoral letters to Timothy and Titus offered encouragement, guidance, and support that were typical of Paul. These men were his associates in Christian ministry, deeply involved in matters affecting the congregations under their care. They faced the danger of falling into destructive patterns of behavior and the threat of mistaken beliefs that would undermine faithfulness to Christ.

Read the letters through at a single sitting. Notice the combination of an underlying kindness with the strong language warning against various false teachings and sinful practices. Both Timothy and Titus are addressed as "my loyal child in the faith" (*I Timothy 1:2* and *Titus 1:4*, respectively). Paul's instruction in *I Timothy 3:1-7* is frequently read at the ordination of bishops, and *I Timothy 3:8-13* is often included in services of ordination for Deacons (BCP, pp. 515, 540).

The short *Letter to Philemon* is a tender appeal on behalf of Onesimus, a runaway slave. Paul asks Philemon to receive him back in love as a Christian brother. We are privileged to read this private letter and to see the evidence of Paul's caring heart. See, for example, the generous words in *Philemon*, verse 7.

O God, our heavenly Father, who raised up your faithful servant Paul, to be a pastor in your Church and to feed your flock: Give abundantly to all pastors the gifts of your Holy Spirit, that they may minister in your household as true servants of Christ and stewards of your divine mysteries; through Jesus Christ our Lord, who lives and reigns with you and the Holy Spirit, one God, for ever and ever. Amen.

Of a Pastor
The Book of Common Prayer, p. 248

TEACHING TIP

The students' relationship with clergy and other church leaders may depend on the size of your congregation. In smaller churches where everyone knows everyone else quite well, students may have a clearer image of the pastoral role that people play for each other. In large congregations, this may not be the case. Look for opportunities to help class members become better acquainted with clergy persons and others who offer pastoral care to understand how these people meet the needs of others.

GATHERING

Write the Collect "Of a Pastor," above, on a chalkboard or newsprint. Use a bright color to underline or highlight the word "pastor" in both places.

As the students arrive, invite them to read the prayer and talk about the meaning of "pastor." Who are the pastors they have known? What do they remember best about each one?

When everyone is present, say:

Let us pray. (Use the Collect "Of a Pastor," or a prayer of your own choosing.)

The chosen student lector reads from the class Bible:

A Reading from the Second Letter of Paul to Timothy, chapter 3, verses 14 through 17.

But as for you, continue in what you have learned and firmly believed, knowing from whom you learned it, and how from childhood you have known the sacred writings that are able to instruct you for salvation through faith in Christ Jesus. All scripture is inspired by God and is useful for teaching, for reproof, for correction, and for training in righteousness, so that everyone who belongs to God may be proficient, equipped for every good work.

Reader: The Word of the Lord.
Response: Thanks be to God.

INTRODUCING THE STORY
(Time: 10–20 minutes)

Begin by reading aloud from The Examination in the service for ordination of a priest (BCP, p. 531), the following words addressed to the person about to become a new priest:

"Now you are called to work as a pastor, priest, and teacher, . . ."

Explain that "pastor" means "shepherd," and a pastor is one who looks after the spiritual well-being of a congregation of Christians. Our understanding of the work of a pastor has its beginnings in the New Testament as Paul served in this capacity. He visited the churches for which he was responsible and he wrote them letters. He also wrote letters to fellow ministers to advise them. (The two letters to Timothy and the letter to Titus are called "pastoral" letters.)

Point out that Paul wrote another, private letter to a man named Philemon. It also shows us Paul's kind, pastoral heart. Display the two portraits of Paul on Poster No. 23 from the Teacher's Packet.

Since this is a very short letter (only about a page in most Bibles), read it aloud or tell the story in your own words. For ideas read the article about Onesimus in the student newspaper, *Covenant Times* (Unit IV, Issue 8).

After the reading or telling of the story, ask: What has happened to cause Paul to write this letter? What does Paul say about himself? Where is he at this time?

How does Paul feel about Onesimus? What does he ask Philemon to do?

How does the letter make you feel about Paul as a person?

Look at the box on page 3 of the student newspaper about the outcome of Paul's letter. Encourage class members to speculate about Philemon's response.

Paul also interceded for another friend. Ask the students to look in their Bibles at *I Timothy 4:12*. What does Paul say about Timothy's youth?

EXPLORING
(Time: 15–20 minutes)

Option 1. Role Play

After discussing Paul's letter to Philemon, ask for volunteers to serve as a panel on a talk show. Possible panelists are: Paul, Onesimus, Philemon, Philemon's wife, and a slave friend of Onesimus, among others. Others in the class will be the audience. The leader or another student can serve as moderator.

Ask the person playing Onesimus to describe his (or her) dilemma. Paul can plead his case, and Philemon can tell his side. Others can add comments when appropriate. The moderator should encourage the audience to ask questions. Explore different endings to the story. At the conclusion, come to a consensus about the way the students believe the story ended.

Option 2. Paul Collage

Supply old magazines, sheets of sturdy construction paper, scissors, and glue. Direct the students to make individual collages devoted to the ministry of Paul. They may cut out pictures, draw illustrations, clip words and phrases, or select bits of color to create their images of the apostle and his work. Display the finished artwork for all to see. Ask the students to explain why they selected the pictures and words to describe Paul.

Option 3. Crossword

Turn in the student newspaper, *Covenant Times*, Unit IV, Issue 8, to the crossword titled "Onesimus." Students may work individually, in pairs, or as a total group.

MUSIC
(Time: 10 minutes)

Listen to both "Christ is made the sure foundation" *(The Hymnal 1982,* 518) and "O Spirit of Life, O Spirit of God" *(The Hymnal 1982,* 505) on the *Children Sing!* tape. Point out that the words of the second hymn are a prayer directed to the Holy Spirit. In the third stanza, the prayer asks "that charity may warm each heart." How does this phrase remind us of Paul's words to Philemon?

CONNECTING/SPEAKING OUT
(Time: 15–20 minutes)

Option 1. Group Discussion
Talk with students about the story of Philemon and Onesimus. Point out that slaves and servants were common in households of Paul's time. Ask: How do you think Onesimus became a Christian? How would his life be different after he returned to his master?

Ask the students to look up the word "compassion" in an English dictionary and list some of the definitions, such as "feeling pity, feeling sorrow for the sufferings or trouble of others, wanting to be helpful, having deep sympathy."

Suggest that the students turn to the *Letter of Paul to Philemon* and work individually or in pairs to find evidence that Paul was compassionate. Ask: What did Paul think about slavery? (An article in the student newspaper suggests that Paul most likely was opposed to slavery.)

Option 2. Current Events
Enlist the students' help in making a list of personal troubles or crises that might occur at any time, such as hospitalization for an illness, a death in the family, a period of unemployment, the loss of a pet, difficulties in school, or a friend's relocation to another area.

Ask: What could a pastor say or do that would be especially helpful? Can anyone be a "pastor" to people in need? What could you say or do to help someone facing one of these difficulties?

REFLECTING
(Time: 10 minutes)

Continue with the method of reflecting described in Session 1. Start by asking class members to uncover their scrolls and prepare to write another letter to Paul.

Encourage the students to consider Paul's pastoral concern for Onesimus, Philemon, young Timothy, and Titus. If Paul were the pastor of their church, what would they want to tell him? ask him? Would they be willing to share a problem with Paul? Why, or why not?

When the writing is completed, instruct the students to add their letters to their scrolls, wrap them in covers, and tie them securely. Place the scrolls together in a safe place.

LEARNING SKILLS
(Time: 10–15 minutes)

Option 1. Class Memory Challenge
Review all the books of the New Testament. Place on a board or newsprint the following headings:
The Four Gospels
The Early Church's History
The Letters of Paul
Other Letters
The Revelation

Invite the students to organize the twenty-seven books under the headings. The Gospels are *Matthew* through *John*; *Acts* is the New Testament history book; the letters of Paul are *Romans* through *Philemon*; the other letters are *James* through *Jude*. The *Book of Revelations* stands alone at the end.

Refer to the chart in the student newspaper, *Covenant Times*, Unit IV, Issue 8. Note again the asterisks after the thirteen letters attributed to the apostle Paul.

Option 2. Learning Scripture
Invite the students to learn, before the next session, *Ephesians 5:1* or *6:18*. See "Learning Scripture" in the student newspaper, *Covenant Times*.

ONGOING PROJECT
(Time: 5–10 minutes)

Rome
Continue this ongoing project as described in Session 1. Distribute supplies for making a travel poster on the city of Rome during the time of Paul.

Share the following information:
Rome is a large city built on seven hills. Its foundations were laid more than 800 years before the

birth of Christ. It was the location of temples, houses, and palaces of the rich and emperors. The people received free wheat, free water, and very inexpensive wine. Admission to races, games, and circuses was free. The huge Circus of Maximus would hold 150,000 people, and the theater of Pompey, 40,000. The city had an efficient government, including police and firefighters. At least thirteen Jewish synagogues were located in Rome.

Note: This is the final session on the apostle Paul. Decide whether to conclude this ongoing project at this session or continue with the suggestions given in Session 9, which is devoted to Pentecost. Will the class members display all their completed posters in the church?

SYMBOL CARD and TREASUREBOOK

Card 35 illustrates the shield of Lydia, along with a Scripture verse, and an explanation on the back.

Suggest that the students review all of Part IV in *Shell Year Treasurebook*. What would they like to add to the book's sections on Paul?

GOING FORTH

Gather the group for dismissal. The teacher or a student will say:

I ask your prayers for peace; for goodwill among nations; and for the well-being of all people.
Pray for justice and peace.
Silence

I ask your prayers for the poor, the sick, the hungry, the oppressed, and those in prison.
Pray for those in any need or trouble.
Silence

[Learners may add their petitions.]

I ask your prayers for all who seek God, or a deeper knowledge of him.
Pray that they may find and be found by him.
From The Prayers of the People
The Book of Common Prayer, p. 386

Teacher: Let us go forth in the name of Christ.
Students: Thanks be to God.

TEACHER'S ASSESSMENT

In this final session on Paul, were the students able to catch a sense of his compassionate heart and kindliness? What observations did they share about the pastoral needs of people in today's Church?

LOOKING AHEAD

Session 9 has been prepared for use on Pentecost Day. Use it on the date most appropriate for your local schedule. It will not matter if this date occurs before Sessions 1-8 have been completed. Consider how to relate the session activities to your congregation's plans for celebrating this feast.

THE APOSTLE PAUL

SESSION 9
PENTECOST: FESTIVAL OF THE SPIRIT

FOCUS

At Pentecost, we celebrate the descent of the Holy Spirit upon the Church. The students should be able to say why Pentecost is a major Feast, and plan for their own celebration of this day.

GETTING READY

After his resurrection, Jesus appeared to his disciples and "breathed on them." He said to them, "Receive the Holy Spirit." (See *John 20:19-22*.) Then, just prior to his ascension into heaven, the risen Jesus said to the apostles, "You will receive power when the Holy Spirit has come upon you; and you shall be my witnesses in Jerusalem, and in all Judea and Samaria, and to the ends of the earth *(Acts 1:8)*."

The Pentecost event, described in *Acts 2*, was seen by the early Church as the fulfillment of Jesus' promise. They had waited for seven weeks to learn what God intended for them, and now their mission was being made clear. Peter declared it in his first sermon—Jesus, the crucified one, had been raised up. He is both Lord and Messiah. (See *Acts 2:29-36*.)

As one of the Principal Feasts of the Church, the Day of Pentecost celebrates the continuing presence of the Holy Spirit among Christian believers.

Pentecost can be a time of great joy. The day has not been subject to the kinds of exploitation typical of the periods surrounding Christmas Day and Easter Day. For that reason, students in church school can enjoy creating their own forms of celebration.

Almighty God, on this day you opened the way of eternal life to every race and nation by the promised gift of your Holy Spirit: Shed abroad this gift throughout the world by the preaching of the Gospel, that it may reach to the ends of the earth; through Jesus Christ our Lord, who lives and reigns with you, in the unity of the Holy Spirit, one God, for ever and ever. *Amen.*

The Day of Pentecost: Whitsunday
The Book of Common Prayer, p. 227

TEACHING TIP

Principal Feasts of the Church, such as the Day of Pentecost, offer opportunities for participation by people of all ages. Be alert to the ways intermediate students can contribute their enthusiasm and talents at your church's Pentecost celebration.

GATHERING

Display Poster No. 24 for Pentecost from the Teacher's Packet that shows various symbols associated with the event.

As the students arrive, ask them to study the poster and locate and explain the symbols it includes. Open a copy of the student newspaper, *Covenant Times* (Unit IV, Issue 9) to page two for an article about Pentecost symbols. Students may want to use a chalkboard or newsprint to write words and phrases about this festival day.

When everyone is present, say:

Let us pray. (Use the Collect "The Day of Pentecost: Whitsunday," above, or a prayer of your own choosing.)

The chosen student lector reads from the class Bible:

A Reading from the Book of Acts, chapter 2, verses 1 through 4.

When the day of Pentecost had come, they were all together in one place. And suddenly from heaven there came a sound like the rush of a violent wind, and it filled the entire house where they were sitting. Divided tongues, as of fire, appeared among them, and a tongue rested on each of them. All of them were filled with the Holy Spirit and began to speak in other languages, as the Spirit gave them ability.

Reader: The Word of the Lord.
Response: Thanks be to God.

INTRODUCING THE STORY
(Time: 10–20 minutes)

Begin by directing the students to turn in *The Book of Common Prayer* to the Calendar of the Church Year, p.15. Note that the Day of Pentecost is one of the Principal Feasts of the Church, ranking alongside Easter Day and Christmas Day. Ask: What do we celebrate on this day? Why is it so important for Christians?

Tell the story found in *Acts 2* about Pentecost. Stress the wonder and mystery of the Pentecost event. A fictional interview with a disciple that is based on the account is in the student newspaper, ***Covenant Times*** (Unit IV, Issue 9).

His story begins with the ascension of Jesus into heaven. Remind the students that the Pentecost event was the fulfillment of a promise from Jesus Christ. Ask them to turn in their Bibles to *John 20:19-22*. When did this appearance of the risen Christ occur? What did Jesus do? What was his promise? How did the disciples react?

Ask the group to help you make a list of all the different places represented at the first Pentecost described in *Acts 2:9-11*. Explain that Jerusalem drew people from all parts of the civilized world at that time. If Pentecost happened in our nation's capital or in your area, what languages would be heard? Is it easier to accept new ideas if they are presented in a language that you understand?

EXPLORING
(Time: 15–20 minutes)

Option 1. Pentecost Celebration

Make plans for a classroom celebration of the Feast of Pentecost (the birthday of the Church). Some possibilities are:

• arranging a birthday party for the Church with a Pentecost cake

• participating in the church's service by carrying a banner in the procession

• arranging a time for interested students to reaffirm their baptismal vows (BCP, pp. 415-419)

• decorating the classroom with red and white balloons and streamers

• choosing a promise from The Baptismal Covenant for concentrated effort during the weeks after Pentecost. (Turn to *The Book of Common Prayer,* pp. 304-305, and convert the "action" questions to declarative sentences. Example: Continue in the apostles' teaching and fellowship, in the breaking of bread, and in the prayers. Make duplicate copies of all the sentences on individual strips of paper. Be sure to have enough strips for all class members and the teacher. Fold the strips and place them in a box or basket. Ask each person to choose a slip, read it, and work that promise.)

• inflating red balloons and attaching slips of paper that contain verses of Scripture and short prayers. The class members can share them with younger children of the church after the Pentecost service. Instruct the recipients to ask an older person to help them read the special messages.

Option 2. Windsock Flames

Obtain materials for creating windsocks. Give each student a piece of red fabric approximately 18 x 18 inches, to be sewn or glued along one side to form a cloth cone. Supply wire for making a circular frame approximately 5.5 inches in diameter. Attach the windsock to the wire frame with glue or stitching. At the bottom of the cone, attach seven streamers of red, approximately 2 inches wide and 24 inches long. Attach string for hanging the completed sock. As it blows in the wind, it will be a Pentecost reminder, with the streamers looking like seven flames.

Note: This project can be done on a simpler scale by preparing rings of wire only, to which the seven streamers of red crepe paper are attached.

Option 3. Fill-in-the-Blank Puzzle

Turn in the student newspaper, *Covenant Times,* Unit IV, Issue 9, to the fill-in-the-blank puzzle titled "Pentecost." Students may work individually, in pairs, or as a total group.

MUSIC
(Time: 10 minutes)

Sing "O Spirit of Life, O Spirit of God" *(The Hymnal 1982,* 505) with the *Children Sing!* tape. Suggest that the students discover how the following words are used in the stanzas: faith, love, word, Father, and Son.

Note that the hymn appears in a section of the hymnal headed "The Holy Spirit." Ask the class members to count how many hymns are in this section.

CONNECTING/SPEAKING OUT
(Time: 15–20 minutes)

Option 1. Group Discussion

Talk with the students about the association of "breath," "wind," and "spirit." In *Genesis 1:2,* "a wind from God swept over the face of the waters." The same word that is used for wind in Hebrew is translated Spirit. Older translations of the Bible read, "The Spirit of God moved over the face of the deep." In the New Testament, the Greek word for breath and spirit is "pneuma." (Note that this is the root for the word, pneumonia. When a person has pneumonia, it is "breath trouble.")

Ask: How is breath essential to life? What happens when it is impaired or absent? Invite the class members to make an analogy of breath to God's spirit. The Church understands the message of Pentecost to be that the Holy Spirit imparts a special quality of life and the power to be God's people in the world.

Option 2. Current Events

Think together as a group about the Church's customs surrounding the Day of Pentecost, such as wearing red clothing, making red decorations for the church, or serving cake with red icing. Ask: Which customs are your favorites?

Explain why Pentecost is sometimes called Whitsunday. This is an English contraction of White Sunday. Pentecost was a traditional day for baptisms and confirmations, when the candidates wore white. What other celebrations in the Church or outside the Church are related to colors? (St. Patrick's Day, Valentine's Day, and Lent, for example.)

REFLECTING
(Time: 10 minutes)

Continue with the procedure for reflecting suggested in Session 1. Distribute the covered scrolls to the students, and invite them to add another letter.

Ask the students to recall that the apostle Paul would have heard from the apostles who were present the story of what happened at the first Pentecost. Throughout his preaching and his writing, he spoke often about the gift of the Holy Spirit. Ask: What would you like to tell Paul about your own church's Pentecost celebration?

When the letter writing is completed, ask the students to place their letters in the scrolls, wrap the scrolls, and tie them securely. (If this is the final session of the Unit, the students should take their scrolls home.)

LEARNING SKILLS
(Time: 10–15 minutes)

Option 1. Class Memory Challenge

As a final review of this Unit's memory challenge, refer to the chart in the student newspaper, *Covenant Times,* Unit IV, Issue 9. If it seems appropriate, you may want to encourage the students to list or recite the names of all the books in both Old and New Testaments.

Option 2. Learning Scripture

The suggested verses to be learned following this session are *Joel 2:28* or *Acts 2:4.* See "Learning Scripture" in the student newspaper, *Covenant Times.*

ONGOING PROJECT
(Time: 5–10 minutes)

Jerusalem

Refer to Session 1 for a description of this ongoing project. Distribute supplies for making a travel poster on the city of Jerusalem.

Share the following information with students as they prepare to work:

The capital city of Jerusalem is called the religious center of the world for Jews, Christians, and Muslims. It was the location of the temple where Jesus prayed. Each year thousands of pilgrims have gathered there for Passover and to observe Holy Week and Easter. Synagogues were scattered throughout the city. The city was surrounded by walls and had magnificent gates. The city had many olive trees and cedars.

If this is the final poster in this series, decide on a place to display the total project.

SYMBOL CARD and TREASUREBOOK

Card 36 depicts the Pentecost flames, and has a Scripture verse, and an explanation on the back.

Throughout the *Shell Year Treasurebook*, the text refers to the work of the Holy Spirit—inspiring the Scriptures of the Old and New Testaments, given to us in Holy Baptism, and directing the work of the apostles. Ask students to go through the entire book to look for references to the Holy Spirit.

GOING FORTH

Gather the group for dismissal. The teacher or a student will say:

I ask your prayers for peace; for goodwill among nations; and for the well-being of all people.
Pray for justice and peace.
Silence

I ask your prayers for the poor, the sick, the hungry, the oppressed, and those in prison.
Pray for those in any need or trouble.
Silence

[Learners may add their petitions.]

I ask your prayers for all who seek God, or a deeper knowledge of him.
Pray that they may find and be found by him.

From The Prayers of the People
The Book of Common Prayer, p. 386

Teacher: Let us go forth in the name of Christ.
Students: Thanks be to God.

TEACHER'S ASSESSMENT

Are the students more aware that the Day of Pentecost is a Principal Feast of the Church? What is their general point of view about this festival in their congregation?

ECC
EPISCOPAL CHILDREN'S CURRICULUM

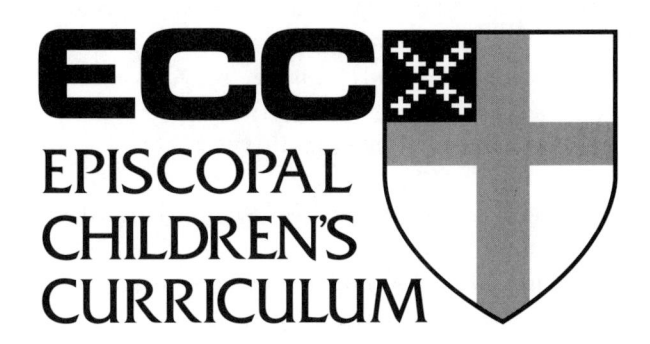

FOUNDATION PAPER

The following statement represents the theological foundation for Episcopal Children's Curriculum, a project of Virginia Theological Seminary, through its Center for the Ministry of Teaching, in collaboration with Morehouse Publishing. Adopted January, 1990.

The aim of Christian education in Episcopal Church parishes and congregations is to assist every member in living out the covenant made in Holy Baptism (BCP, p. 304). Hence, the common ministry of teachers and learners focuses on matters of both faith and practice:

Faith in God who made heaven and earth, in Jesus Christ the Son of God, and in the Holy Spirit who is Lord and giver of life. Practice of worship and prayer, of repentance and obedience, of loving service to all persons, and of active pursuit of God's justice and peace in the world.

The content of our faith and practice is continually reexamined and corrected as we search Holy Scripture and the preserved tradition of the Church. All Christians have access to these sources and are invited to discover for themselves not only the record of God's action in former times but also God's living presence in our contemporary world; in that sense, every member of the church is engaged in theological reflection.

In every generation we consider afresh what it means to speak of the one God who created everything, who is still at work in Christ to "make all things new," that is always breaking into every dimension of our existence. Teachers of children, youth, and adults in the Church play a vital role in helping learners to approach all of life with an attitude of openness in order to discover and proclaim God's presence in relation to every event and movement. Our roles as teachers and learners require critical, discriminative thinking; Christian education's aim is to assist all members of the Church to discern the signs and spirits of the age and to bring sound theological judgment to bear upon what we observe and experience.

• We participate in worship with the prime intention of honoring God as transcendent. We acknowledge our sinfulness and confess our need of forgiveness. We give thanks for the good news of the gospel—that in Christ we receive pardon for all our offenses and are made worthy to stand before God.

In the liturgical life of the Church, we are confronted again and again with the story of God's creative and saving action in the world, revealed supremely in the life and work of Jesus Christ, our risen and ascended Lord. By continual participation in the prayers and rites of the Church, we are engrafted further into its holy fellowship and formed as the living church—glorifying God in the company of apostles and saints who have gone before us, and with all our brothers and sisters in Christ at home and throughout the world.

Participation in the Church's common life of worship is absolutely primary for effective Christian education. But so also is participation in Christ's ministry to individuals in need and to the structures of society when they produce oppression, discrimination, and misery rather than health and wholeness for all of God's people. Thus, we respond in our daily life and work to the saving gospel proclaimed by the church, and to the challenge to take part in carrying out the Church's mission throughout the world.

• At the same time, we engage in a constant process of explaining to ourselves and others where we came from, who we are as baptized persons gathered at the Lord's Table, and what we are called to be and to do in this present time.

Foundation

We strive for greater knowledge of, and the ability to share:
- the whole story of God's revelation as we receive it from Holy Scripture
- the lively and continuing tradition of the Church's history and heritage
- and the practices that are morally and ethically appropriate among contemporary followers of Jesus Christ

The Bible, Christian theology, church history, and current issues in the world are to be faithfully explored in our struggle to follow the leading of the Holy Spirit and to discover the will of God for our time.

There can be no substitute for serious efforts to teach and learn the Biblical narrative and the story of the Church in all their fullness.

The Church's ministry of teaching is an urgent endeavor undertaken by God's faithful people who renounce sin and evil, who turn to Christ as Savior, and who put their whole trust in the grace and love of God living together as redeemed sinners in the community of the thankful.

Our common life in the Church is not only the locus but also the vehicle of Christian education. Knowing that the Church is called to be a sign to the world of the reign of God that is to come, we engage in our work as teachers and learners so that we may become a people known to bear one another's burdens and to offer comfort and aid to all who suffer and are in need.

We seek also to foster well-informed and active membership in visible structures of the congregations and dioceses as they pursue concrete acts of witness and mission to the world. We work together with our neighbors who are engaged in many kinds of work as they seek to serve the common good of humanity and to work for peace and justice.

Immersion in the Church's faith and practice through regular participation and repeated explanation becomes, therefore, the foundation for Episcopalians' work of Christian education.
The educative task in a parish or mission is a joint effort of clergy, parents, sponsors and others in the congregation. We cannot rely solely on organized classes for the instruction and nurture of individuals. With the help and support of the whole congregation, parents—by word and example, prayers and witness—seek to bring up their children in the Christian faith and way of life.

It is incumbent on a congregation to provide opportunities for children, youth, and adults to study and learn with their peers. Well-planned congregational structures for Christian education contribute much to the Church's vitality. Parishes that foster strong ministries of teaching for all their members are most likely to grow and to take on meaningful activities of Christian mission. The work of evangelization—reaching out to persons who are not yet baptized or confirmed in the Church—is best undertaken in parishes with strong programs of Christian education.

Christian education is Biblical, theological, historical, liturgical, spiritual, and ethical in content and character. But we do not teach in a setting extracted from the contemporary scene; we are set down in the world's midst and must learn its language systems in order to communicate and interpret our faith within it. The insights and wisdom of every available discipline devoted to the pursuit of truth about our human situation offer valuable resources for our endeavor.

Members of a congregation, as it gathers for worship and study, bring with them the ways of speaking that are common to their everyday encounters. Teachers in the Church are aware that they must provide bridges between the Word of God (known to us in Jesus Christ, the Bible, and the Church) and the everyday life of learners. Persons who teach are involved in a continual back-and-forth movement between the peculiar language of God's people and the pervasive languages of contemporary society. Toward that end, they are well served by knowledge gained from the social sciences in such areas as these:
- Research and information on patterns of human growth and stages of development that affect how we learn at each age level.
- Theories of group process and behavior that affect the climate of any formal effort to educate persons or to maintain institutions.

- Styles of pedagogy and models for teaching offered as options in schools and classrooms.
- Methods of objective evaluation of the progress of individuals and groups in an educational setting.
- Forms of media used in human communication, with assessment of their relative strengths and weaknesses.

At the very least, the following requisites for a steady program of teaching and learning in the Church will include:

- Committed and prayerful teachers who are dedicated to giving their very best talents and efforts to the enterprise.
- A community of people constantly concerned and willing to support and aid the church's ministry of teaching.
- Appropriately designed material for both teachers and pupils who study the Bible, the Church's story, and the full range of customs and practices of the Anglican and Episcopal traditions in particular.
- Conscious effort on the part of editors, writers, and teachers to relate subject matter to contemporary life issues, in ways appropriate to each age level, with special emphasis on the fostering of individuals' ability to make moral and ethical decisions that reflect their Christian faith.
- Ongoing discussion among teachers (in teams and small groups) concerning the nature of effective Christian education and their own roles.

Effective curriculum resources for Christian education in the Episcopal Church will include the following:

1. Teachers' background material for their personal enrichment as they prepare to teach from the Bible, the *Book of Common Prayer*, and other sources for interpreting the Church's faith and practice.
2. Helpful discussions of the age-level characteristics of learners.
3. Specific suggestions for teaching procedures.
4. Attractive materials to be shared with learners (such as texts and take-home items).

All rights reserved.
Virginia Theological
Seminary, January, 1990

- Notes -

- Notes -

- Notes -